Julia Cresswell is a specialist in the history of language and medieval literature and has an MA and Doctorate in the field. She has worked as a researcher into the history of words for the *Oxford English Dictionary* and on dictionaries of quotations and has always spent part of the year teaching undergraduates. She divides her time between teaching undergraduates and adult education classes, looking after a small academic library and writing.
She lives in Oxford.

By the Same Author

The Penguin Dictionary of Clichés

Scottish First Names

A Dictionary of Allusions

Collins Gem Dictionary of Irish First Names

The Hutchinson Dictionary of Business Quotations (written with Anna Leinster)

Collins Pocket Reference First Names

Guinness Book of British Place Names (written with Fred McDonald)

Bloomsbury Dictionary of First Names

Collins Gem Dictionary of First Names

THE WATKINS
DICTIONARY
OF ANGELS

Julia Cresswell

WATKINS PUBLISHING
LONDON

This edition published in the UK 2006 by
Watkins Publishing, Sixth Floor, Castle House,
75–76 Wells Street, London W1T 3QH
Distributed in the United States and Canada by
Sterling Publishing Co., Inc.
387 Park Avenue South, New York, NY 10016-8810

1 3 5 7 9 10 8 6 4 2

Designed and typeset by Jerry Goldie

Printed and bound in Great Britain

Library of Congress Cataloging-in-Publication data available

ISBN-10: 1-84293-205-5
ISBN-13: 9-781842-932056

www.watkinspublishing.com

CONTENTS

ACKNOWLEDGEMENTS

Finally, I come to the acknowledgments. I should like to thank Michael Mann, who had the idea of writing the book, and his editorial team. Also Ruby Radwan for talking to me about Islam, and Emilie Savage Smith for passing on some of her great expertise in Arabic culture and for suggesting some very useful books, and Philip Pullman for giving permission to quote from his works. I could not have found much of the information I needed without access to the Bodleian Library's Oriental Reading Room; help that will not, alas, be there for others in the future as the Reading Room is to close. Last but not least, thank you to my family, Philip and Alexander, for the many and various forms of support they gave me while writing this book, not to mention all the cups of tea.

INTRODUCTION

Where do They Come From – A Brief History of Angels

When you start to write a book on angels, you suddenly realise how all-pervasive angels are in our culture. You see them all around you; not just in churches and art galleries, but in everyday decorations such as old carvings on buildings, supporting a coat of arms, or even on greetings cards. Even our language is full of angels, whether in the inane lyrics of a popular song, in proverbs ('Fools rush in …') or in the lowly world of sweet foods.

Where does the idea of angels come from? It seems to be an almost inevitable companion to the idea of a supreme or superior God. Once people's idea of the Divine progressed beyond that of a little local god, attached to a single person, place, family or tribe, they seem to have felt the need for some kind of intermediary between themselves and this awesome superior figure. Certainly, from India to Europe we find the idea of beings whose job is to help communication between the divine and the human. The same process seems to have happened with the tribes of Israel, as they passed through the difficult mental process involved in changing their understanding of the nature of their God from a tribal god to a universal supreme being. This is an enormous intellectual leap, and with it comes a problem. If you are used to thinking in terms of your God being one of many (even if a jealous one, who wants you to have no other), but who focuses solely on your people, it seems reasonable to feel close to Him and able to communicate with Him – and there is good evidence in the Bible to show that this is how the God of the Jews started out. However, if He is the one all-powerful God, then your relationship with Him, and your ability to communicate with Him, becomes more problematical. The solution to this big gap is the intermediary, who can act as a means of communication in both directions. The greater the emphasis on monotheism, the greater seems to be the need to find some way of personifying the forces of nature. In some religions it may be the minor deity; in others an ancestor spirit which takes this role. For still others, and not just in some branches of Christianity, it may be a saint. For many religions coming out of the Middle East, angels of some sort were the answer.

In the earlier books of the Bible there is not much lore about the angels. They usually appear in the form of men or fire, but there is not felt to be much need to elaborate about them. Their nature is ambiguous, and continued to be so, not least because in both the Old and New Testaments the basic words used for angel, *malak* and *angelos,* mean 'messenger' and can be used with reference to angels or humans. It was largely left to commentators on the Testaments to develop ideas further.

It was not until the Jews came into contact with the belief systems of the Babylonians during their Exile that angelology really took off. As they came into contact with the beliefs of that area, their concepts of heaven and angels expanded and developed. The religion of the Persians was dualistic, believing in powers of good and bad, and this helped the development of the idea of the power of evil and the fall of the angels. The range of ways of imagining angels was also expanded by the iconography of Persian art, and it is to this we owe the original concept of the Cherubim and the Chariot of the Lord (discussed in the text under the entry for Merkabah). It is to the period of Exile that we also owe the visions of heaven as a hierarchy, the various degrees of angels attendant on God reflecting the structure and bureaucracy of the Persian court. It is because of this extensive influence of the Persian court that so much attention has been given in this work to the beliefs of Zoroastrianism, for this is a continuation of the belief system in place in Babylon. These comments regarding outside influences on the concept of what constitutes an angel or heaven should not be considered derogatory, or to suggest any falling away from an original truth. All such descriptions are, after all, merely attempts to put into words the inexpressible, and it is inevitable that the cultural environment influences the ways in which people try to do this.

Other entries in this book will show the way in which Western Christianity's concept of the appearance of angels, which is profoundly different from the earlier Middle Eastern one, was fundamentally influenced by Greek and Roman iconography. Even today we are influenced by the ideas of the past. One has only to consider the trappings of Christmas. The importance of the birth in the stable-cave at Bethlehem and the role of the star which guided the

Magi (often interpreted as Zoroastrians) owes much to the iconography of Mithraism, one of the dominant religions in the Roman world of the first century. In subsequent centuries we have added to our social customs surrounding the feast, much taken from Germanic paganism. Thus we have transformed Saint Nicholas, once a Turkish bishop, into Santa Claus, a Winter Spirit whose northern home is far from his original homeland, and whose standard red-and-white costume goes back to a soft-drinks advertisement. But just because you can trace the use of mistletoe back to Druid customs, it does not mean that anyone using it as part of the Christmas festivities is actually following Druidic beliefs. In the same way, the extraordinary way that any pool of water in a public place immediately gets coins thrown into it does not mean that people who deposit the coins, with at most a feeling that it is good luck, are consciously participating in a tradition of making sacrifices in water that goes back to at least the Bronze Age.

Another important source of inspiration for angel lore was the text of the Bible itself. Saul Olyan, who has made an extensive study of the sources of angel names, has written of the 'parallel between angelic exegesis of divine attributes and cultic terminology in Second Temple, rabbinic and Hekalot texts and the older, pan-Near Eastern tendency to divinize attributes of the gods and items of the cult, including the temple itself'. Put in more accessible language, this means that as the text of the Bible was studied more and more closely, there was a tendency to read more and more into the words. What at one time was seen as simple description or poetic metaphor was now interpreted as referring to angels. As he has shown, this was particularly likely to happen where the text contained rare or unique words, particularly if their origin was not clear. Hand in hand with this was a general tendency in all religions in the area to turn different aspects of the religion into personifications, either as aspects of Godhead or as angels.

Names, Ranks and Numbers – Where do Angel Names Come From?

Although calculations of the exact number of angels vary, there is general agreement that the number is vast, if not infinite. Human nature being what it is, it was almost inevitable that people would want to put names to at least some of them. The Bible and the Koran do not actually have very much to say about angels in detail, or by name. However, there is a wide variety of other sources for these names which have been drawn on for this book. Individual sources are listed in detail in the Bibliography.

The most important source is a group of books known as the **Pseudepigrapha**. These are sometimes known as Apocryphal books, but that term is best kept for that group of texts known as the **Apocrypha** which were not accepted as canonical for inclusion in the Bible, but which were still felt to have some authority. The Old Testament Pseudepigrapha, on the other hand, are post-biblical. They consist of a collection of texts attributed to people who feature in the Old Testament, but obviously not written by them. The current authoritative edition consists of sixty-five different works. Many of these are rich in angel lore, particularly those visionary texts known as **Merkabah** or **Hekalot** ('palaces') texts, which tell of visions of heaven in terms of a series of palaces populated by ranks of angels, of which the most important are the three different books of Enoch, referred to as *1, 2* and *3 Enoch*. These pseudepigraphal works present many problems for the student. They are often fragmentary, have survived in a wide range of languages which no one scholar can hope to master, and the material itself is often very difficult to understand. We are lucky that we now have the material translated into English by the foremost scholars. Further material on angels is found in the **Talmud**, those written texts which embody the **Mishnah** or oral teachings of Jewish commentators on the Bible.

The mysticism of the Pseudepigrapha later developed into that of the **Kabbalah** of the Middle Ages. This represented a fundamental change of attitude towards angels. As the *Jewish Encyclopedia* puts it, 'In the Talmud, angels were the instruments of God; in the Middle Ages, the instruments of man, who, by calling their names, or by other means, rendered them visible.' The Kabbalah itself is not a fixed body of material, although there are two prime texts: *The Zohar* and the *Sefer Yetzirah* or *Book of Creation*. For our purposes *The Zohar* is the more important text. An understanding of Kabbalah demands deep and complex study, and no attempt has been made to go into details of belief in this book. To speak very broadly, there are two aspects: one which leads to contemplation of the nature of the Divine, and one which deals with more mundane things. Recently, there has been much promotion of what has come to be called 'Practical Kabbalah'. This overlaps heavily with our third main class of material, books of **conjuration** or **magic**. These evolve from the idea also found in the Kabbalah, that the ability to name the right angel in the right way gives you power over them, and that in this way their power can become available to the namer.

But where do the actual forms of the names come from? Angelic names can be of various kinds and fall into four main groups. The first group contains those modelled on biblical names such as Michael and Gabriel. They are made up of a stem element, often a vocabulary word, combined with the ending -*el*, traditionally said to mean 'God'. These are often based on the function of the angel so that Baraqiel, the angel of lightning, is from *baraq*, the Hebrew for lightning. Similarly, names ending in -*yah* come from the Hebrew for 'Lord'. Names ending in -*iel* actually present more problems of interpretation than is generally recognised. The ending can be interpreted as either meaning 'God is my –' or '– of God', so that Hanniel can be understood as 'Favour of God' or 'Divine Favour', and Gabriel as 'Man of God' or 'Divine Man'. Alternatively, the ending can be interpreted as *i* = my + *el* = God, which works fine for Malkiel, 'My King is God' or 'Divine King', but is not an acceptable interpretation for Abdiel which would come out as 'God is my servant'. The actual origin and significance of the form is obscure, although it is evident that it soon became traditional. Because of the doubts in the interpretations of these names, many of the definitions traditionally given for their meanings will not be found in this book, as they are very dubious.

The second group of names is formed on patterns of number magic, such as is found in the Kabbalah. Since all numbers and letters are held to have mystic values, they can be combined to form sacred names. This mechanical combination of letters explains some of the unpronounceable or all-but-unpronounceable names found, such as Pdgnar and Fromezyn. Thirdly, some names come not from Hebrew but from foreign words, particularly Greek. Under Roman domination Jewish writers were part of the rich intellectual life of the Empire, and were influenced by, and in turn influenced, the flow of ideas. Many of the most important texts (including the New Testament) were actually written in Greek, the common language of the Eastern Mediterranean, and it is not surprising that as a result, some of the angel names were formed from that language. Finally, since much visionary material would have been composed in a trance state or similar unusual state, some may be from glosso-lalia, otherwise known as speaking in tongues.

Why do Angel Names Take so Many Forms?

The reason why one angel may have many different forms to its name stems from one of two causes. Either it is because of problems presented by the original language in which the text was written; or else it comes from the fact that these names have been handed down either orally or through manu-scripts. In practice, much of the confusion probably results from combinations of the two.

One fundamental problem with the languages is that they may not contain the same sounds as English, and many use a different alphabet. Certain letters in Arabic and Hebrew can be transcribed into English in different ways, depending on the system used. This explains the variations we find between K and Kh, Ch, G and Gh, which often represent guttural sounds that we do not have in English. Many of our angel names come from Semitic languages – principally Hebrew, but also Arabic, Aramaic and Syriac. These languages depend on three-consonant roots, which are modified, mainly by vowels, to change the meaning. Thus the Arabic root s-l-m, 'be at peace', is the source of the greeting *Salam* (being at peace), of *Muslim* (literally, 'one who causes to be at peace', hence one who submits to God) and *Islam* (submitting to God). The closeness of Hebrew and Arabic can be seen from the Hebrew *Shalom* which is the equivalent of *Salam*, and the forms of names from the same root, Solomon and Suliman. (Those who want to go into this further should read Guy Deutscher's excellent 2005 book, *The Unfolding of Language*.) When these languages are written down, the root letters are given greater prominence than the modifying letters. Vowels may be indicated by dots above or below the line, or omitted altogether. This means that the exact interpretation of the word can be obscure or easily altered. When the word is a name, rather than a word we can guess from context, the confusion is magnified. When you add on top of this that the person copying this down may not be fully familiar with the language, then the opportunities for confusion can easily been seen. A further consideration is that it is only in the last 200 years or so that we have developed the idea of correct spelling. Until then, in many languages it was quite acceptable to write as you pronounced, spelling varying according to the way different regions pronounced words, or even according to individual whim.

On top of the problems presented by the languages, there are the variations that come from the fact that these names are transmitted to us by manuscripts. Everyone who has ever copied out a piece of writing will know how easy it is to introduce changes in what you write down. Imagine this multiplied over hundreds of years. With angel names we again hit the problem of reading unfamiliar words. When we read we anticipate from the context what the next word is likely to be. This is particularly important when reading handwriting. But with angel names we cannot do this. The fact that the sources are handwritten presents particular problems. A word like 'minimum' is easy enough to read when printed, but when hand-written all those 'm's, 'i's and 'u's run into each other, and unless you know the word you are expecting, it is difficult to tell where one letter begins and another ends. In addition, over the centuries handwriting changes, and at different periods different letters can be confused. In medieval manuscripts written in spiky Gothic letters, 'c', 'r' and 't' can be easily confused, and in another style of writing 'b', 'h' or 'k' can be muddled. There is a fourteenth-century form of 'r' that later copiers confused with a 'z'. For many centuries 'v' and 'u' were interchangeable, 'v' being used at the beginning of the word, and 'u' in the middle regardless of what sound they represented. The same situation applied to 'i' and 'j'. In English spelling 'i' and 'y' were at times interchangeable for the same sound. Finally, some of the manuscripts may have been dictated, adding all sorts of opportunities for mishearing. I have tried to point out the various possible confusions in some of the entries, and readers might like to turn to the entry for Uachayel as an example.

There are yet two further sources of confusion. No student of angels can hope to master all the difficult languages involved. Thus, they are dependent on the expert editor and translator. Different scholars make different decisions as the information available to them expands over the years. This means the same angel may have different names in different editions (and it should never be forgotten that editors too are copying manuscripts and, however careful they are, may introduce new errors). Angels may even disappear from one edition to another. See the entries for Dabriel and Ithoth for examples of this. Finally, books that revealed secrets, as many of our texts did, were carefully guarded. Even texts posted on the internet may contain the warnings that their contents should not be revealed or copied, based on the warnings found in the original manuscripts. One such reads: 'Permission is hereby granted to make one handwritten copy for personal use, provided the master binds his executors by a strong oath (juramentum) to bury it with him in his grave. Beyond this, whoever copies this sacred text without permission from the editor will be damned.' Texts involving magic secrets may actually have had the names deliberately altered so that the master kept control of the secret powers.

What Angels are in this Text?

There are thousands of angels' names to be found in the many sources. No book could possibly contain them all, and anyway, many of them are simply parts of long lists, with no further information on them. Someone writing on angels has, therefore, to be selective. There are obviously some angels who are far too important not to go in, and I hope I have included them all. I have included all the angels from the major Pseudepigrapha. I have included the fallen angels from the books of Enoch, but have not listed the many other fallen angels, unless there has been a good reason to do so, although I have included many that some say are still heavenly angels, but others say are fallen. I have also salted the text with a number of purely literary angels, simply to add a bit of variety, and because it is interesting to see how the concept of angel is used creatively. These angels pretty well selected themselves. The problems came when deciding which angels to include thereafter. I decided to use British Library Sloane Manuscript 3826, which I have referred to in the text as the Sloane Manuscript *Book of Raziel*, as my base text. This may at first seem a rather surprising choice. It is not a particularly important text, and has lain largely undisturbed in the British Library since it formed part of the foundation collection in the mid-eighteenth century. What, then, was its attraction? Part of it was the very neglect it has suffered. This means it has a lot of material that has not been incorporated into other books, for it was largely unread until a transcription was made available on the internet by Don Karr in 2003. Even so, it is not an easy work to read or understand. The manuscript has not been properly studied by any expert in manuscripts or language. As a result the best date that is currently available is 'most likely from the sixteenth century'. Now I am no expert in early Hebrew, so cannot comment on the Jewish texts, but I have spent getting on for forty years studying and teaching the earlier forms of English, so that neither the difficult English, nor the Latin sections presented me with a problem. However, someone without this experience would find the work hard going, so I could use my experience to bring new material to the general public. I would suggest that although the manuscript may be sixteenth century, some of the language is rather old-fashioned for that date, except perhaps for an old person writing in the early sixteenth century. I would guess that the text is a reworking of an earlier one, pushing the origin of the material back into the Middle Ages. As well as the unusual material, I felt this work would give the reader a feel for the sort of text earlier people with a shared interest in angels had to work with. As the entries will show, there are many obscurities and corruptions in the text, but it has the advantage of also being idiosyncratic, and conveying an idea of the chanciness of what has and has not survived from the past. If there appear to be too many entries from this one text I apologise, but it does give the reader an idea of the almost remorseless quality of the lists of angels in some texts. A final advantage is that it shares a common source for its lists of angels of the months and weeks with another important text, the *Liber Juratus*. I do not think the connection can be direct – there are too many differences and corruptions between the two versions – but I do believe that at some point they shared a common ancestor for this section. This means that I have been able to illustrate the way in which the forms of the names vary. In the entries, the form from the Sloane *Raziel* comes first, and the *Liber Juratus* form comes second. All comments on the function of the angels come from *Raziel*, for the *Liber Juratus* simply lists the names. Information on the other texts read for this work will be found in the Bibliography.

Technical Words and Languages

I have tried throughout to keep the book as free as possible from technical terms and specialist language, but it is impossible to avoid them all. Rather than explain them each time they are used, here is a brief list of the religions, terms and languages used in the book.

Religions, etc.

Akkadian refers to an ancient people living to the north of Babylonia (now northern Iraq), their language, culture and religion.

Chaldeans The Chaldeans were another branch of the Babylonian Empire; so famous as sorcerers that the word came to mean 'magician'. The term is also used of an early branch of the Christian Church, with a few followers still left in the Middle East.

Coptic The Copts are inhabitants of Ethiopia and Egypt. They were very early converts to Christianity, as well as having had pre-Christian contacts with Judaism. It is thanks to early Coptic scholars that some texts have survived, notably the most important and, until recently, only version of *1 Enoch*, which survives in a medieval manuscript in the Ge'ez dialect of Coptic.

Gnosticism Gnostics followed a belief system which drew on many cultural roots, particularly those of the eastern Mediterranean. As P Alexander, editor of *3 Enoch*, writes, '"Gnosticism" is notoriously difficult to define, for there are many variations in detail between the various Gnostic systems, but a typical system would speak of God as a transcendent, supreme power; of a second power (sometimes called the demiurge) that created the world; of a series of spheres (or aeons) separating man from the supreme power, each under the control of a hostile spirit (or archon); of the divinity of the human soul and its ascent to the supreme power; and the secret knowledge (gnosis) by which this ascent is to be achieved.' There were many branches and sub-sects, among whom where the **Ophian** or **Ophitic** Gnostics, who attached special import-ance to the serpent. Much of what we know of the Gnostics comes from writings of the early Church Fathers, who saw Gnosticism as a particular threat to the development of Christianity. At the same time many Jewish and Christian writers were heavily influenced by the ideas of Gnosticism.

Kabbalah As explained above, the term has been used very loosely in this book, to cover a wide range of beliefs found in mystic Judaism that developed in the Middle Ages.

Mandaeans This is a small Gnostic sect, heavily influenced by Christianity, which still survives in Iraq, although many of its followers have now been driven into exile. They are also known as the Nasoreans.

Neo-Platonism This is a belief system or philosophy which derives largely from the writings of Plotinus (AD 205–70) and his followers. Plotinus, in his turn, based his ideas, as the name suggests, on the writing of the Athenian philosopher Plato (427–347 BC), which was combined with Middle Eastern mysticism in an attempt to build an intellectual basis for a sound moral and religious life.

Qumran Scrolls The Qumran or Dead Sea Scrolls are manuscript materials found in the area to the north-west of the Dead Sea since 1947, stored in jars and preserved by the desert climate. They mostly date from around the beginning of the Christian era, and although fragmentary, preserve much new material on the history of Jewish mysticism at this date.

Samaritans The Samaritans are a small sect still living near Jerusalem who branched off from Judaism many centuries ago. Their beliefs are based on the same texts as Judaism, but their religious practices differ.

Yezidis A small sect of Kurdish speakers whose religion shows similarities to Zoroastrianism, Christianity, the Sufi branch of Islam, and Gnosticism, although it would be difficult to prove in which direction each influence flowed. They have mistakenly been called devil worshippers, because they believe that Satan repented, was reconciled with God, and returned to his original rank in heaven.

Zoroastrianism Zoroastrians or, as they are called in India, Parsees, follow the teachings of the Persian prophet Zoroaster, or Zarathustra, who lived towards the end of the second millennium BC. The belief system, which draws heavily on even earlier beliefs, is dualistic, believing in two powers: one good, one evil. The religion has had an influence on many later religions.

Languages

Aramaic The language that developed from Hebrew, and was spoken in Palestine and the surrounding countries at the beginning of the Christian era. Syriac is a branch of Aramaic.

Coptic A language, of which there are several distinct dialects, which descends from Ancient Egyptian. See further under religions, above.

Hebrew The language of the Old Testament and of Jewish scholarship.

Persian The language of Zoroastrianism. It is an Indo-European language, spoken in the ancient Persian Empire, in what is now Iran and surrounding countries. The religious texts, the *Avesta*, are written in a form of Old Persian called Avestan; a later form of the language (Middle Persian) is known as Pahlavi, while the modern form is known as either Persian or Farsi.

Slavic or **Slavonic** A language, or rather now a group of languages, of Eastern Europe. In the Middle Ages, Old Church Slavonic was the language of learning in the region, and it is the only language in which *2 Enoch* has survived.

Using This Book

The angels in this book are listed in alphabetical order. If other angels are dealt with in the same entry there will be a cross-reference within the alphabetical list, unless the angels are very minor, and only significant as followers of another angel. If there is an independent entry for an angel who is referred to within an entry, then the name appears in small capitals.

For convenience, angels are referred to as 'he', and the human race as Mankind or simply Man without any implication of gender, unless there is a particular reason to use 'she'.

I have tried to be even-handed in my treatment of the source material, merely reporting the views of others. This means that the book may contain material that some readers disagree with, and certainly contains contradictory material, but this is unfortunately unavoidable if the book is to treat the subject thoroughly.

Julia Cresswell

A–Z
of Angels

A

Aadon, **Aaron**, **Aarom** Angels of the second lunar month according to the *Liber Juratus* and the Sloane manuscript *Book of Raziel*, with the power to grant your wishes.

Aal One of the Angels of Wednesday, the day of Mercury, according to the *Liber Juratus* and the Sloane manuscript *Book of Raziel*. Among his many companion Wednesday angels are **Aaniturla** (found in the *Liber Juratus* as **Danyturla**) and **Aaon** or **Aaen**.

Abaddon, **Abadon**, **Abbadon** This name comes from the Hebrew word for 'destruction', or 'place of destruction', and the earliest biblical uses of the name refer to the bottomless pit, the abyss. However, in Job 28:22, 'Destruction and death say, We have heard the fame thereof with our ears,' which shows a transitional stage where Abaddon (here translated as 'Destruction') has begun to move towards personification, and by Revelation 9 Abaddon has become a fully-fledged angel. This passage describes how the fifth angel sounded its trumpet and a star (stars are usually interpreted in this text as falling angels) falls from heaven to earth 'and to him was given the key of the bottomless pit. And he opened the bottomless pit; and there rose a smoke out of the pit, as the smoke of a great furnace: and the sun and the moon were darkened.' St John describes the demons 'with tails like unto scorpions' that come out of the pit and continues, 'And they had a king over them, which is the angel of the bottomless pit, whose name in the Hebrew tongue is Abaddon, but in the Greek tongue hath his name Apollyon.' In Chapter 20, St John appears to describe the same figure when he says 'And I saw an angel come down from heaven, having the key of the bottomless pit and a great chain in his hand. And he laid hold on the dragon, that old serpent, which is the Devil, and Satan, and bound him a thousand years.' This seems to set up a conflict between the idea of Abaddon as an angel who leads demons and as one who binds Satan. There are various solutions that have been proposed. Either Abaddon is not the angel who holds the key to the pit; or we are talking about two different angels in the two different passages (and MICHAEL, as the traditional defeater of the dragon, has been identified by some as the angel in Chapter 20); or in Chapter 9 Abaddon is leading the demons that are sent to punish Mankind and in doing so is simply performing God's will, as he is in Chapter 20.

Abaddon is variously called an, or even the ANGEL OF DEATH (a title also given to SAMAEL and in Islam to IZRAIL) and the Angel of the Pit or Abyss, and is usually seen as demonic rather than benevolent. His alternative name, Apollyon, means 'destroyer' in Greek and technically has no connection with the name of the Greek god Apollo, although once Apollyon was firmly identified as a demon (often considered synonymous with Asmodeus or Belial) it was convenient to have a close identification between paganism and hell.

Abagtha see HARBONAH

Aban In Zoroastrianism, Aban is one of the YAZATAS, the equivalent of angels.

She is female and personifies water (the meaning of her name) and rainfall. She resides in the starry regions and goes under a number of alternative names, the most important of which is **Aredvi Sura Anahita**, meaning 'strong immaculate Anahita. She is **Arduisur** in Avestan, **Apas** or **Api** in Middle Persian and **Ap** in Pahlavi. She works alongside SPENTA ARMAITI, and the eighth month in the Persian calendar, which runs from 23 October to 21 November, is named Aban after her, as is the ninth day of each month.

Abariel An angel whose name appears on the Second Pentacle of the Moon in *The Key of Solomon* which claims, 'This serveth against all perils and dangers by water, and if it should chance that the Spirits of the Moon should excite and cause great rain and exceeding tempests about the Circle, in order to astonish and terrify thee; on showing unto them this Pentacle, it will all speedily cease.'

Abasdarhon The angel of the fifth hour of the night in the *Lemegeton*. His chief followers are **Meniel, Charaby, Appiniel, Deinatz, Nechorym, Hameriel, Vulcaniel, Samelon, Gemary, Vanescor, Samerym, Xantropy, Herphatz, Chrymas, Patrozyn, Nameton, Barmas** or **Barmos, Platiel, Neszomy, Quesdor, Caremaz, Umariel, Kralym** and **Habalon**.

Abdals A group of Angels in Islamic lore. Said to number seventy, the abdals (meaning 'substitutes') are known only to God and fulfil the essential task of permitting the world to continue in existence. They are not immortal, however, and when one of them dies their number is kept constant by God, who secretly appoints a replacement.

Abdiel Abdiel features as a Seraph in the *Sepher Raziel*, but is best known from Milton's *Paradise Lost*, where he features in Books Five and Six. He is among the angels who listen to Lucifer's harangue that leads to the revolt of the angels, but is infuriated by what he hears and flies off in disgust to report what is going on. He alone is not seduced by Lucifer's words (as Milton puts it, 'faithful only hee; among innumerable false, unmov'd,/Unshak'n, unseduc'd,') and his righteousness is enshrined in his name, which means 'servant of God'. In Book Six, Abdiel fights with the rest of the heavenly host against the rebel angels. In the form of a 'flaming seraph' he puts the FALLEN ANGELS ARIEL, ARIOC and RAMIEL to flight, and strikes Satan himself with his sword. This fighting prowess means that the angel also gave its name to a whole class of mine-laying ships in use in the Second World War. HMS *Abdiel* itself served with particular distinction until sunk in 1943. A namesake was in use in the British navy until 1990.

Abdisuel, Abdizriel, Abdizuel A MOON ANGEL who rules over the twelfth mansion of the moon. His zodiac sign is Leo, he encourages fertility and is a supporter of captives and servants. However, he works against sailors.

Abecaisdon, Abercaysdon One of the angels of the seventh lunar month according to the *Liber Juratus* and the Sloane manuscript *Book of Raziel*, which says that if they are named 'in each thing that thou wilt do … thou shalt profit'.

Abedel, **Abdyel** An angel of the first lunar month according to the *Liber Juratus* and the Sloane manuscript *Book of Raziel*.

Abel In most reference works on angels, Abel is described as an angel who judges the dead, as seen in the *Testament of Abraham*. However, if the text is read carefully, it is found that while both Adam and Abel sit on thrones in heaven and seem to have been glorified (they are described as wondrous, glorious and frightening), there is no suggestion that they are angels. In Chapter Thirteen Abel is explicitly described as 'the son of Adam, the first-formed, who is called Abel, whom Cain the wicked killed. And he sits here to judge the entire creation, examining both righteous and sinners.' The later confusion may have come from poor texts or translations.

Abezethibou A demon in the *Testament of Solomon*, who was once an angel in heaven, but is now a one-winged demon 'plotting against every wind under heaven'. It was he who hardened Pharaoh's heart when Moses demanded he let his people go; and he assisted **Jannes** and **Jambres** (usually described as Egyptian magicians, but sometimes described as angels, in which case they may be linked with HARUT and MARUT). These two worked against Moses in his attempt to free Israel.

Abiel The angel that rules the fifteenth degree of Cancer under CAEL and the fifteenth degree of Leo under OL, according to the *Lemegeton*.

Abinel An angel presiding over Thursday, the day of Jove, according to Sloane manuscript *Book of Raziel*.

Ablaieil, **Ablayeyll** An angel presiding over Friday, the day of Venus, according to the *Liber Juratus* and the Sloane manuscript *Book of Raziel*. **Abneyrin** is another Friday angel in these works.

Abnisor An angel of the third lunar month according to the Sloane manuscript *Book of Raziel*, whose naming brings benefits. He is **Abuifor** in the *Liber Juratus*.

Abrac An angel of the fifth lunar month according to the *Liber Juratus* and the Sloane manuscript *Book of Raziel*, who if invoked brings benefits. He does not appear in the *Liber Juratus* list.

Abragin An angel of the second lunar month according to the Sloane manuscript *Book of Raziel* with the power to grant wishes.

Abramacyn According to the *Liber Juratus* and the Sloane manuscript *Book of Raziel*, this is one of the GUARDIAN ANGELS with special care of Monday (Luna) who should be invoked to aid works started on that day. **Abranocyn** or **Abranoryn** and **Abrasachysyn**, **Abrasasyn** are fellow Monday angels.

Abrasiel see BARAQIEL

Abrastos In the Sloane manuscript *Book of Raziel* an angel with power over water.

Abraxas Some say that the proper name of this being is **Abrasax**, and it also occurs as **Abraxis**. The accounts of who and what Abraxas are are immensely varied and, depending on which system you wish to follow, he can be seen as a god, an angel or, by orthodox

Christians, a demon. The most important role of Abraxas is in Gnosticism. For Gnostics, Abraxas is the supreme power who unites both the dark and the light. In the Kabbalah he is the prince of AEONS. Abraxas stones, engraved gems used as amulets, are frequently found. These show him with the head of a cockerel (or occasionally a hawk) which symbolises the sun, because of the cock's crowing to greet it. He has a human body (sometimes winged) and a pair of snakes instead of legs. He sometimes carries a whip and a shield. In numerology the Greek letters of his name add up to 365. As well as the obvious links with the days of the year, this also led to the idea that he was the 365th and highest AEON; and among the Persians that he was the source of 365 emanations. This, among other things, also led to much use of his name in magic. Indeed it has been claimed, unprovably, that his name is the source of the word 'abracadabra'.

Abri, Abry One of the angels of the seventh lunar month according to the *Liber Juratus* and the Sloane manuscript *Book of Raziel*, which says that if they are named 'in each thing that thou wilt do … thou shalt profit'. **Abrid**, an angel of the summer equinox invoked by occultists and used on amulets against the evil eye, may be another form of the name.

Abrigriel An angel cited by Alma Daniel, Timothy Wyllie and Andrew Ramer in their influential 1992 book *Ask Your Angels* as a 'transformation angel'.

Abrinael A MOON ANGEL who rules the twenty-fourth mansion of the moon.

He works in the sign of Aquarius, and is supportive of married couples and brings victory to soldiers; but is hostile to the operation of effective government.

Abris, Abrys An angel of the third lunar month according to the *Liber Juratus* and the Sloane manuscript *Book of Raziel*, whose naming brings benefits.

Abrisaf, Abrysaf In the *Liber Juratus* and the Sloane manuscript *Book of Raziel*, an angel of the eleventh lunar month. If invoked in the relevant month, he will ensure success in your enterprise.

Absafyabitan An angel of the second lunar month according to the Sloane manuscript *Book of Raziel*, with the power to grant wishes.

Absamon An angel of the second lunar month according to the *Liber Juratus* and the Sloane manuscript *Book of Raziel* with the power to grant wishes.

Abson An angel of the west of the first heaven in the Sloane manuscript *Book of Raziel*.

Acceriel In the Sloane manuscript *Book of Raziel*, an angel with power over water.

Acciriron This is one of the angels presiding over Saturday, the day of Saturn or Sabat, according to the Sloane manuscript *Book of Raziel*. If invoked appropriately and in a state of purity, they will aid you.

Acclamations see APPARITIONS

Accusing Angel An angel whose function is to accuse the dead of their sins before the judgement seat. SATAN, whose name means 'the adversary', is the most usual accusing Angel, but the role is also taken by DUBIEL, MASTEMA, SAMMAEL and SEMYAZA, among others.

Acdiel In the Sloane manuscript *Book of Raziel* an angel with power over fire and flame.

Achael The angel that rules the twenty-fourth degree of Gemini under GIEL, according to the *Lemegeton*.

Achaiah In the Kaballah, Achaiah, whose name means 'trouble', is one of eight SERAPHIM. He is the angel of patience, and the discoverer of the secrets of nature. He is also said by some angelologists to be the GUARDIAN ANGEL of those born between 21 and 25 April under Taurus. In this role he is described as an angel of perspicacity, giving aid in solving problems.

Achiel The angel that rules the twenty-first degree of Gemini under GIEL, according to the *Lemegeton*.

Achlas, **Athlas** An angel of the second lunar month according to the *Liber Juratus* and the Sloane manuscript *Book of Raziel*, with the power to grant wishes.

Acia, **Acya** An angel of the first lunar month according to the *Liber Juratus* and the Sloane manuscript *Book of Raziel*.

Aciel An angel of the east of the fifth heaven in the Sloane manuscript *Book of Raziel*.

Aczonyn, **Aezonyn** According to the *Liber Juratus* and the Sloane manuscript *Book of Raziel*, this is one of the GUARDIAN ANGELS with special care of Monday (Luna), who should be invoked to aid works started on that day.

Adail see ADOIL

Adar see ATAR

Addriel In the Sloane manuscript *Book of Raziel*, an angel of the twelfth lunar month. If invoked in the relevant month, he will ensure success in your enterprise.

Adernahael see ADNACHIEL

Adi An angel of the third lunar month according to the Sloane manuscript *Book of Raziel*, whose naming brings benefits. In the manuscript this angel is followed by **Ysar**. In the *Liber Juratus* these appear as one angel, **Adyysar**.

Adiamenyn, **Adyanienyn** According to the *Liber Juratus* and the Sloane manuscript *Book of Raziel*, this is one of the GUARDIAN ANGELS with special care of Monday (Luna), who should be invoked to aid works started on that day.

Adiel, **Adyell** An angel of the third lunar month according to the Sloane manuscript *Book of Raziel*, whose naming brings benefits. In the *Lemegeton* he is one of the zodiac angels.

Adimus One of the seven REPROBATED ANGELS. It is surprisingly difficult to find any information about him, but Thomas Heywood, in *The Hierarchy of* *the Blessed Angels* (1635), says he was an angel who was condemned by God to eternal damnation.

Adityas Angel analogues in Hinduism. They are personifications of the ruling principals of the universe. They are the sons of the goddess Aditi, whose name means 'boundlessness' and who embodies unlimited space and consciousness, and hence eternity. In earlier texts they were said to be eight, but later the number was given as twelve, to correspond to the months of the year. They are usually listed as **Amsa** (the share of the gods); **Aryaman** (generous nobility); **Bhaga** (due inheritance), **Daksa** (ritual skill); **Mitra** (constancy in friendship), **Pusan** (prosperity); **Sakra** (courage); **Savitr** (power of words); Tvastr (skill in craft and technique); **Varuna** (fate); **Vishnu** (cosmic law); **Vivasvat** (social law). The term is also extended to mean any god.

Adnachiel According to Thomas Heywood's *Hierarchy of the Blessed Angels* and others, the angel who rules the order of ANGELS, a job which he shares with PHALEG. He also rules November and the sign of Sagittarius. The name is also found as **Advachiel** and **Adernahael**.

Adnibia An angel of the second lunar month according to the Sloane manuscript *Book of Raziel,* with the power to grant wishes.

Adniel, Admyel An angel of the first lunar month according to the *Liber Juratus* and the Sloane manuscript *Book of Raziel.*

Adnyam An angel of the fourth lunar

month according to the Sloane manuscript *Book of Raziel* who, if invoked, brings benefits.

Adoil, Adail Not a true angel, but a primordial 'great AEON', the source of light, depicted in *2 Enoch* 25. There it is shown as a spiritual being, distinct from God, but used in the creation of the universe. There has been much scholarly debate on the meaning of the name. While it could mean 'light or creation' or 'his eternity', scholars cannot even agree as to which language the word comes from. While many analyse it as a Hebrew word, others see it as coming from Greek or the Slavonic of the surviving text, or even a mixture of the two. See also under ARCHAS.

Adonaeus, Adonaios, Adonaiu, Adnaeus This is the name of one of the great ARCHONS in Gnostic belief. He represented the sun. The name comes from the same root, *adonai* meaning 'God', as does the name Adonis, the dying god of the winter sun, beloved of Aphrodite/Astarte. He was adopted from the religion of the Palestine region into the Greek religious system, and from there, because of his reputation for beauty, adopted into general English use.

Adonai Adonai occurs in most texts as one of the Names of God; but in some texts he is an angel. In some versions of Gnosticism Adonai or ADONAEUS is the name of one of either seven or twelve (depending on which text you follow) angels created by the god IALDABOATH 'in his own image'. He is also said to be one of the seven ANGELS OF THE PRESENCE who created the world in Phoenician mythology. In magic workings the name is used particularly in exorcisms of fire.

Adoniel An angel found in magical texts. In the *Testament of Solomon* he controls the demon Metathiax who causes pains in the kidneys, while he is an angel of the ninth lunar month in the *Liber Juratus* and the Sloane manuscript *Book of Raziel*, which says that if they are named 'in each thing that thou wilt do … thou shalt profit'. He is one of the angels whose name is used in the Fourth Pentacle of Jupiter which 'serveth to acquire riches and honour' in *The Key of Solomon*. In the *Lemegeton*, Adoniel is an attendant angel on SARANDIEL, angel of the twelfth hour of the night.

Adrapan see PAMYEL

Adriel, **Hadriel**, **Hadraniel** Meaning 'honour, splendour', this angel appears in Hebrew texts as Hadriel or Hadraniel, but in Greek magical papyrus as Adriel. In the Sloane manuscript *Book of Raziel* Adriel is an angel with power over the north, but in some Hebrew texts he is described as an angel who guards the gates of either the south or the east wind. As **Adrael** he is found as an angel serving in the first heaven. He is also a MOON ANGEL who rules the seventeenth mansion of the moon in the sign of Scorpio. He makes love long lasting; strengthens buildings, improves bad fortune and helps seamen. As Hadraniel, *The Zohar* tells us that when he 'proclaims the will of the Lord, his voice penetrates through 200,000 firmaments' and 12,000 flashes of lightning come from his mouth. In some texts this angel is identified with METATRON.

Adroziel see JEFISCHA

Adtriel An angel with power over the west, according to the Sloane manuscript *Book of Raziel*.

Advachiel see ADNACHIEL

Adzdiel The angel of the planet Venus (Noga), according to the Sloane manuscript *Book of Raziel*.

Adziriel, **Adziryell** An angel of the first lunar month according to the *Liber Juratus* and the Sloane manuscript *Book of Raziel*.

Aebel see ANUSH, MINISTERING ANGELS

Ael An angel presiding over Thursday, the day of Jove, according to the *Liber Juratus* and the Sloane manuscript *Book of Raziel*. He is AOL in the *Liber Juratus*. See also under IAOEL.

Aeon An angelic rank in early Hebrew writing, where Aeons are the embodiment of God's thoughts. In Gnosticism, one of a series of spheres separating Man from the supreme power ruled by emanations from God, also called Aeons. These are (usually) numbered at 365 with ABRAXAS at their head and PISTIS-SOPHIA ruling the lower thirty that encompass our world. Ideas are very varied in Gnosticism, and sometimes Aeons are ruled by a hostile spirit called an archon. The Greek form of the word is **Aion**, and is found in the New Testament meaning 'eternity'. Concepts linking the word with religion seem to have existed all round the eastern Mediterranean, for although we know very little about the rituals in Greek mystery religions, we do know that at the temple set up in Alexandria in Egypt to provide resident Greeks with a substitute for the famous mysteries of Eleusis, there was a night-time ceremony in which the daughter of the fertility goddess Demeter, Kore (Greek for 'the maiden'), a goddess of spring and rebirth gave birth to a child called Aion. Kore is better known by the name of Persephone, and in this manifestation is both a goddess of the underworld, and of rebirth and spring. Kore, in the form **Core**, appears as an angel of spring in the *Heptameron* and the *Liber Juratus*. Aeon can also be used to refer to the great primordial being from which the universe was created, such as ADOIL and ARCHAS.

Aesal An angel of the eighth lunar month according to the *Liber Juratus* and the Sloane manuscript *Book of Raziel*, which says that if named 'in each thing that thou wilt do … thou shalt profit'.

Af see APH

Afarit see IFRIT

Affafniel An angel of anger in the *Sefer Raziel*, who has sixteen faces. **Affariel** in the Sloane manuscript *Book of Raziel* and the *Liber Juratus*, who is an elemental angel with power over the earth, is probably a mistranscription of the same name.

Affry, **Affrye** An angel of the second lunar month according to the *Liber Juratus* and the Sloane manuscript *Book of Raziel* with the power to grant wishes.

Afrit see IFRIT

Agalmaturod In *The Key of Solomon*, an angel whose name is invoked when preparing materials for the practice of magic.

Agni see ATAR

Agrasinden, **Agrasnydyn** According to the Sloane manuscript *Book of Raziel* and the *Liber Juratus*, this is one of the GUARDIAN ANGELS with special care of Monday (Luna), who should be invoked to aid works started on that day.

Agrat bat Mahlat In Talmudic literature and in *The Zohar*, Agrat bat Mahlat is one of the three brides of SAMAEL, the other two being **Lilith** and **Naamah** (discussed under HARUT AND MARUT). These three are regarded as angels of prostitution, with a fourth such angel, **Eisheth Zenunim**, sometimes added to the list. Like so many dark angels, Agrat bat Mahlat has been taken up by various alternative cultures, and her name is in regular use among fantasy writers and gamers and has even been used as the title of a song.

Aguel In the Sloane manuscript *Book of Raziel*, an angel of the first heaven, and of the twelfth lunar month. If invoked in the relevant month, he will ensure success in your enterprise.

Ahura Berezant see APAM NAPAT

Ahura Mazda see AHURANI, AMESHA SPENTAS, DEVAS

Ahurani A female YAZAD (Zoroastrian angel) presiding over water and thus fertility. She watches over both rainfall and standing water, and is invoked for health, healing, prosperity and growth.

Historically, she may go back to an ancient Persian goddess, and has links with the water nymphs found in both Greek and Slavic myth, but her name is closely linked to Zoroastrianism, for it means 'She who belongs to Ahura' and she is described as either the wife or daughter of the Zoroastrian God, **Ahura Mazda.**

Ahura, **Ahuras** see ASURAS

Aiel The angel who rules Aries according to the *Lemegeton*. Elsewhere, he is an angel of the air, ruler of Sunday and resides in the fourth heaven.

Ailoaeus, **Ailoaios** This is one of the great ARCHONS in Ophian Gnosticism. He is keeper of the second gate, which leads to the AEON or sphere of the ARCHONS. Since the name also appears as **Ailoein** it probably derives from the Hebrew *Elohim*, 'God'. Ailoaeus represents the planet Mercury.

Aion see AEON

Airyaman YAZAD (Zoroastrian angel) of friendship and healing. His name comes from the same root as that of the Hindu god Aryaman, and he has much the same characteristics.

Aishim In the Kabbalah, the Aishim are found as an order of angels. Their name means 'the flames' and derives from Psalm 104:4 'who maketh his angels spirits, his ministers a flaming fire'. People exploring the internet should also be warned that the name has been used for an adult computer game. There is some confusion between the name Aishim and the ISHIM, despite the fact that one is flame and the other ice.

Ajel The angel that rules the third degree of Leo under OL, according to the *Lemegeton.*

Aker One of the nine 'angels who are over the consummation', in other words at the end of the world, in the Greek *Apocalypse of Ezra.*

Akhshti YAZAD (Zoroastrian angel) personifying peace.

Akriel Generally considered an angel who is invoked in cases of infertility and, as a secondary function, against imbecility. From this, recent angelologists have developed the more positive view that Akriel is an angel who inspires intellectual achievements and improves memory.

Alachuc see DARDARIEL

Aladiah In modern angelology, this is the GUARDIAN ANGEL of those born under Taurus between 6 and 10 May, who is considered an angel of renewal. This means he is supportive of those who want to let go of the past and start all over again, finding new opportunities. He also helps healing in oneself and others. He is also one of the seventy-two SHEMHAMPHORAE angels who bear a mystic name of God.

Alael, **Ahiel** An angel presiding over Thursday, the day of Jove, according to Sloane manuscript *Book of Raziel.*

Alaphar see DARDARIEL

Alapion An angel of the element earth, under the planet Cocab (Mercury), to be invoked when working under this planet, according to the Sloane manuscript *Book of Raziel*.

Alatiel An angel of the element water, under the planet Cocab (Mercury), to be invoked when working under this planet, according to the Sloane manuscript *Book of Raziel*. He may be related to **Alat**, an angel who stands guard in the seventh heaven.

Albedagryn According to the Sloane manuscript *Book of Raziel*, this is one of the GUARDIAN ANGELS of Sunday (Solis) who should be invoked to aid works started on that day. He is **Elbedagrin** in the *Liber Juratus*.

Albion's Angel The poet, artist and mystic William Blake (1757–1827) had his own ideas about the nature of angels and the Divine, and expressed many of them in his works. The Angel of Albion (Albion is an old name for Britain) appears in a picture *Breach in the City – in the Morning after Battle* which is in the front of his book *Visions of the Daughters of Albion*.

Alfrael see ORIEL

Alga An angel whose name is invoked in magic rites. It is also one of the many names of God, being the first letter of the Hebrew 'Thou art mighty for ever'. The word can be inscribed on the blade of a magician's sword and on other magical instruments. In Kabbalah, Alga is an angel of the Seal invoked in conjurations of the Reed.

Al-Harith see IBLIS

Alimiel According to the *Lemegeton*, this is an angel who is invoked for fertility in animals, plants and women.

Alimon In magical rites Alimon, with his assistants **Tafti** and **Reivtip**, are invoked for protection from sharp instruments, gunshot and other weapons of war. In the form **Almyon** in the *Liber Juratus* and the Sloane manuscript *Book of Raziel* he is one of the angels presiding over Saturday, the day of Saturn or Sabat, who must be invoked in a state of purity if he is to help you.

Alisaf, **Alysaf** An angel of the eighth lunar month according to the *Liber Juratus* and the Sloane manuscript *Book of Raziel*, which says that if they are named 'in each thing that thou wilt do … thou shalt profit'.

Alkanosts In Russian folklore, Alkanosts are spirits, sometimes described as angels, with birds' bodies and the heads of beautiful women. They are reminiscent of the sirens of Greek myth, and in many accounts behave in the same way, tempting men to their doom. They can, however, be more benign. In the nineteenth-century Russian composer Rimsky-Korsakov's late opera *The Legend of the Invisible City of Kiezh and the Maiden Fevronia*, Alkanost and Sirin feature as nature spirits who take the soul of the dying Fevronia to the city she has saved from destruction for a spiritual marriage with her betrothed.

Al-Khidr see GREEN MAN

Almarizel, **Almariziel**, **Almas** see BARIEL

Almemel A water angel under Sabaday (Saturn), to be invoked when working under this planet, according to the

Sloane manuscript *Book of Raziel*.

Almodar see TARTYS

Almonoyz see SERQUANICH

Almux An angel of the third lunar month according to the Sloane manuscript *Book of Raziel*, whose naming brings benefits. The name appears as **Almur** in the *Liber Juratus*.

Alscini An angel of the south of first heaven in the Sloane manuscript *Book of Raziel*.

Alserin, **Alseyryn** An angel presiding over Friday, the day of Venus, according to the *Liber Juratus* and the Sloane manuscript *Book of Raziel*.

Alsfiton, **Alfyton** This is one of the angels presiding over Saturday, the day of Saturn or Sabat, according to the *Liber Juratus* and the Sloane manuscript *Book of Raziel*. If invoked appropriately and in a state of purity, he will aid you.

Alson An angel of the eighth lunar month according to the *Liber Juratus* and the Sloane manuscript *Book of Raziel*, which says that if named 'in each thing that thou wilt do … thou shalt profit'.

Altim, **Altym** One of the angels of the seventh lunar month according to the *Liber Juratus* and the Sloane manuscript *Book of Raziel*.

Alzeyeil, **Alzeyeyll** An angel presiding over Friday, the day of Venus, according to the *Liber Juratus* and the Sloane manuscript *Book of Raziel*.

Amael An angel of hope and a PRINCI-PALITY who resides in the third heaven. This angel is particularly popular with spiritualists and those interested in the paranormal. In the *Liber Juratus* he is the ruling angel of Venus.

Amahraspandan see AMESHA SPENTAS

Amalym see OSMADIEL

Amantuliel An angel of the fifth lunar month according to the Sloane manuscript *Book of Raziel*, who if invoked brings benefits.

Amarahspands see AMESHA SPENTAS

Amariel, **Amaryel** The angel with power over the third month according to the *Liber Juratus* and the Sloane manuscript *Book of Raziel*, through whose power a man may know his future.

Amaros see ARMAROS

Amator In *The Key of Solomon*, an angel whose name is invoked when the master is putting on the white linen vestments of powers before practising magic.

Ambayerin, **Ambayeyryn** An angel presiding over Friday, the day of Venus, according to the *Liber Juratus* and the Sloane manuscript *Book of Raziel*.

Ambriel Ambriel is the angel of the month of May or Gemini. According to which text you use, he is either the chief officer of the twelfth hour of the night or a subordinate one under SARANDIEL. He is invoked to ward against evil and, in the Kabbalah, he is invoked for conjuring under the seventh seal of

Mars. The name may also be found as **Amrael**, who appears as an angel of the fourth lunar month in the Sloane manuscript *Book of Raziel* and in the *Liber Juratus*.

Amdalycyn, **Amdalysyn** According to the the *Liber Juratus* and the Sloane manuscript *Book of Raziel*, this is one of the GUARDIAN ANGELS with special care of Monday (Luna) who should be invoked to aid works started on that day.

Ameinyn, **Aneynyn** One of the angels of Wednesday, the day of Mercury, according to Sloane manuscript *Book of Raziel* and the *Liber Juratus*.

Amelson see NARCORIEL

Ameniel see SAMAEL

Amerany see SABRATHAN

Ameratat The name of this Zoroastrian AMESHA SPENTA, who is also found as **Amordad**, **Amurdad** or **Amoordad**, means 'immortality'. In modern Persian it is shortened to **Mordad** (which is also the name of a month), a contradiction in terms since this means 'death', the 'a' in front of the full form of the name making it negative, thus 'deathless'. She presided over the plant life of the earth with its powers of regeneration. She is closely linked to HAURVATAT, and together they represent the completion of human development and the final achievement of our life on earth. Indeed, so closely have Ameratat and Haurvatat been linked that they have been called twins, for it is taught that it is only through the wholeness of Haurvatat that immortality can be achieved. It is thought that the name of

the Muslim angel Marut (see HARUT AND MARUT) may be derived from her. The Persian fifth month, Mordad or **Murdad**, runs from 23 July to 22 August, and her name is also given to the seventh day of the month.

Amesha Spentas This term translates as 'Beneficent Immortals' and in Zoroastrianism these are the highest spiritual beings created by **Ahura Mazda** (also called **Ohrmazd** or **Ormazd**), the Supreme Being. They are thus usually equated with ARCHANGELS, although more strictly they should be seen as personifications of aspects of the divinity, and of human virtues to aspire to. They are VOHU MANO, ASHA VAHISHTA, KHSHATHRA VAIRYA, SPENTA ARMAITI, HAURVATAT and AMERETAT, and with Ahura Mazda, the Lord of wisdom, they form the seven Holy Immortals that protected the first seven creations when the material world was made. They are respectively the protectors of animals, fire, sky, waters, earth and plants. The first three are masculine as these are regarded as masculine elements; the second three are feminine as they rule over female elements, although each rules over moral and spiritual planes as well as aspects of the physical world. (See individual entries for more details.) Each Amesha Spenta has an eternal arch-enemy in the **Daevas** (demons, see under DEVA) headed by **Ahriman** (the antagonist of Ahura Mazda). Amesha Spenta is the form of the name in the original Avestan writings, but in the later Pahlavi writing it becomes **Amahraspandan** or **Amarahspands**. Each Amesha Spenta has a month of the Persian calendar named after him or her.

Ameyl, **Amayl** According to the *Liber Juratus* and the Sloane manuscript *Book of Raziel* this is one of the GUARDIAN ANGELS of Sunday (Solis), who should be invoked to aid works started on that day. **Ammiel**, subordinate to MENDRION, angel of the seventh hour, is probably the same.

Amides In *The Key of Solomon*, *Lemegeton* and *Heptameron*, an angel whose name is invoked when the master is putting on the white linen vestments of powers before practising magic.

Amiol, **Amyel** One of the angels of Wednesday, the day of Mercury, according to the Sloane manuscript *Book of Raziel* and the *Liber Juratus*.

Ammiel see MENDRION

Amneal, **Aumeal** One of the angels of Wednesday, the day of Mercury, according to the *Liber Juratus* and the Sloane manuscript *Book of Raziel*.

Amnediel A MOON ANGEL who rules the eighth mansion of the moon in Cancer. He encourages love and friendship and good feeling among travellers. He drives away mice and confirms the imprisonment of captives.

Amnixiel A MOON ANGEL who rules the twenty-eighth mansion of the moon in Pisces. He benefits harvests and merchants, but causes the loss of treasure. He helps keep travellers safe in dangerous places, brings joy to the married and strengthens prisons. However, some list him among the FALLEN ANGELS.

Amonazy see ZAAZENACH

Amor In *The Key of Solomon*, an angel whose name is invoked when the master is putting on the white linen vestments of powers before practising magic.

Amordad, **Amoordad**, **Amurdad** see AMERTAT

Amrael see AMBRIEL

Amriel see SERQUANICH

Amurael An angel of the element earth, under the planet Noga (Venus), to be invoked when working under this planet, according to the Sloane manuscript *Book of Raziel*.

Amutiel A MOON ANGEL who rules the nineteenth mansion of the moon in Scorpio. He is a destructive force, for he supports the sacking of towns, causes refugees and supports the destruction of seamen and captives.

Amyel In the *Liber Juratus* and the Sloane manuscript *Book of Raziel*, an angel of the thirteenth lunar month (March). If invoked in the relevant month, he will ensure success in your enterprise. He is also described as the angel of Thursday, the day of Jupiter.

Amynyel In the Sloane manuscript *Book of Raziel* an angel with power over fire and flame.

Amyter, **Amasya** An angel of the fifth lunar month according to the *Liber Juratus* and the Sloane manuscript *Book of Raziel*, who if invoked brings benefits.

Anachiel One of the angels whose name is used in the Third Pentacle of Saturn, 'good for use at night when thou invokest the Spirits of the nature of Saturn' in *The Key of Solomon*. The name was used by the American poet Longfellow for the angel of Saturn in the first edition of his *The Golden Legend* in 1851, but in later editions he used the name **Orifel**.

Anael, **Anafiel** see HANIEL

Anaghra Raocha Also known as **Anagranand Aneran**, this YAZAD (Zoroastrian angel) is a personification of the 'endless light', roughly equating to the Zoroastrian heaven. The thirtieth day of the month in the Zoroastrian religious calendar is named after him.

Anahid see HARUT AND MARUT

Anahita see ABAN

Anakim see NEPHILIM

Ananchel, **Ananehel** By tradition, Ananchel is supposed to be an angel sent by God to make Esther attractive to the king of the Persians. The biblical *Book of Esther* tells how Esther, taken as a wife by the king to replace his disobedient wife Vashti, was able to save the Jews in exile in Persia from a plot to exterminate them.

Ananel One of the GRIGORI, 'a chief of ten', according to *1 Enoch* 6.

Anapiel YHWH, **Anafiel**, **Anapel**, **Anaphiel**, **Aniel**, **Aniy(y)el** see HANIEL

Anapion see MENDRION

Anauel An angel who protects businessmen, commerce and bankers. As the GUARDIAN ANGEL of those born between

31 January and 4 February he is considered an angel of coordination, who protects from accidents and illness, reinforces intelligence and memory and supports communicators.

Anaya An angel of the first lunar month according to the *Liber Juratus* and the Sloane manuscript *Book of Raziel*.

Anayenyn, **Anaenym** According to the the *Liber Juratus* and the Sloane manuscript *Book of Raziel*, this is one of the GUARDIAN ANGELS with special care of Monday (Luna) who should be invoked to aid works started on that day.

Anazachia One of the angels whose name is used in the Third Pentacle of Saturn, 'good for use at night when thou invokest the Spirits of the nature of Saturn' in *The Key of Solomon*.

Ancarilyn One of the angels of Wednesday, the day of Mercury, according to the Sloane manuscript *Book of Raziel*. Confusion between 'n' and 'u' and 'c' and 't', common between the two manuscripts, means the name is **Autarylyn** in the *Liber Juratus*.

Ancason An angel of the first lunar month according to the Sloane manuscript *Book of Raziel*. At some point 'n' and 'ri' have become confused, and the name appears as **Aricasom** in the *Liber Juratus*.

Ancuyel An angel presiding over Thursday, the day of Jove, according to Sloane manuscript *Book of Raziel*. The list of Thursday angels differs significantly between *Raziel* and *Juratus*, but the equivalent angel in *Liber Juratus* seems to be **Anenyel**.

Andas An angel of the third lunar month according to the *Liber Juratus* and the Sloane manuscript *Book of Raziel*, whose naming brings benefits. In other writings Andas is an attendant on **Varcan**, who rules the angels of the air on Sunday.

Anebynnyl According to the Sloane manuscript *Book of Raziel*, this is one of the GUARDIAN ANGELS of Sunday (Solis) who should be invoked to aid works started on that day.

Aneran see ANAGHRA RAOCHA

Angel of Death The concept of a spirit that attends the dying person has a long history. The spirit of death can be terrible, especially when bringing mass death, or kindly, helping the sick and elderly to make a good death and easing the soul into the next life. Indeed, some have ascribed this kindly role of angel of death to the GUARDIAN ANGEL. In the *Testament of Solomon* the angel of death is identified by the Greek term *kosmokratores*, 'world rulers', or *kosmokratores tou skotous*, 'world rulers of darkness'. Kosmokratores were originally Greek spirits who control parts of the cosmos, but Hellenised Rabbis adopted the term to refer to evil spirits, particularly the angel of death. THANATOS is the embodiment of death in Greek tradition. A further Greek concept linked with the Angel of Death is the PSYCHOPOMP, literally 'conductor or guide of the soul'. The psychopomp guides the soul to its fate. In the Religions of the Book this is usually to some form of heaven or hell, depending on their behaviour on earth. In the pagan religions the most common psychopomp was CHARON for the

Greeks or Romans, although HERMES and even Apollo could have the same role, while the best-known psychopomp of the Egyptians was Anubis. The role of the angel of death can be divided up into four main aspects. Taking the souls from the body; judging it; leading it to its fate; and guarding it in the afterlife. MICHAEL is the most prominent of the angels who lead the souls of the dead to the afterlife and later to their fate, although RAPHAEL is also given this role at times. He is also one who weighs in the balance, although this duty is given to many other angels, such as DOKIEL and PURIEL. In Zorastrianism MITHRA is one of the judges of the dead and RASHN weighs souls. As a fierce and punishing force the angel of death is sometimes identified as SAMAEL, elsewhere as ABADDON, or APH among others. In Islam ISRAFIL is the main angel of death, but there is also a separate class of Angels of Death (see under MALAIK), and MUNKIR AND NAKIR judge those in the tomb. See also under ANGELS OF DESTRUCTION, ANGELS OF PUNISHMENT, ANGELS OF TORMENT.

Angel of Justice see ANGEL OF LOVE

Angel of Love According to Jewish legend, as an example to Mankind to take advice from others, however exalted a person might be, God consulted the angels about the creation of Mankind. The Angel of Love supported the idea, because Mankind would be affectionate and loving. The **Angel of Truth** was against it, because Man would be full of lies. For this, God cast him down to earth. When the other angels objected to this, God said, 'Truth will spring back out of the earth.' The **Angel of Justice** favoured the creation of Mankind, so that justice could be practised on the earth, but the **Angel of Peace** objected on the grounds that Man would be quarrelsome.

Angel of Peace see ANGEL OF LOVE

Angels As a class in the hierarchy of angels, as opposed to a general term, angels are the lowest rank of angels, the furthest from God in the surrounding choirs, and thus the ones who can most easily interact with man. In various sources their number is said to be so vast as to be infinite. Although we are so familiar with the depiction of angels as winged figures with halos that it is difficult to envisage them in any other form, in the Bible they are nearly always described as looking like ordinary men. Indeed, there are a number of passages where theologians debate as to whether the 'man' should be interpreted as literally a man, an angel or as a manifestation of God Himself. This is further aggravated by the fact that the word for angel, *mal'ak* in Hebrew, *angelos* in Greek, both meaning 'messenger', can be and is used literally of a person bearing a message. Although referred to frequently in the Bible, very few angels are actually named there. Angels perform many different functions. Angels act as divine agents, execute judgement, lead, protect and heal, and intercede with God on behalf of humans. One of the primary functions of angels is to act as GUARDIAN ANGELS. Although some would like to see these as a separate class of angel, many are emphatic that they do not constitute a separate choir. Angels in Islam do not fit into the same sort of hierarchy as in Judeo-Christianity, but perform much the same functions. For angels as a

general term see the Introduction.

Angels of the Animosities see
MASTEMA

Angels of Darkness Term used of
FALLEN ANGELS in the *Key of Solomon* and elsewhere.

Angels of Destruction In Jewish tradition the role of these angels is to punish the wicked in the world and to be warders of the souls in hell. The tortures they inflict on these souls are to purify them. The most famous instance of their role as punishing angels is in Exodus 12 when the first-born of the Egyptians are destroyed, but those of the Israelites saved. In MERKABAH literature, Angels of Destruction sometimes try to stop the visionary from seeing his vision of the heavens. Some say the Angels of Destruction are confined at the far end of the heavens, from which they may never stir. Thus their activities are curtailed, while the ANGELS OF MERCY encircle the Throne of God. Others locate Angels of Destruction on the fifth earth, guarding the souls of the wicked in Sheol. There they beat the wicked with fiery scourges. In one tradition, when judgement is given in the great court of heaven the Angels of Destruction go out with the unsheathed sword of God to execute judgement on the wicked. There are 12,000 Angels of Destruction, ruled by Kemuel, or Qemuel (see under CAMAEL) in many sources, although others number them at 40,000 or 90,000. *3 Enoch* gives their chief as SIMKIEL, while other Angels of Destruction have been named as URIEL, HARBONAH, AZRIEL, APH, KOLAZONTA, HEMAH and ZAAPIEL. Sometimes the idea of the Angel of

Destruction is expressed in terms of a baleful star.

Angels of the Face Angels who are close to the presence of the Lord and often called or conflated with ANGELS OF THE PRESENCE. The angels most frequently given this title are METATRON, MICHAEL, JAHOEL, SURIEL, Yefehfiah (see under YEPIPYAH), ZAGZAGAEL and URIEL. Sometimes there is only one Angel of the Face. In Jewish legend there is a story that on the second day of Creation, God was angered when some of the waters refused to be parted from the dry land. He summoned the Angel of the Face and ordered him to destroy the newly made earth. The angel opened his eyes wide, and scorching fires and thick clouds rolled forth from them. However, the angel persuaded God to relent, and Creation continued.

Angels of Mercy In Jewish tradition, the Angels of Mercy have immediate access to the Throne of God (compare ANGELS OF DESTRUCTION). Among those named as Angels of Mercy are UZZIEL, RAHMIEL, RACHMIEL, GABRIEL, MICHAEL, **Zadkiel** (see SACHIEL) and ZEHANPURYU. In one Islamic tradition, after a person is buried, Angels of Mercy come for the soul of believers and take them from the grave to be birds in the trees of paradise. The souls will be united with the bodies at the resurrection. Sometimes these angels are named as MUNKA AND NAKIR. The souls of the unbelievers are taken by the ANGELS OF PUNISHMENT.

Angels of Mons see MONS, ANGELS OF

Angels of Paradise According to *2 Enoch*, paradise is found in the third heaven, and is the place where the Lord goes to rest. This garden is guarded by 300 bright angels. When a just man appears before the gates of paradise, the clothes in which he was buried are taken off him, and Angels of Paradise array him in seven garments of clouds of glory, and place upon his head two crowns. They utter praises before him and say to him, 'Go thy way, and eat thy bread with joy.' And they lead him to a place full of rivers, surrounded by 800 kinds of roses and myrtles. Particular angels who have been named in association with paradise include GABRIEL, JOHIEL, MICHAEL, SHAMSHIEL, ZEPHON and ZOTIEL.

Angels of the Presence and Angels of Sanctification These are the two senior classes of angels in the *Book of Jubilees*, written in the second century BC. This text also lists a number of nature angels: the angels of the spirit of fire; of the spirits of the winds; of the spirit of the clouds and darkness and snow and hail and frost; of the resoundings and thunder and lightning; of the spirits of cold and heat and winter and springtime and harvest and summer; and of the spirits of all his creatures which are in heaven and earth. The author of *Jubilees* does not include any of the more familiar ranks of angels, nor is he interested in names. Even when writing of the GRIGORI he does not name them. He names only one FALLEN ANGEL, MASTEMA. On the other hand, he does give some more unusual information about angels, such as the fact that they are born circumcised, so are able to join in all the rites of Israel. Some authorities say there are twelve Angels of the Presence, others give the number as seventy, while others say that they were expelled from heaven for revealing God's purpose to Mankind. The concept of Angels of the Presence, also called Princes of the Presence, seems to come from the way in which the Bible gives special figurative treatment to the concept of the Presence of God, which later developed into the concept of special angels. At first, MICHAEL and/or METATRON were given the title of the particular Angel of the Presence, but this title was later transferred to the ARCHANGEL PENUEL. Other angels who have been given the title are ASTANPHAEUS, JAHOEL, **Phanuel** (see PHANAEL), SABAOTH, SANDALPHON, SARAQAEL, SURIEL, URIEL, YEPIPYAH, ZAGZAGAEL. There is little to distinguish Angels of the Presence from those of Sanctification, and the same names can occur in lists of both.

Angels of Punishment In a process known as the Punishment of the Tomb (*Adhab al-Kabr*) in Islamic tradition, the souls of the dead are questioned in the grave as to their faith. The virtuous believer is received by the ANGELS OF MERCY, but the Angels of Punishment haul the faithless off to hell where they are beaten with iron whips which cause flames.

Angels of Sanctification see ANGELS OF THE PRESENCE

Angels of the Sun In *2 Enoch* 11 we are told that the course of the sun and moon are in the fourth heaven. 'And by day fifteen myriads of angels attend it, and by night a thousand … six-winged ones issue with the angels before the sun's wheel into the fiery flames, and a hundred angels kindle the sun and set it alight.' Ginzberg tells us that ninety-six angels accompany the sun on his daily journey, in relays of eight every hour, two to the left of him, and two to the right, two before and two behind. Strong as he is, he could complete his course from south to north in a single instant, but 365 angels restrain him by means of as many grappling irons. Every day one loosens his hold, and the sun must thus spend 365 days on his course. The progress of the sun in his circuit is an uninterrupted song of praise to God. And this song alone makes his motion possible. Therefore, when Joshua wanted to bid the sun stand still, he had to command silence. His song of praise hushed, the sun stood still. *The Zohar* gives a different view of how the sun functions, saying that every dawn the angel who rules the sun uses the power of the holy name which is inscribed on his forehead to open the windows of heaven. There are a number of angels associated with the sun, including RAPHAEL, MICHAEL and GALGALIEL.

Angels of Torment In the third heaven is both paradise and a place of torment. *2 Enoch* tells of a vision in which the narrator is led by two angels to the northern side of heaven where he is shown a terrible place. It is dark except for 'murky fire constantly flaming aloft, and there is a fiery river coming forth, and that whole place is everywhere fire, and everywhere there is frost and ice, thirst and shivering, while the bonds are very cruel, and the angels fearful and merciless, bearing angry weapons, merciless torture.' Enoch is told that this is the place prepared for sinners.

Angel of Truth see ANGEL OF LOVE

Angels, Creation of In Jewish tradition, angels were created on the second day, after the basic creation of the universe, so that men could be sure that they had not helped God in the creation of the universe, and God was the sole creator. A more detailed account of the Creation of the Angels is found in *2 Enoch* 29 where God tells Enoch that on the second day, 'For all my own heavens I shaped a shape from the fiery substance. My eye looked at the solid and very hard rock. And from the flash of my eye I took the marvellous substance of lightning, both fire in water and water in fire; neither does this one extinguish that one, nor does that one dry out this one. That is why lightning is sharper and brighter than the shining of the sun, and softer than water, more solid that the hardest rock. And from the rock I cut off a great fire, and from the fire I created the ranks of the bodiless armies – ten myriad angels – and their weapons are fiery and their clothes are burning flames. And I gave orders that each should stand in his own rank.' In Jewish myth, water is the prime element from which creation emerged ('And the Spirit of God moved upon the face of the waters' says Genesis 1:2), but the Chaldeans believed that fire was the source of everything, which may explain the Creation of Angels from fire. Alternatively, the image here may be of angels being sparked from the rock, just as fire can be created by making sparks with flints. The view of the Creation of Angels in Islam is rather different, for there, tradition says that angels were created from light, while the DJINN were created from fire. Western Christianity tends to think of angels in terms of light as well.

Angels, Fall of the There are two distinct traditions of the Fall of the Angels. While there is no story about angels being expelled from heaven in the Old Testament, it is a frequent theme in non-Bible religious writing. In one tradition, the angels are the sons of God who look upon the daughters of men and find them irresistible and so fall, as in Genesis 6. These are the WATCHERS or GRIGORI, and in many accounts their sins are not so much sexual as imparting knowledge to Mankind, much as Prometheus does in Greek legend. The leader of the Grigori is given various names including AZAZEL, MASTEMA and SEMYAZA. The theme of angels who cannot resist the attraction of women is also found in Islam, where HARUT AND MARUT are exposed to the sort of trials that Mankind meet, and fail miserably. Another story is of an angel who considers he could be higher than God, and tries to usurp his place. This is found in *2 Enoch* 29, 'But one of the order of the archangels deviated, together with the division that was under his authority. He thought up the impossible idea, that he might place his throne higher than the clouds which are above the earth, and that he might become equal to my power. And I hurled him out from the height, together with his angels. And he was flying around in the air, ceaselessly above the Bottomless.' This in Enoch takes place on the second day of creation, although in Byzantine traditions SATAN's rebellion took place on the fourth day. In Christian doctrine the tradition of the angel who tried to set himself above God was combined with the passage in Isaiah 14:12, 'How art thou fallen from heaven, O Lucifer, son of the morning! How art thou cut down to the ground, which did weaken the nations!' Here 'Lucifer' means 'light-bringer' (that is, the morning star) and the passage is usually interpreted as referring to the fall of Nebudnezzar. However, in the past it was combined with the tradition of the arrogant angel, and Lucifer became a synonym for Satan. Much energy has been spent identifying which choir the angels who fell belonged to, and how many (anything up to a third of the angels, with numbers given from 200 to 133,306,668) fell. The themes of angels seduced by the wonders of being able to experience the senses of Mankind, and of the rebel angel, have been popular with writers. Satan's rebelling and fall was written up in poetry as early as the ninth century in Anglo-Saxon verse. And of course, one of the greatest works of literature on angels, Milton's *Paradise Lost* (1667), deals with this topic. Islam has no such stories, as obedience is held to be an essential quality of angels, and they are incapable of going against God's will. Rebellion is found only among the DJINN, and in IBLIS in particular.

Angels, Nature of Accounts of the nature of angels vary vastly from culture to culture and age to age. So wide is the range of ideas that it could fill a whole book by itself and it is impossible to go into it in any depth in this sort of book. However, a brief account can be given here. First, it is important to realise that our modern, Western image of angels, at least in popular culture, is very different from early accounts. We tend to portray angels as either somewhat effete humans – willowy, sexually ambiguous but beautiful, dressed in robes, with colourful wings; or as shimmering manifestations of light. Alternatively, they are shown as chubby, winged babies (PUTTI). These ideas come principally from classical art and the way spirits such as NIKE, EROS or THANATOS were shown. In earlier times angels were not necessarily humanoid – see the HAYYOT and CHERUBIM. They were often of vast size, described as large enough to stretch from earth to heaven, or with wings that cover the sky. They could be made from flame, and have multiple wings and eyes. Sometimes we find interesting evidence in texts as to how angels were perceived. They are swift, for *2 Enoch* 30 says Man's intelligence is created from the swiftness of the angels. Ginzberg, summarising Jewish legends, says, 'The angels that are fashioned from fire have forms of fire, but only so long as they remain in heaven. When they descend to earth, to do the bidding of God here below, either they are changed into wind, or they assume the guise of men. There are ten ranks or degrees among the angels. The ministering angels, those who come in contact with the sublunary world, now repair to their chambers to take their purification bath. They dive into a stream of fire and flame 7 times, and 365 times they examine themselves carefully, to make sure that no taint clings to their bodies. Only then they feel privileged to mount the fiery ladder and join the angels of the seventh heaven, and surround the throne of God with Hashmal and all the holy Hayyot. Adorned with millions of fiery crowns, arrayed in fiery garments, all the angels in unison, in the same words, and with the same melody, intone songs of praise to God.' Turning to sixteenth-century England, the Sloane manuscript

Book of Raziel tells us (in my modernised version of the text) 'Hermes [Trismagismus] said that the spirits which appear in this world be these. Some truly be heavenly and the prophet calls them Angels, and they be bright and clear as flame or a star as we have said. Others be of the air and of many colours green bright and other such and of many shapes. And others be fiery and they be bright and red. And others be watery and they be white and as bright as tin or iron burnished or quicksilver. Others be that come near to men and be like to a white cloud or to a white cloth. And others be dark and dim and of various forms which are called Devils.' It is claimed that angels do not eat human food, even when they appear to. When MICHAEL, GABRIEL and RAPHAEL visited Abraham and Sarah (Genesis 18) in the form of three men, and appeared to eat with them, the food was really consumed by heavenly fire. Angels are not always shown as friendly towards Mankind. Many versions of the fall of Satan-figures are linked to his refusal to bow down to Adam; there are stories of a general hostility towards the creation of Mankind by angels, and many mystic texts have angel figures actively trying to prevent the soul entering heaven, and even trying to stop the Law being revealed to Moses.

Angra Mainya see DEVAS, VOHU MANU

Anhael An angel of the west of the fifth heaven in the Sloane manuscript *Book of Raziel*.

Aniel, **Aniyel**, **Aniyyel** see HANIEL

Animistics Some say that Animistics are an order of angel, others that they are somewhere halfway between angel and human. They are ISSIM, a Hebrew word meaning 'nobles, lords, princes', and if not angels are at least above those on the earth. Henry Cornelius Agrippa, writing on *Ceremonial Magic,* says that they are blessed souls, inferior to the hierarchies of angels, but 'have their influence on the sons of men, and give knowledge and the wonderful under-standing of things'. METATRON is said to rule the Animistics.

Anitor In *The Key of Solomon* and other texts, an angel whose name is invoked when the master is putting on the white linen vestments of power before practising magic.

Anixiel, **Amixiel** A MOON ANGEL who rules the third mansion of the moon in Aries. He supports sailors, hunters and alchemists.

Anmael A leader of the FALLEN ANGELS, who may be identical with SEMYAZA, as he is said to have made the same bargain to reveal the true name of God to a woman in return for sexual favours.

Anmanineylyn, **Amnanyneylyn** In the *Liber Juratus* and the Sloane manuscript *Book of Raziel* this is one of the GUARDIAN ANGELS with special care of Monday (Luna) who should be invoked to aid works started on that day.

Anpiel Anpiel is the GUARDIAN ANGEL of birds. He resides in the sixth heaven, where he is also involved in the trans-mission of prayers from earth to heaven. Ginzberg gives his name as the angel who takes Enoch to heaven.

Anqnihim According to the Sloane

manuscript *Book of Raziel*, this is one of the GUARDIAN ANGELS of Sunday (Solis).

Anrylin An angel presiding over Friday, the day of Venus, according to Sloane manuscript *Book of Raziel*. In the *Liber Juratus* it appears as **Ourylyn**.

Ansiel Ansiel means 'the constrainer' and his name is invoked in magic against forgetting and stupidity.

Ansuil see AUSIUL

Antquiel, **Antquyel** An angel presiding over Thursday, the day of Jove, according to the *Liber Juratus* and the Sloane manuscript *Book of Raziel*.

Anulus An angel of the west of the second heaven in the Sloane manuscript *Book of Raziel*.

Anunna, **Anunnaku** Although Gustav Davidson, quoting a work on Chaldean Magic, says of Anunna, 'in Akkadian theology, the anunna are angels who are almost always terrestrial spirits', others say that Anunna is the Sumerian name for the sky and earth gods, the assembly of the high gods, and especially for the deities of a local pantheon. The name means 'those of princely seed'. The Akkadian term is **Anunnaku**, who are the gods of the underworld and judge the dead, although in many ways there are similar to the Anunna. The name means 'offspring of Anu'. In this, their role is closer to angels, for Anu is the Mesopotamian god of the firmament, who has many similarities with the God of Genesis. They thus effectively share a name with the BENE ELIM whose name means 'sons of God'.

Anush According to *Yalkut Reubeni* of 1660, Anush, **Aebel** and **Shetel** were three MINISTERING ANGELS whose function was to serve Adam, roasting his meat and cooling his wine.

Aol see AEL, IAOEL

Ap, **Apas**, **Api** see ABAN

Apam Napat In Zoroastrianism, Apam Napat is the male YAZAD (angel) of waters (although among Hindus he is regarded as a god). His name means 'son of the waters' and comes from the same root, the Indo-European word for 'cloud, heaven', as the Greek god of the sea, Neptune. He is also called **Ahura Berezant** and **Burz Yazad**.

Aph, **Af** This name means 'anger' in Hebrew, and this angel is the manifestation of Divine Anger. He is often linked with HEMAH, whose name means 'wrath'. Their functions are often linked to the passage in Deuteronomy 9:19, which says, 'For I feared the anger (*ap*) and the rage (*hema*) with which the Lord was enraged against you to destroy you,' although the pairing of these two words, particularly in the context of God's anger against Israel, is so common in the Old Testament as to be close to a cliché. In Jewish tradition, Aph is one of the ANGELS OF PUNISHMENT and governs the death of mortals, while *The Zohar* describes him as one of three angels in Gehena who punish those who commit idolatry, incest and murder. Others have called him one of the ANGELS OF DESTRUCTION. He has a special place in legends of Moses, and Ginzberg tells us that when he returned from exile to Egypt to demand the release of the Israelites,

'Moses was but half-hearted about his mission. He travelled leisurely, thinking: "When I arrive in Egypt and announce to the children of Israel that the end of the term of Egyptian slavery has come, they will say, 'We know very well that our bondage must last four hundred years, and the end is not yet,' but if I were to put this objection before God, He would break out in wrath against me. It is best for me to consume as much time as possible on the way thither." God was ill pleased with Moses for this artifice, and He spake to him, saying, "Joseph prophesied long ago that the oppression of Egypt would endure only two hundred and ten years." For his lack of faith Moses was punished while he was on the road to Egypt. The angels Af and Hemah appeared and swallowed his whole body down to his feet, and they gave him up only after Zipporah, nimble as a bird, circumcised her son Gershom, and touched the feet of her husband with the blood of the circumcision. The reason why their son had remained uncircumcised until then was that Jethro had made the condition, when he consented to the marriage of his daughter with Moses, that the first son of their union should be brought up as a Gentile. When Moses was released by the angels, he attacked them, and he slew Hemah, whose host of angels, however, held their own before the assailant.' Elsewhere, Aph is described as exceedingly tall and made of chains or red and black fire. See also under KEZEF.

Aphael, **Apha** An angel found in certain Coptic Christian texts as an Angel of the Presence of God. The name may well come from the Aramaic word *appa*, a translation of the Hebrew word for 'face', and thus be the equivalent of

the angel PENUEL.

Aphiel The angel that rules the ninth degree of Cancer under CAEL and the ninth degree of Leo under OL, according to the *Lemegeton*. **Apheieyl**, an angel presiding over Friday, the day of Venus, according to Sloane manuscript *Book of Raziel*, is probably an alternative spelling of the same name.

Apollyon see ABADDON

Apparitions In the angelic hierarchy of Robert Fludd, found in his *Utriusque cosmi majoris et minoris historia*, Apparitions, **Acclamations** and **Voices** are the three primary groups of angels.

Appiniel see ABASDARHON

Aquyel see ARAKIEL

Arac An angel of the ninth lunar month according to the *Liber Juratus* and the Sloane manuscript *Book of Raziel*, which says that if they are named 'in each thing that thou wilt do … thou shalt profit'.

Araciel see ARKIEL

Araebel An angel of the sixth hour, serving under **Samil** according to the *Lemegeton*, but in the form **Arabyel**, an angel of the sixth lunar month according to the *Liber Juratus* and the Sloane manuscript *Book of Raziel*, which says that if he and his colleagues are named 'in each thing that thou wilt do … thou shalt profit'.

Arael An angel said in the *Testament of Solomon* to be able to control the demon Sphandor who causes paralysis.

37

It has been suggested that the name may actually be a form of the name URIEL.

Arafit see IFRIT

Arakiba One of the GRIGORI, 'a chief of ten', according to *1 Enoch* 6.

Arakiel, Araqiel, Araquiel, Araciel In the *Sibylline Oracles* Araquiel is one of the five angels (the others being AZAEL, RAMIEL, SAMIEL and URIEL) who lead souls to judgement. However, in Charles' translation of *I Enoch* 8 he is one of the GRIGORI who taught Mankind the 'signs of the earth'. In the more modern translation of *1 Enoch* in Charlesworth's *Pseudepigrapha,* the name appears as **Kokarerel** or in some manuscripts **Kokabel**, and no mention is made of Arakiel. This same work explains 'the signs' as meaning miraculous signs. Two angels found in the Sloane manuscript *Book of Raziel,* **Arariquiel**, an angel of the ninth lunar month and **Aquyel**, both of whom if named 'in each thing that thou wilt do … thou shalt profit', may be the same angel.

Aralim see ERELIM

Aramaiti see SPENTA ARMAITI

Arapiel YHWH, Araphiel One of the great angels in heaven according to *3 Enoch*, a guardian of the second hall of the seventh heaven.

Araqiel, Araquiel see ARAKIEL

Arariel Arariel is seen by some as an ANGEL OF PUNISHMENT and as a warrior, but he is primarily seen as an angel who can cure stupidity. He is also classed by Talmudists as one of the seven angels with dominion over the earth, with a special power over water, who is therefore a bringer of luck to fishermen.

Araton or **Aratron** An OLYMPIC SPIRIT who rules 49 of the 196 provinces, rules the first hour of Saturday and gives true answers. In the Sloane manuscript *Book of Raziel,* he is an angel of the first lunar month.

Arauchiah One of the angels whose name is used in the Third Pentacle of Saturn. 'Good for use at night when thou invokest the Spirits of the nature of Saturn' in *The Key of Solomon.*

Archangels The name means 'chief angels' in Greek and they are, according to Dionysius the Areopagite, the messengers who bear divine decrees. The *Testament of Adam* explains that Archangels are the second order of angels, whose role is to direct the affairs of all creation, with the exception of Mankind who is looked after by the angels. Ginzberg tells us that they encircle the Divine Throne in the form of fiery mountains and flaming hills. They are also in charge of heaven's armies in the battle against hell, and act as supervisors to GUARDIAN ANGELS. The word archangel occurs twice in the New Testament: in Jude 9, where MICHAEL is referred to as the archangel who 'contended with the devil' and in 1 Thessalonians 4:6, where there is a reference to 'the archangel's call' that will come on the day the lord returns from heaven. The only two angels mentioned by name in the main body of the Bible, Michael and GABRIEL are Archangels. RAPHAEL, who features in the *Book of Tobit* (classed by many among the *Apocrypha*) is also an Archangel. These three are considered saints who can intercede for the person praying by the Roman Catholic Church. In Islam, there are four archangels; MIKAL and DJIBRIL are named in the Koran as Archangels, and it is usually assumed that ISRAFIL and IZRAIL are the other two. *1 Enoch* names seven: SURUEL (or URIEL) 'one of the holy angels – for he is of eternity and of trembling'; RAPHAEL, 'one of the holy angels, for he is of the spirits of man'; RAGUEL, 'one of the holy angels who take vengeance for the world and for the luminaries'; MICHAEL, 'one of the holy angels, for he is obedient in his benevolence over the people and the nations'; SARAQAEL, 'one of the holy angels who are set over the spirits of Mankind who sin in the spirit'; GABRIEL, 'one of the holy angels who oversee the garden of Eden, and the serpents, and the cherubim'. Some manuscripts add REMIEL, 'one of the holy angels, whom God set over those who rise' and that these are 'the names of the angels seven', which is often accepted as the traditional number of angels. The Kabbalah considers the Archangels to be METATRON, RAZIEL, TZAPHQIEL, TADQIEL, **Khamael** (SAMAEL), MICHAEL, HANIEL, RAPHAEL, GABRIEL and, to bring the list up to the requisite ten, METATRON again. Each one corresponds to one of the SEFIROTH. **Anael** (HANIEL), BARAKIL, JEHUDIEL, **Orphiel**, PHANAEL, SEALTIEL and ZADKIEL, have also been classed as Archangels.

Archas, **Arkhas**, **Arukhas** The primordial AEON or being from which God made the solid part of the universe according to *2 Enoch* 26. After God has created the heavens from ADOIL, he tells

Enoch, 'I called out a second time into the lowest things, and I said, "Let one of the invisible things come out solid and visible." There came out Arukhas, solid and heavy and very black. And I saw how suitable he was. And I said to him, "Come down low and become solid! And become the foundation of the lowest things!" and he came down and became solid. And he became the foundation of the lowest things. And there is nothing lower than the darkness, except nothing itself.' Although Laurence interpreted the name as 'Spirit of Creation', the same problems of interpretation bedevil this name as those discussed at ADOIL.

Archiel see HANIEL

Archistrategos, **Archstratege** A Greek title meaning 'commander-in-chief of an army', usually given to MICHAEL, often described as 'commander-in-chief of all the regiments of heaven', the angel that leads the troops of heaven against the forces of SATAN. He shares this role with RAPHAEL in the Greek *Apocalypse of Ezra*, where both Michael and Raphael also serve as guides in the vision.

Archon The Greek word *archon* means 'ruler, magistrate', and has been used widely to cover a range of different spiritual beings. In the Greek translation of the Old Testament 'archon' is used to translate thirty-six different Hebrew terms dealing with positions of authority. As a class of angels Archons are equated with AEONS, ARCHANGELS, PRINCIPALITIES (*archai* in Greek) and demons. It is also used in some writings as a term for SATAN, who is *archon ton daimonion* or 'Ruler of the Demons', or

SEMYAZA. In Gnostic texts Archons are rulers of the various heavens, often hostile to the souls that aspire to reach the face of God. They often share names with angels found elsewhere. The Ophians, for example, according to the *Contra Celsum* of Origen (third century AD), named them, in ascending order of heaven, HORAEUS, AILOAEUS, ASTAPHAEUS, ADONAEUS, SABAOTH, IAO and IALDABOATH (these names appear in a wide variety of spellings such as **Oreus, Oraios, Ailoaios, Astaphaios, Adnaeus, Adonais, Jao, Jaldaboath,** depending on which manuscript and which transliteration tradition is used). They can only be passed if the soul can address them by the correct name, recite the correct formula and show them the correct symbol. This seems to derive from the much earlier Babylonian concept of the soul ascending through the seven planets to the god Anu. According to the *Testament of Adam*, Archons control the weather.

Ard see ASHI VANGHUHI

Arda Fravash see FRAVASHIS

Ardiel, Adryel In the *Liber Juratus* and the Sloane manuscript *Book of Raziel*, an angel of the thirteenth lunar month (March). If invoked in the relevant month, he will ensure success in your enterprise.

Ardifiel, Ardesiel A MOON ANGEL who rules the tenth mansion of the moon, in Leo. He supports love and good feeling, strengthens buildings and helps against enemies. Since he shares the same features, he may well be he same angel as ADRIEL.

Arduisur see ABAN

Ardwahisht see ASHA VAHISHTA

Aredvi Sura Anahita see ABAN

Arehanah One of the angels whose name is used in the Fifth Pentacle of Saturn 'which chaseth away the Spirits which guard treasures' in *The Key of Solomon*.

Arel Angel of fire and one of the angels whose name is used in the Seventh Pentacle of the Sun which, 'If any be by chance imprisoned or detained in fetters of iron, at the presence of this Pentacle, which should be engraved in Gold on the day and hour of the Sun, he will be immediately delivered and set at liberty' in *The Key of Solomon*.

Arelim see ERELIM

Arfaniel, Arfanyel In the *Liber Juratus* and the Sloane manuscript *Book of Raziel* an elemental angel with power over the earth.

Arfig An air angel under Sabaday (Saturn), to be invoked when working under this planet, according to the Sloane manuscript *Book of Raziel*.

Aribiriel One of the angels of Wednesday, the day of Mercury, according to Sloane manuscript *Book of Raziel*. He has become **Aryhyryel** in the *Liber Juratus*.

Ariel The name Ariel means 'lion of God'. In angel literature Ariel takes on a wide range of roles, from being one of the chief angels 'of the loveliest form' to a ruler of hell. Thomas Heywood describes him in the *Hierarchy of the Blessed Angels* as one of the seven princes who rule the waters and as 'Earth's great Lord'. Others say he helps RAPHAEL in healing. In Milton's *Paradise Lost* he is a FALLEN ANGEL routed by the faithful ABDIEL. Magic texts show him as a lion-headed angel. He appears in the Sloane manuscript *Book of Raziel* as **Arieil**, one of the GUARDIAN ANGELS of Sunday (Solis) who should be invoked to aid works started on that day. He is also the angel that rules the twelfth degree of Cancer under CAEL and the twelfth degree of Leo under OL, according to the *Lemegeton*. **Aryel**, an angel of the second lunar month in the Sloane manuscript *Book of Raziel*, is presumably the same name. Some people nowadays also identify a female counterpart, **Arielle**. As the guardian angel of those born under Scorpio between 8 and 12 November he is held to be an angel of revelation, who helps foresee the future and discover hidden truths, both worldly and spiritual. He helps the fulfilment of ambitions and effective work and helps towards success in life. Because of the similarity of sound there is some confusion between ANAEL, URIEL and Ariel. The character of Ariel in Shakespeare's *The Tempest* is unlikely to be directly influenced by the angel name, but is more likely a play on 'air, airy', a reflection of the spirit's airy nature.

Arioc, Arioch Arioc is one of the FALLEN ANGELS put to flight by ABDIEL in Milton's *Paradise Lost*. The origin of Arioch seems to be from a character in the Bible. In the Book of Daniel he is a man appointed by Nebuchadnezzar to put the wise men of Babylon to death,

which makes the name a good candidate for a demon. Milton did not originate the name for a fallen angel, for in Thomas Nashe's *Pierce Pennilesse, His Supplication to the Divell* published in 1592, seventy-five years before *Paradise Lost,* he is 'the great Arioch that is termed the spirit of revenge'. The name has been taken up by Michael Moorcock, who uses it in his *Elric* novels as the patron chaos lord of Elric and his ancestors. There is some confusion between this fallen angel and ARIUK, also known as Arioc or Arioch.

Ariuk and Mariuk Angels appointed by God to watch over the descendants of Enoch, according to *1 Enoch*. The name also appears as ARIOC or Arioch, which can cause some confusion.

Arkhas see ARCHAS

Armaiti see SPENTA ARMAITI

Armapy see PAMYEL

Armaqnieyeyl According to the *Liber Juratus* and the Sloane manuscript *Book of Raziel*, this is one of the GUARDIAN ANGELS of Sunday (Solis) who should be invoked to aid works started on that day.

Armariel In the Sloane manuscript *Book of Raziel* an angel with power over water.

Armaros, Amaros One of the GRIGORI, 'a chief of ten', according to *1 Enoch* 7, who taught Mankind 'the resolving of incantations'.

Armen One of the GRIGORI, according to *1 Enoch* 26.

Armiel see DARDARIEL

Armisael Armisael is found in the
Talmud as an angel who aids conception
and helps ease the pain of childbirth.
The latter is done by repeating Psalm 20
nine times, and if this repeatedly proves
ineffective, the angel can be appealed to
directly with 'I conjure you, Armisael,
angel who governs the womb, that you
help this woman and the child in her
body to life and peace. Amen, Amen,
Amen.' To many people, however, the
name is better known in a sinister role
in the Japanese anime television series
Neon Genesis Evangelion first aired in
1995. In this series, based on its creator's
experience of depression and psycho-
therapy, in the near future earth is
invaded by monstrous beings known as
angels, and Armisael is the fastest,
stealthiest and most agile of these.

Armmyel see VATHMIEL

Armosiel see JEFISCHA

Armosy see ORIEL

Arnebiel see SANIEL

Arobolyn, **Arobylyn** An angel
presiding over Friday, the day of Venus,
according to the *Liber Juratus* and the
Sloane manuscript *Book of Raziel*.

Arsabon One of the angels of the
seventh lunar month according to the
Liber Juratus and the Sloane manuscript
Book of Raziel, which says that if they
are named 'in each thing that thou wilt
do … thou shalt profit'.

Arsaferal, **Arsafael** An angel of the
eighth lunar month according to the
Liber Juratus and the Sloane manuscript
Book of Raziel.

Arshishwang see ASHI VANGHUHI

Arshtat, **Ashtad** A female YAZAD personifying rectitude, Arshtat or Ashtad
presides over justice. The twenty-sixth
day of the month in the Zoroastrian
religious calendar is named for her. In
hymns she is invoked together with
RASHNU, the Yazad of the final
judgement as 'The very straight Rashnu
and Arshtat, who further the world,
who augment the world'. She is also
closely associated with AMERETAT.

Artaqifa One of the GRIGORI according
to *1 Enoch*.

Arukhas see ARCHAS

Aryel see ARIEL

Arylin, **Arylyn** According to the *Liber
Juratus* and the Sloane manuscript *Book
of Raziel* this is one of the GUARDIAN
ANGELS with special care of Monday
(Luna) who should be invoked to aid
works started on that day.

Aryor In the Sloane manuscript *Book of
Raziel*, an angel of the tenth lunar
month. If invoked in rites his name will
ensure good results. As so often, there is
confusion between 'c' and 'r' in the manuscripts of *Raziel* and the *Liber Juratus*,
and in the latter it appears as **Acyor**.

Arzaf An angel of the eighth lunar
month according to the *Liber Juratus*
and the Sloane manuscript *Book of
Raziel*.

Asael see AZAEL

Asaf see ASAPH

Asaliah In the Kabbalah Asaliah is an Angel of Justice (see under ANGELS OF TRUTH) and one of the VIRTUES under RAPHAEL. He is also one of the seventy-two SHEMHAMPHORAE. Elsewhere, he is said to be the GUARDIAN ANGEL of those born under Scorpio between 13 and 17 November. In this capacity he reinforces understanding and intellect, clarifying thought and rendering it accurate, and generally reinforces intellectual capacity.

Asaph, **Asaf** An angel with power over water and of the fourth lunar month of the Hebrew calendar, Tammuz. According to *The Zohar*, during the night he leads the hosts of angels who sing hymns to God (HEMAN leads the morning chants and JEDUTHUN the evening ones) He is said to have composed Psalms 50 and 73 through to 83 and to be the father of medicine. He is an angel of the fourth lunar month according to the Sloane manuscript *Book of Raziel*.

Asaphin, **Asaphyn** According to the *Liber Juratus* and the Sloane manuscript *Book of Raziel*, this is one of the angels with special care of Monday (Luna) who should be invoked to aid works started on that day.

Asbeel A leader of the GRIGORI who, in *1 Enoch*, led the others astray by advising them to seduce the daughters of men. The name is interpreted as meaning 'deserter from God'.

Asbogah, **Azbugay YWHW** The angel whose task it is to reward the righteous when they have been judged in the celestial law court according to *3 Enoch*.

He clothes the new arrivals in heaven with righteousness. He is one of the eight great princes of the throne of judgement and ranks even above METATRON. The name, meaning 'strength', is also found as one of the secret names of God. He is invoked for 'healing of all illness and all hurt and all evil spirit'.

Asdon An angel of the first lunar month according to the Sloane manuscript *Book of Raziel*.

Asel The angel that rules the third degree of Gemini under GIEL, according to the *Lemegeton*.

Asha Vahishta Meaning 'Highest Asha', representing ultimate righteousness and truth and justice, this is the AMESHA SPENTA (Zoroastrian archangel) presiding over Asha (a term covering Divine Law, righteousness, justice and many other concepts). He is lord of fire and noontime heat. Asha Vahishta is also known as **Ardwahisht** and **Ordibehesht**. He was the second Amesha Spenta created and is the most prominent of the male Amesha Spentas because he is the principal adversary of the DAEVAS.

Ashi Vanghuhi Meaning 'good blessings, rewards', this is the female YAZAD (Zoroastrian angel) presiding over blessings. She is also known as **Ashishwangh**, **Arshishwang** and **Ard**. The twenty-fifth day of the month in the Zoroastrian religious calendar is named for her. She works in tandem with SPENTA ARMAITI.

Asiel see AZAEL

Asirac In the Sloane manuscript *Book of Raziel*, an angel of the tenth lunar month. If invoked in rites his name will ensure good results. The name is **Asyzat** in the *Liber Juratus,* while **Aslaqwy**, another tenth-month angel appears as **Aslaom.**

Asman YAZAD (Zoroastrian angel) presiding over the sky. The sky was the first of the worldly creations of the God Ohrmazd, followed by water, earth, plants, animals and Mankind.

Asmiel see VEQUANIEL

Aspiramo One of the angels of the seventh lunar month according to the Sloane manuscript *Book of Raziel*. The equivalent in the *Liber Juratus* is **Asyramon.**

Asrael Asrael is the title of the 1888 opera by the Italian composer Alberto Franchetti (1860–1942). In a plot that owes much to Wagner's *Lohengrin* and Bioto's *Mefistofele* this is an epic account of Christian Love, in the person of the angelic nefta and the spirit of evil found in Asrael. **Nefta** loves Asrael and prays to be sent to earth to rescue his soul. After various episodes set in a vaguely medieval world Nefta succeeds. Asrael is also the title of a massive symphony written by the Czech composer Josef Suk and first performed in 1905. The death of close members of his family lies behind it. Asrael is an alternative form of the name AZRAEL.

Asrafil see ISRAFIL

Asroilu YHWH In *3 Enoch,* a mighty angel and 'head of every session of the heavenly academy'. A similarly-named angel, **Asroili'i'el** (where '-el', like YHWH, indicates 'God'), is found in *Hekalot Rabbati.* **Asrieylin**, one of the angels with special care of Monday in the Sloane manuscript *Book of Raziel,* may be another form of the name, particularly as in manuscripts combinations of the letters 'i', 'u' and 'n' are easily confused.

Asron One of many angels who guard the gates of the east wind.

Assiel An angel of healing found in the *Book of Raziel* and elsewhere.

Astagna, Astrgna An angel of the west of the fourth heaven in the Sloane manuscript *Book of Raziel*. In the *Heptameron* and elsewhere he is resident in the fifth heaven and rules on Tuesday.

Astaphaeus, Astanphaeus, Aastaphai, Astaphaios Astaphaeus is one of the seven great ARCHONS or ELOHIM in Gnostic belief, who guards the third gate leading to the AEON of the Archons. Astaphaeus is the Archon of the planet Venus, and the name derives from Astaphe, a goddess whose name and picture is found engraved on Gnostic gem stones and used in magic spells. Astanphaeus, a variant form of the name, is one of the ANGELS OF THE PRESENCE, and an angel of the planet Mercury.

Asteraoth, Astaroth, Asteroth In the *Testament of Solomon* we are told that this is the angel that can thwart the evil star known as Power, who raises up tyrants and topples kings. Surprisingly, this appears to be a form of the name Ashtoreth or Astarte, the Canaanite fertility goddess. The connection may be that Ashtoreth was one of the false gods that Solomon is said to have followed in his old age and been punished for (I Kings 11:5). Astaroth, or Asteroth, appears as a FALLEN ANGEL in a number of books of magic, and as **Astoreth** in *Paradise Lost*. He is said to feel unjustly punished by God, and to believe that he will return one day to heaven. When conjured he is said to manifest in the form of a beautiful angel riding on a dragon and carrying a viper in his right hand. He can be made to give true answers to questions about the past, the present and the future, but his breath is so foul that the magician needs to use his magic ring to protect his face. Asteroth is said to be skilled in the liberal sciences, but to engender laziness. He is also said to be a grand duke in hell, when he acts as a treasurer, and commands forty legions of demons. There is disagreement about his rank before he fell: some say he was one of the SERAPHIM, but others say a prince among the THRONES.

Astrocon see NARCORIEL

Astrofiel see BERATIEL

Asuras Asuras are the nearest thing in Hinduism to FALLEN ANGELS. Although they were once considered gods, in later developments in mythology it was said that as their numbers increased they became proud and jealous of the DEVAS, and fought them. This led to their becoming classed as demons, but if they repent they can become benefactors of Mankind. Asuras are also called **Ahuras**, but the use of this word needs to be carefully distinguished from the use of Ahura in Zoroastrianism where it is used of many of the highest, including **Ahura Mazda** ('Lord Wisdom') the great creator God.

Asymeylyn, **Asymolyn** An angel of the day of Mars (Tuesday) with power over 'red metal' in the *Liber Juratus* and the Sloane manuscript *Book of Raziel*.

Asyriel see OMIEL

Aszre, **Aszrus** An angel of the first lunar month according to the *Liber Juratus* and the Sloane manuscript *Book of Raziel*.

Ataphiel see BARATTIEL

Atar, **Adar** Atar is the YAZAD (Zoroastrian angel) presiding over fire and purity. He is referred to as 'the Son of **Ahura Mazda**' in the *Avesta*, and appears as **Agni** in the Indian *Rig-Veda*. He is one of the most important of all Yazads, and in Avestan mythology he is shown as having a special relationship with the legendary king Takhmorup (Tahmoureth) and with Yima Khshaeta (Jamshid) whom he helps to overcome many obstacles. The name also takes the forms **Atesh** and **Atash**, and as **Azar** has the ninth day of the month and the ninth month of the year (22 November to 21 December) named after him in the Zoroastrian religious calendar.

Atarguniel see ATRUGIEL

Atel In *The Heptameron*, an angel who resides in the fourth heaven and who has dominion over the air and the Lord's Day and who must be invoked from the east.

Atesh see ATAR

Atheniel A MOON ANGEL who rules the twenty-seventh mansion of the moon in Pisces. He increases harvests and income and heals infirmities. However he is also a general cause of mischief, works against buildings, endangers seamen and prolongs prison sentences.

Athiel The angel that rules the eighteenth degree of Cancer under CAEL as well as the eighteenth degree of Leo under OL, according to the *Lemegeton*.

Atliel, Ataliel A MOON ANGEL who rules the fifteenth mansion of the moon in Libra. He helps in the digging of pits and extracting of treasure, but impedes travellers and incites divorce and quarrels and the destruction of buildings and enemies.

Atragon An angel of the east of the fourth heaven in the Sloane manuscript *Book of Raziel*.

Atrugiel YHWH In *3 Enoch*, one of the great princes of heaven. The name is also found as **Atrugiel**, **Atarguniel** and **Atruggiel**.

Attarod see TISHTRYA

Auphanim One of the ten choirs of the Holy Angels, according to the *Key of Solomon*. It is a form of the word OPHANIM.

Aurion This is one of the angels presiding over Saturday, the day of Saturn or Sabat, according to the Sloane manuscript *Book of Raziel*. If they are invoked appropriately and in a state of purity, they will aid you. **Unryon** appears in the same place in the *Liber Juratus*.

Ausiul, Ansuil The angel who rules Aquarius according to the *Lemegeton*.

Authorities A rank of angels who have jurisdiction over the heavenly bodies: the sun, the moon and the stars, according to the *Testament of Adam*. Elsewhere they are equated with other choirs of angels – some say POWERS, some VIRTUES while Dionysius the Areopagite says they are the same as DOMINIONS and St John of Damascus says they rank sixth in the hierarchy, below Powers. The concept of the Authorities comes from several passages in the New Testament where the word authorities (Greek *exousiai*) is used in ways that can be interpreted to mean denizens of heaven.

Avatar (plural **Avatars** or in Sanscrit **Avatara**) In Hinduism avatars (the word comes from the Sanskrit meaning 'descent') are the earthly incarnations of the divine. Since they can act as intermediaries between man and the gods, they perform a function similar to that of angels.

Ayayeylin An angel presiding over Friday, the day of Venus, according to the Sloane manuscript *Book of Raziel*. He is **Mayeylyn** in the *Liber Juratus*.

Aymeylyn, Aymsylyn According to the *Liber Juratus* and the Sloane manuscript *Book of Raziel* this is one of the GUARDIAN ANGELS with special care of Monday (Luna) who should be invoked to aid works started on that day.

Aza see AZZAH

Azael A MOON ANGEL who rules the twenty-fifth mansion of the moon in

Aquarius. Like AMUTIEL he supports besieging of cites and encourages revenge. He destroys enemies and causes divorce, helps in spells against sex and prevents people carrying out their duties. He does, however, help messengers. He needs to be distinguished from the FALLEN ANGEL AZAEL or Aziel.

Azael, **Asael**, **Asiel**, **Aziel** In *3 Enoch*, a trio of angels, UZZAH, AZZAH and Azael oppose Enoch's elevation to METATRON, although when God stands firm, they prostrate themselves to him. They are described as laying charges against Enoch, which associates them with the Satan-figure SAMAEL who is described as 'Prince of the Accusers'. These three are also credited with corrupting Mankind by teaching them sorcery. In *1 Enoch 6* Asael is identified as one of the GRIGORI, 'a chief of ten'. Many aspects of Azael should be identified with AZAZEL, but not everything he does is malign; in the *Testament of Solomon* it is Azael who thwarts and binds the demon Lix Tetrax, who causes destructive winds and whirlwinds, creates divisions among men, starts fires, particularly in fields, and makes households non-functional, particularly in summertime. When he gets the chance he will slither under the corners of houses to gain entry. He also has power over the type of fever that lasts for a day and a half. In *The Zohar,* Azzah and Azael are FALLEN ANGELS who sleep with Naamah, Lamech's daughter, and thereby engender the **Sedim**, Assyrian guardian spirits. The angels are punished by being chained in the desert until Judgement Day. Elsewhere, Azael is said to guard treasure and teach witchcraft. This is said to be so powerful that its

exponents are said to be able to call the sun, moon and stars down from the heavens. (Compare HARUT AND MARUT.)

Azar see ATAR

Azarel This angel appears in *The Key of Solomon,* in the Fifth Pentacle of the Moon, used for destroying enemies and summoning souls from Hades. Since he is used for such dark purposes, it is not unreasonable to associate the name with angels such as AZAEL and AZAZEL.

Azariel A MOON ANGEL who rules the twenty-fourth mansion of the moon in Taurus. He is a disruptive angel, causing quarrels, the destruction of buildings, wells and mines. However, in the Talmud he is the angel governing the waters of the earth.

Azazel, **Azazil** In stories of the GRIGORI in *1 Enoch*, Azazel appears as something of a Prometheus figure, for he taught Mankind the celestial secrets of how to make knives, arms, shields and coats of mail. He showed them metals and how to work them into bracelets and all sorts of trinkets, the use of eye make-up and how to ornament themselves with the rarest and most precious jewels and all sorts of paints, thus introducing Mankind to sensual allurements. To punish him for revealing these divine secrets, RAPHAEL was told to put the FALLEN ANGEL Azazel into chains, cast him into a pit of sharp and pointed stones in the desert Dudael, and to cover him with darkness. He was to remain like this until the great Day of Judgement, when he would be thrown into the fiery pit of hell, and the earth would be healed of the corruption he had introduced to it. As he would not repent from his sins when God destroyed the NEPHILIM, the sacrifice of the Scapegoat was introduces (see Leviticus 16). Two he-goats were sacrificed in the Temple on the Day of Atonement, the one for God, that He pardon the sins of Israel, the other for Azazel, that he bear the sins of Israel. Many of the stories told of Azazil are also told of SEMYAZA. In origin, Azazel may well have been the name of a demon of the desert. Azazel appears in Muslim tradition as Azazil. The stories of Azazil are very similar to those of the Jewish traditions found in texts such as the *Book of Enoch* and *Apocalypse of Abraham*, but rather than being associated with AZZAH, he is associated with HARUT AND MARUT. Some traditions say that Azazil was the name of IBLIS before his fall.

In the *Apocalypse of Abraham* the birds that descend on Abraham's first ever sacrifice to the true God in Genesis 15 are identified with Azazel, and he is also said to be the one who tempted Adam and Eve. In Robertson Davies' 1981 novel *The Rebel Angels,* Azazel and Samahazai (see under SEMYAZA) are on earth in the forms of Clem Hollier and Simon Darcout, professors of the College of St John and the Holy Ghost, known as 'Spook'. This novel draws on an old Gnostic myth in which Samahazai reveals all the secrets of heaven and creation to King Solomon, after which he and his followers are expelled from heaven. As Davies then says, 'And did they mope and plot vengeance? Not they! They weren't sore-headed egotists like Lucifer. Instead they gave Mankind another push up the ladder, they came to earth and taught tongues and healing and laws and

hygiene – taught everything.' Azazel plays an important role in *1 Enoch* and in a number of texts from Qumran. Although the name is usually said to mean 'God Strengthens' the actual meaning is obscure. The word only occurs in the Bible once, in Leviticus 16:8, and its exact meaning is unknown.

Azbugay YWHW see ASBOGAH

Azday, **Azdai** Azday is an angel of the ninth lunar month according to the *Liber Juratus* and the Sloane manuscript *Book of Raziel*. Azdai is also the name of an angel found in a Mandaean inscription.

Azeruel A MOON ANGEL who rules the sixteenth mansion of the moon in Scorpio. While he supports the ransoming of captives, he works against journeys, marriage, harvests and trade.

Azigor, **Azyger** An angel of the third lunar month according to the *Liber Juratus* and the Sloane manuscript *Book of Raziel*.

Aziriphale This convincing-sounding angel name was created by Terry Pratchett and Neil Gaiman for their 1990 novel *Good Omens*. In this work, a gripping and comic parody of the 1976 *Omen* film combined with a paean of praise for the English countryside and the joys of a normal childhood, Aziriphale takes the role of a GUARDIAN ANGEL of Mankind, so soft-hearted that he gives Adam and Eve the flaming sword with which they were to be kept out of paradise so that they can keep warm. He and Crawley, the devil who is on permanent duty in the world, have been working with humans for so long that they have drawn close together and now sometimes have difficulty remembering where their responsibilities lie.

Azrael, **Azrail** see IZRAIL

Azraieylin, **Azrayeylyn** An angel presiding over Friday, the day of Venus, according to the *Liber Juratus* and the Sloane manuscript *Book of Raziel.*

Azriel One of the ANGELS OF DESTRUCTION, who is invoked to ward off evil. He is located in the north side of heaven. However, in the Sloane manuscript *Book of Raziel,* he is an angel of the twelfth lunar month. If invoked in the relevant month, he will ensure success in your enterprise.

Azzah, **Aza**, **Azza** In *3 Enoch,* a trio of angels, UZZAH, Azzah and AZAEL, oppose Enoch's elevation to METATRON, although when God stands firm, they prostrate themselves to him. They are described as laying charges against Enoch, which associates them with the Satan-figure SAMAEL, who is described as 'Prince of the Accusers'. These three are also credited with corrupting Mankind by teaching them sorcery. Azzah is said elsewhere to have passed on knowledge to Solomon. He is also known by the name SEMYAZA. See also AZAEL.

B

Baajah The angel that rules the fifteenth degree of Capricorn under CASUJOJAH and the fifteenth degree of Aquarius under AUSIUL, according to the *Lemegeton.*

Baalberith see BALBERITH

Bacharachyn, **Bachramyn** According to the *Liber Juratus* and the Sloane manuscript *Book of Raziel,* this is one of the angels with special care of Monday (Luna) who should be invoked to aid works started on that day.

Bachiel, **Bakiel** The angel that rules the twentieth degree of Taurus under TUAL and the twentieth degree of Gemini under GIEL, according to the *Lemegeton.* He may be the same as **Baciel**, an angel of the fourth heaven in the *Heptameron.*

Bachmyel In the Sloane manuscript *Book of Raziel* an angel with power over water.

Bactanael An angel of the south of the first heaven in the Sloane manuscript *Book of Raziel.*

Bacyel An angel of the north of the fourth heaven in the Sloane manuscript *Book of Raziel.*

Badeilyn, **Badeykyn** According to the *Liber Juratus* and the Sloane manuscript *Book of Raziel* this is one of the angels with special care of Monday (Luna) who should be invoked to aid works started on that day.

Bael In the Sloane manuscript *Book of Raziel* an elemental angel with power over the earth.

Bagdial In Isaac Bashevis Singer's *Collected Short Stories* there is a story called 'The Warehouse' in which a tubby angel called Bagdial hands out cards which entitle new arrivals in the lower heavens to claim a new body.

Bagiel The angel that rules the twelfth degree of Virgo under VOIL, according to the *Lemegeton*.

Bahamut In Islamic myth, this is an enormous fish. On its back stands **Kujarta**, the giant bull. On his back is a rock of ruby, and on this rock stands a nameless angel who supports the world on his shoulders. Bahmut and the Old Testament Behemoth (usually interpreted as a hippopotamus) appear to be from the same root. Bahamut is a popular creature with gamers.

Bahman, **Bahrman** see VOHU MANO

Bahoraelin, **Bahoraely** An angel presiding over Friday, the day of Venus, according to the *Liber Juratus* and the Sloane manuscript *Book of Raziel*.

Baiedalin, **Bayeykyn** According to the *Liber Juratus* and the Sloane manuscript *Book of Raziel*, this is one of the GUARDIAN ANGELS with special care of Monday (Luna) who should be invoked to aid works started on that day.

Bakiel The angel that rules the tenth degree of Gemini under GIEL, according to the *Lemegeton*.

Balam, **Balan** In magic, this is a fallen DOMINION who now heads forty legions from hell. He can be conjured, when he appears with three heads, one each of a man, a ram and a bull, with the tail of a serpent and eye of fire. He manifests naked and riding on a bear, with a goshawk on his wrist. He has a hoarse voice, but can be made to speak truthfully about the past, the present and the future, and he is also said to have the power to make you invisible and to inspire wit.

Balberith, **Baalberith**, **Beal**, **Berith**, **Elberith** Once a Prince among the choir of CHERUBIM, Balberith is now counted among the FALLEN ANGELS in hell, where he is both lawyer and pontiff, one of his chief tasks being the witnessing of signatures between humans and the devil. It is Balberith who was said to be the chief devil afflicting nuns in a convent in Aix-en-Provence in 1611, according to one of the possessed, Sister Madeleine Demandolx de la Palud. This witch trial was significant as being the first in France where the testimony of one of the possessed was taken into account. Prior to this, such testimony had been dismissed on the grounds that demons were well known to be liars.

Baldoi In *The Key of Solomon*, an angel whose name is invoked when preparing materials for the practice of magic.

Balganarichyn, **Balganaychyn** According to the *Liber Juratus* and the Sloane manuscript *Book of Raziel*, this is one of the GUARDIAN ANGELS with special care of Monday.

Baliel One of the angels of the eighth lunar month in the Sloane manuscript

Book of Raziel. Alternatively, he can be the angel that rules the tenth degree of Libra under JAEL, according to the *Lemegeton,* or an angel of the first heaven, ruling Monday according to the *Heptameron,* which says he should be called on for the north.

Balquiel is called the angel of the planet Mars (or Madin) in the Sloane manuscript *Book of Raziel.*

Balthamos and **Baruch** Two angels that appear in Philip Pullman's *The Subtle Knife* and *The Amber Spyglass* (Books Two and Three of the *His Dark Materials* trilogy). Generally, like C S Lewis's ELDIL (elements of the trilogy are a response to Lewis's work) they are only visible as a shimmering, but in Chapter Two of the *Spyglass* Will, the hero, stirs up the fire they are sitting by so that the smoke 'had the effect of outlining their bodies so that he could see them both clearly for the first time. Balthamos was slender; his narrow wings were folded elegantly behind his shoulders, and his face bore an expression that mingled haughty disdain with a tender, ardent sympathy, as if he would love all things if only his nature could let him forget their defects. But he saw no defects in Baruch, that was clear. Baruch seemed younger, as Balthamos had said he was, and was more powerfully built, his wings snow-white and massive. He had a simpler nature: he looked up to Balthamos as the fount of all knowledge and joy. Will found himself intrigued and moved by their love for each other.' A distinctive element in the nature of Pullman's angels is described by Will, when he says 'Angels wish they had bodies. They told me that angels can't understand why *we*

don't enjoy the world more. It would be sort of ecstasy for them to have our flesh and our senses.' When Baruch is killed taking information to Lord Azriel to help him establish a republic of heaven, Balthamos goes to pieces, but finally manages to carry on with his self-appointed task of aiding Will. One of the vital pieces of information that Baruch takes is that he was once the brother of METATRON, who is a man taken up into heaven, and that this leaves Metatron, who has taken over the real power in heaven, susceptible to the charms of the flesh, just as the GRIGORI were. Pullman has great fun in his books playing with angel lore. The forces of heaven reside in The Clouded Mountain, also known as The Chariot (see MERKABAH), and he deals subtly with great debates, such as whether the angels who visit Abraham in Genesis really eat. See also BARUCH, XAPHANIA.

Balthioul, **Balthial**, **Bathiel** Distress, the evil star that causes men to lack moderation, is thwarted by Balthioul according to *The Testament of Solomon.*

Balyer An angel of the south of second heaven in the Sloane manuscript *Book of Raziel.*

Bangiel The angel that rules the thirteenth degree of Libra under JAEL, according to the *Lemegeton.*

Banorsasti, **Banorsasty** In the *Liber Juratus* and the Sloane manuscript *Book of Raziel*, an angel of the eleventh lunar month.

Baraaniel In the Sloane manuscript *Book of Raziel* an elemental angel with power over the earth.

Baradiel, **Bardiel** According to *3 Enoch* this is the princely angel in charge of the third heaven, Sehaqim. Together with NURIEL he has dominion over hail. The name is also found as Bardiel and **Barchiel**.

Barakel, **Baraqijal** One of the GRIGORI who taught Mankind astrology according to *1 Enoch*. The name looks suspiciously like that of BARAQIEL.

Baraqiel, **Barkiel**, **Barquiel**, **Barbiel** In *3 Enoch* Baraqiel is called the angel of the lightning (the name comes from the Hebrew for 'lightning' combined with the word for 'God'). He is also in charge of the second heaven, Raqia. Barquiel is described as the angel that governs the seventh hour of the day in the *Lemegeton*. He is attended by the angels **Abrasiel, Farmos, Nestorii, Manuel, Sagiel, Harmiel, Nastrus, Varmay, Tulmas, Crosiel, Pasriel, Venesiel, Evarym, Drufiel, Kathos** and many more. **Barachiel** or **Barasiel**, an angel of the element air in the Sloane manuscript *Book of Raziel,* is probably a form of the same name, although the manuscript also has Barquiel as an angel of the fifth heaven. In other texts he is described as either one of the seven ARCHANGELS or as one of the four chief SERAPHIM, as ruler of the confessors and a prince of the second and third heaven. He is widely described as an angel with connections to the planets, the zodiac and the calendar, and said to be the angel of Jupiter (as is SACHIEL), of February, and of either Scorpio or Pisces. Under the name Barkiel he is one of the guards of the gates of the east wind, and if he is also Barbiel (in some fifteenth-century manuscripts 'k' and 'b' are not easy to distinguish) he is one of

the angels ruling the twenty-eight mansions of the moon as well as ruler of October. However, there are also accounts of an evil Barbiel, a FALLEN ANGEL who was once either a VIRTUE or an ANGEL, and now serves as one of the seven Electors of Hell under ZAPHIEL. As a MOON ANGEL he is said to rule the ninth mansion of the moon, transitional between Cancer and Leo, to hinder harvests, to cause quarrels and impede travellers.

Barattiel, **Ataphiel** In *3 Enoch* Barattiel is a mighty Prince, who supports the highest heaven, Arabot, on his fingertips. The name is also found in some versions as **Ataphiel**.

Barbiel see BARAQIEL

Barcalin, **Barkalyn** An angel presiding over Friday, the day of Venus, according to the *Liber Juratus* and the Sloane manuscript *Book of Raziel.*

Barchiel, **Bardiel** see BARADIEL

Barfiell The angel with power over the eighth lunar moth in the *Liber Juratus.*

Bargar An angel of the second lunar month according to the *Liber Juratus* and the Sloane manuscript *Book of Raziel,* with the power to grant wishes.

Barginiel see MAMAEL

Barhil, **Barhyl** In the *Liber Juratus* and the Sloane manuscript *Book of Raziel* this is one of the angels of Sunday who should be invoked to aid works started on that day.

Bariel One of the angels whose name is

used in the Fourth Pentacle of Jupiter which 'serveth to acquire riches and honour' in *The Key of Solomon*. In the *Lemegeton* Bariel is the angel governing the eleventh hour of every day, who has, among his many servants, the angels: **Almarizel** or **Almariziel, Prasiniel, Chadros, Turmiel, Lamiel, Menafiel, Menasiel, Demasor, Omary, Helmas, Zemoel, Almas, Perman, Comial, Temas** and LANIFIEL. According to the *Liber Juratus* and the Sloane manuscript *Book of Raziel* he is one of the angels of Wednesday, the day of Mercury.

Barilagni, Barylaguy In the *Liber Juratus* and the Sloane manuscript *Book of Raziel*, an angel of the thirteenth lunar month (March). If invoked in the relevant month, he will ensure success in your enterprise.

Barkiel see BARAQIEL

Barman see VOHU MANO

Barmas, Barmos see ABASDARHON

Barnayeyl, Barneyeyl An angel presiding over Friday, the day of Venus, according to the *Liber Juratus* and the Sloane manuscript *Book of Raziel*.

Barquiel see BARAQIEL

Barsfilin, Barsslylyn One of the Wednesday angels in the *Liber Juratus* and the Sloane manuscript *Book of Raziel*.

Baruch Baruch appears in the Bible as the secretary (and by implication literary executor) of the Prophet Jeremiah. This led to three Pseudepigraphal works being ascribed

to him, with *3 Baruch* in particular which describes his experiences in heaven being an important source of information on angels. There is also an angel called Baruch (the name means 'blessed') described as guardian of the Tree of Life and in Gnosticism an angel sent to 'succour the spirit in man'. In the *Lemegeton* he is an aerial spirit. See also under BALTHAMOS AND BARUCH.

Baruchiel In the *Testament of Solomon*, the angel who thwarts the evil star of Strife. The name appears to come from the Hebrew for 'blessed'.

Barya'il An angel of the Muslim seventh heaven.

Bashir see MUBASHSHIR AND BASHIR

Basilon and **Basilion** see ORIEL

Bastelyn, Bastaylyn A Tuesday angel in the *Liber Juratus* and the Sloane manuscript *Book of Raziel*.

Basy An angel of the north of the first heaven in the Sloane manuscript *Book of Raziel*.

Batarel One of the GRIGORI, 'a chief of ten' and one of 200 FALLEN ANGELS, according to *1 Enoch*.

Bath Qol, Bath-Kol, Bat Qol In the Kabbalah, a female angel, whose name means 'daughter of the voice' or 'heavenly voice'. She is associated with prophecy and appears in the form of a dove. She is said to have visited Rabbi Simeon ben Yohai, the reputed author of *The Zohar,* who spent twelve years as a hermit in a cave in Israel in the second century. Bath-Kol is also a name given to the voice that called upon Cain, after he had murdered his brother, asking, 'Where is thy brother, Abel?'

Bathiel see BALTHIOUL

Batriel An angel of the south of the second heaven in the Sloane manuscript *Book of Raziel*. This would appear to be the same as **Batarel**, one of 200 FALLEN ANGELS found in the *Book of Enoch*, who is known to be invoked in magic.

Bazazath An angel in the *Testament of Solomon*, who has the power to control a destructive, fire-breathing, dragon-shaped demon called Obizuth. He is also said to be an ARCHANGEL and can appear under the name of **Bazazarath** or **Raphael-Bazazath**.

Beal see BALBERITH

Beburos One of the nine 'angels who are over the consummation' (i.e. the end of the world) in the *Greek Apocalypse of Ezra*, about which nothing more is known.

Becar An angel of the eighth lunar month in the *Liber Juratus* and the Sloane manuscript *Book of Raziel*.

Beel An angel presiding over Thursday, the day of Jove, according to the *Liber Juratus* and the Sloane manuscript *Book of Raziel*. This work also says he is the chief angel of Saturn (although this role is elsewhere given to CASSIEL), and therefore a Saturday angel. Saturn angels are described as clothed with darkness, tall and thin and having power over cold, dry winds. Beel is also found is manuscripts as a spelling for Bel, the demon or pagan god in Daniel.

Beerel One of the angels of Wednesday in the *Liber Juratus* and the Sloane manuscript *Book of Raziel*.

Befranzy see PAMYEL

Belon This is one of the angels presiding over Saturday, the day of Saturn or Sabat, according to the Sloane manuscript *Book of Raziel*. If invoked appropriately and in a state of purity, they will aid you.

Ben Nez A winged angel whose role is to use his pinions to keep back the force of the south wind, which, according to Jewish legend, blows directly from the regions of fire near hell. Were it not for Ben Nez, Ginzberg tells us, Mankind would be consumed by the heat.

Benad Hasche Female angels allegedly venerated in Arabic culture, mentioned by Thomas Moore in the preface to his 1823 collection of narrative poems, *Loves of the Angels*.

Bene Elohim (**Bene Elim** singular) A general term for angels used in the Old Testament, literally meaning 'sons of god'. In some later texts this came to be seen as the name for a separate order of angels, thus we find **Beni Elohim** for one of the ten choirs of the Holy Angels, according to the *Key of Solomon*, which distinguishes them from the ELOHIM. Their exact status is subject to conflicting accounts, although most agree that their main function is to sing the praises of God. Some say they are a division of the angels known as THRONES, and others that they are ISHIM or ARCHANGELS. As 'sons of God' they have also been identified with the GRIGORI ('The sons of God looked upon the

Daughters of Men, and saw that they were fair'). *The Zohar* ranks them ninth in the hierarchy of the angels, although others put them eighth. *The Zohar* also says their leader is HOFNIEL, although others say it is AZAZEL.

Benenil, **Benenonyll** One of the Wednesday angels in the *Liber Juratus* and the Sloane manuscript *Book of Raziel*.

Bengariel An angel of the element air, under the planet Cocab (Mercury), to be invoked when working under this planet, according to the Sloane manuscript *Book of Raziel*.

Bengiel The angel that rules the eleventh degree of Pisces under PASIL, according to the *Lemegeton*.

Beniel An angel presiding over Thursday, the day of Jove, according to the Sloane manuscript *Book of Raziel*. Elsewhere, he is credited with the power of conferring invisibility.

Benit, **Benyh** An angel of the first lunar month according to the Sloane manuscript *Book of Raziel*.

Beratiel According to the *Lemegeton*, the angel of the twelfth hour of the day, attended by **Camarom** or **Camaron**, **Astrofiel**, **Penatiel**, **Demarac** or **Demarae**, **Famaras**, **Plamiel**, **Nerastiel**, **Fimarson**, **Quirix**, **Sameron**, **Edriel**, **Choriel**, ROMIEL, **Fenosiel**, **Harmary**.

Beriel, **Berriel**, **Beryel**, **Beryel** In the *Liber Juratus* and the Sloane manuscript *Book of Raziel*, an angel of the twelfth lunar month. Also, in *Raziel*, of the element air and of the element earth.

The angel that rules the eleventh degree of Taurus under TUAL, according to the *Lemegeton*. Some claim that the name is the same as that of the demon **Belial**.

Berion, **Beryob** One of the angels of Wednesday, the day of Mercury, in the *Liber Juratus* and the Sloane manuscript *Book of Raziel*.

Berith see BALBERITH

Betabaat An angel of the east of the second heaven in the Sloane manuscript *Book of Raziel*.

Bethaz, **Bethtaez** According to the Sloane manuscript *Book of Raziel*, this is one of the angels of Sunday.

Bethnael A MOON ANGEL who rules the twenty-first mansion of the moon, in Capricorn. An angel who supports the underdog, he helps to cure illness and aids the escape of prisoners and servants.

Bethor Bethor appears in the *Three Books of Occult Philosophy* of Cornelius Agrippa with the following impressive statistics: he rules over 42 provinces and 42 kings, 35 princes, 28 dukes, 21 councillors, 14 servants, 7 envoys and 29,000 legions of spirits, each legion having a head-count of 490. He is also an OLYMPIC SPIRIT who rules 42 of the 196 provinces and ruled the events of the world between 60 BC and AD 430.

Betiel The angel that rules the twentieth degree of Aries under AIEL, according to the *Lemegeton*.

Bevael The angel that rules the fourteenth degree of Scorpio under

JOSEL and the eleventh degree of Sagittarius under SUIAJASEL, according to the *Lemegeton*.

Biael The angel that rules the first degree of Aries under AIEL, according to the *Lemegeton*.

Bidukht see HARUT AND MARUT

Bigtha see HARBONAH

Binah In the *Key of Solomon* identified as one of the angels who preside over the ten SEFIROTH. Elsewhere she is identified with SOPHIA (the name means 'understanding' or 'intelligence'), and in the *Book of Concealed Mystery* she is called 'the sea'.

Biqa see KASBEEL

Biraquel The angel with power over the fifth lunar month according to the Sloane manuscript version of *The Book of Raziel*, through whose power a man may know his future. He is **Beraquiel** in the *Liber Juratus*.

Biztha see HARBONAH

Boel In *The Zohar*, Boel is one of the seven exalted THRONE angels of the first heaven. He holds the four keys to the four corners of the earth. With these he can unlock the gates to the Garden of Eden and if the guardian CHERUBIM, set there to prevent the return of man, permit passage, the angels can then meet there. An angel of the sixth lunar month in the *Liber Juratus* and the Sloane manuscript *Book of Raziel*. He is also an angel of Wednesday. Elsewhere, he is described as the angel who governs the planet Saturn.

Borachiel According to the *Lemegeton*, this is an angel who is invoked for fertility in animals, plants and women.

Borayeyl, **Borayeyll** A Friday angel in the *Liber Juratus* and the Sloane manuscript *Book of Raziel*.

Borhai An angel of the third lunar month according to the Sloane manuscript *Book of Raziel*. The name becomes **Borzac** in the *Liber Juratus*.

Bortaz An angel of the west of the fifth heaven in the Sloane manuscript *Book of Raziel*.

Boxoraylon, **Bornaylon** This is one of the angels presiding over Saturday, the day of Saturn or Sabat, according to the *Liber Juratus* and the Sloane manuscript *Book of Raziel*.

Braliel An angel of the east of the fourth heaven in the Sloane manuscript *Book of Raziel*. The entry for Braliel is followed immediately by **Braaliel**, although one would normally take this form as a variant spelling.

Bramiel see JEFISCHA

Brandiel see PAMYEL

Branielin, **Bramiel** In the *Liber Juratus* and the Sloane manuscript *Book of Raziel*, one of the angels with special care of Monday.

Brasiel see SANIEL

Briathos An angel found in the *Testament of Solomon* who can control a dog-shaped demon.

Briel, Breell An angel presiding over Thursday, the day of Jove, according to the *Liber Juratus* and the Sloane manuscript *Book of Raziel*. He is also an angel invoked on amulets to protect those giving birth.

Brofilyn, Brofylyn An angel of the day of Mars (Tuesday) with power over 'red metal' in the *Liber Juratus* and the Sloane manuscript *Book of Raziel*.

Brumiel see SAMAEL

Bufanotz see NARCORIEL

Burz Yazad see APAM NAPAT

Busasejal One of the GRIGORI according to *1 Enoch*.

Byeniel In the Sloane manuscript *Book of Raziel* an elemental angel with power over the earth.

Byny An angel of the fifth lunar month in the *Liber Juratus* and the Sloane manuscript *Book of Raziel*. It may be the same name as BINAH.

C

Cabriel Thomas Heywood, in his *Hierarchy of the Blessed Angels,* describes Cabriel as 'the president' and as governing Aquarius. In the *Book of Raziel* he is one of six angels placed over the four parts of heaven. He is also an angel of the element fire, under the planet Mars, in the same work. The name is also found as **Cabrael** and **Kabriel**, who is also described as an attendant of SARANDIEL. As a MOON ANGEL see under GABRIEL.

Cabrifiel An angel presiding over Thursday, the day of Jove, according to the Sloane manuscript *Book of Raziel*. The initial 'C' becomes an 'R' in the *Liber Juratus* and the name appears as **Rubyeyel**.

Cabyn A Tuesday angel according to the Sloane manuscript *Book of Raziel*, but a Friday one in the *Liber Juratus*.

Cacitilyn A Tuesday angel in the *Liber Juratus* and the Sloane manuscript *Book of Raziel*.

Cael In the Sloane manuscript *Book of Raziel*, an angel of the twelfth lunar month. The angel who rules Cancer according to the *Lemegeton*.

Cahatel, Cahet(h)el Cahatel is considered one of the eight SERAPHIM and one of the seventy-two SHEMHAM-PHORAE angels. He rules over agricultural produce and is invoked to increase or improve crops. As the GUARDIAN ANGEL for those born under Taurus between 26 and 30 April he is considered the angel of the home, who brings serenity and tranquility to a family. He is said to secure success in anything that relates to the sea and water.

Caiel see CAMAEL

Caisaat, Caysaac An angel of the first lunar month according to the Sloane manuscript *Book of Raziel*.

Cajaiel The angel that rules the twentieth degree of Pisces under PASIL, according to the *Lemegeton*.

Cakaziel An angel of the element fire, under the planet Noga (Venus), to be invoked when working under this planet, according to the Sloane manuscript *Book of Raziel*.

Cakiel The angel that rules the ninth degree of Aries under AIEL, according to the *Lemegeton*.

Calcas An angel of the east of the fourth heaven in the Sloane manuscript *Book of Raziel*.

Calchihay, Chalchyphay One of the angels of the ninth lunar month according to the *Liber Juratus* and the Sloane manuscript *Book of Raziel*, which says that if they are named 'in each thing that thou wilt do … thou shalt profit'.

Caliel, Calliel One of the seventy-two SHEMHAMPHORAE angels, Caliel is a THRONE of the second heaven, who brings prompt help against adversity. As a GUARDIAN ANGEL of those born under Gemini between 16 and 21 June, he is said to be an angel of joy who

harmonises thought and action, and helps avoid impulsiveness.

Calipon This is one of the angels presiding over Saturday, the day of Saturn of Sabat, according to the Sloane manuscript *Book of Raziel*. The name is **Calyrxon** in the *Liber Juratus*.

Calloyel An angel of the south of the second heaven in the Sloane manuscript *Book of Raziel*.

Calnamia One of the angels of Wednesday, the day of Mercury, according to the Sloane manuscript *Book of Raziel*. He does not appear in the *Liber Juratus*.

Calodaemon see DAEMON

Camael, Caiel, Camiul, Camniel, Camuel, Cancel, Kemuel, Khamael, Qemuel Camael's most important role is as one of the SEFIROTH of the Tree of Life in the Kabbalah. He is also classed as chief of the POWERS and the ruler of Mars (a role also given to SAMAEL, an angel with whom he shares other features). Elsewhere, he is one of seven angels who stand in the presence of God, or else he is leader of 12,000 ANGELS OF DESTRUCTION. He is also said by some to have been the angel who wrestled with Jacob (see Genesis 10) although some say this is PENIEL. Camael is even thought by some to have been the angel who appeared to Jesus in his agony in the Garden of Gethsemane, although most say this is GABRIEL. Another legend says that he was destroyed by Moses for trying to prevent him receiving the Torah from God. This is not the only malign act attributed to him, for in some traditions he is said to be a Count Palatine of Hell. In this role, when invoked he appears in the form of a leopard crouched upon a rock.

Camarom, Camaron see BERATIEL

Camary see PAMYEL

Camb An angel of the fifth lunar month according to the Sloane manuscript *Book of Raziel*.

Cambiel One of the angels said to rule Aquarius, and an angel of the ninth hour. See also NARCORIEL.

Cambriel see NARCORIEL

Camiel The angel that rules the fourth degree of Aquarius under AUSIUL, according to the *Lemegeton*. This is probably yet another aspect of CAMAEL.

Camirael An angel of the element air, under the planet Noga (Venus), to be invoked when working under this planet, according to the Sloane manuscript *Book of Raziel*.

Camiul, Camniel see CAMAEL

Camosiel see SANIEL

Camuel see CAMAEL

Cananyn One of the angels of Wednesday, the day of Mercury, found in the *Liber Juratus* and the Sloane manuscript *Book of Raziel*.

Cancel see CAMAEL

Candanagyn According to the *Liber Juratus* and the Sloane manuscript *Book of Raziel* this is one of the GUARDIAN ANGELS with special care of Monday (Luna), who should be invoked to aid works started on that day.

Caneloas In *The Key of Solomon*, an angel whose name is invoked when preparing materials for the practice of magic.

Canesylyn, Canofylyn An angel presiding over Friday, the day of Venus, according to the *Liber Juratus* and the Sloane manuscript *Book of Raziel*.

Canyel, Cannyel In the Sloane manuscript *Book of Raziel*, an angel of the tenth lunar month. This manuscript also says that he is an angel of the day of Mars (Tuesday). He is **Canueyl** in the *Liber Juratus*.

Caphriel, Capciel, Capeiel, Capiel, Capziel see CASSIEL

Caran, Caram According to the *Liber Juratus* and the Sloane manuscript *Book of Raziel,* this is one of the GUARDIAN ANGELS of Sunday (Solis) who should be invoked to aid works started on that day.

Carbiel, Carbyel, Carbiol An angel of the second lunar month according to the *Liber Juratus* and the Sloane manuscript *Book of Raziel,* with the power to grant wishes. He is also described there as one of the angels presiding over Thursday, the day of Jupiter, and as angel of the element air, under the planet Madin (Mars), to be invoked when working under this planet. In the *Lemegeton* he is a mighty prince ruling the west and north, with many dukes under him.

Carcas see HARBONAH

Carciel, **Carcyelel**, **Carcoyel** In the *Liber Juratus* and the Sloane manuscript *Book of Raziel*, an angel of the sixth and twelfth lunar months. If invoked in the relevant month, he will ensure success in your enterprise. He is also found in the east of the second heaven.

Cardiel In the Sloane manuscript *Book of Raziel*, an angel of the twelfth lunar month. He is also listed as an attendant of DARDARIEL, angel of the eleventh hour of the night in the *Lemegeton*, and is cited by Davidson as 'an angel invoked in special rites, as in the conjuration of the Sword' in ceremonial magic.

Caremaz see ABASDARHON

Caretaking Angels A class of GUARDIAN ANGEL and CHILDBED ANGEL headed by TEMELUCH, who look after 'infants of untimely birth' and the offspring of adulterous unions.

Caribifin, **Carybyfyn** One of the angels of Wednesday in the *Liber Juratus* and the Sloane manuscript *Book of Raziel*.

Cariel In the Sloane manuscript *Book of Raziel* an angel with power over fire and flame.

Carman see DARDARIEL

Carmiel An angel of the east of the second heaven in the Sloane manuscript *Book of Raziel*, although the name is also given there as an angel in the north of the third heaven.

Carpaliel An angel of the south of the first heaven in the Sloane manuscript *Book of Raziel*.

Carszeneyl, **Carfzoneyll** A Tuesday angel in the *Liber Juratus* and the Sloane manuscript *Book of Raziel*.

Cartalion An angel of the third lunar month found in the Sloane manuscript *Book of Raziel*, whose naming brings benefits.

Cartemat An angel of the second lunar month according to the *Liber Juratus* and the Sloane manuscript *Book of Raziel* with the power to grant wishes.

Casfrubyn, **Caffrnbryn** According to the *Liber Juratus* and the Sloane manuscript *Book of Raziel* this is one of the GUARDIAN ANGELS with special care of Monday (Luna) who should be invoked to aid works started on that day.

Cashiel The angel that rules the fourth degree of Capricorn under CASUJOJAH, according to the *Lemegeton*. He should perhaps be identified with CASSIEL.

Casmiroz see DARDARIEL

Casmuch An angel of the third lunar month according to the *Liber Juratus* and the Sloane manuscript *Book of Raziel*.

Cassiel, **Casiel**, **Caziel**, **Cashiel**, **etc.** Cassiel is a multi-faceted angel. Some say he is ARCHANGEL of Saturn, and an angel of contemplation, to be invoked when attempting meditation, and also called on for peace, harmony and serenity, and when we need the wisdom of the Recording Angels. Others say he is Lord of the CHERUBIM, sombre and mighty, which is reflected in his name, which means 'Knowledge of God', or that he is an angel of time. He is the angel that rules the third degree of Sagittarius under SUIAJASEL, according to the *Lemegeton*. Davidson calls him the angel of solitudes and tears, a prince of the powers and a ruler of the seventh heaven as well as an angel of temperance and one of the three angels of Saturday, with URIEL and MACHATAN. He appears in various guises in the Sloane manuscript *Book of Raziel* and as **Casiel**, is an angel of the first lunar month. As **Capiel** or **Capeiel** he is again one of the angels presiding over Saturday in the same work. If invoked appropriately and in a state of purity, they will aid you. Capiel resides in the east of the fourth heaven. As **Capziel** he is the angel of the planet Saturn. **Caphriel**, **Capciel** and KAFZIEL, the names used for an angel of the element fire under the planet Noga (Venus), and yet again an angel of Saturday, are other forms of the name, while another name, **Zaphkiel**, has been attributed to him by other sources. In fiction, Cassiel also features in Wim Wenders' 1987 film *Wings of Desire* (see under DAMIEL).

Cassilon, Cassylon This is one of the angels presiding over Saturday according to the *Liber Juratus* and the Sloane manuscript *Book of Raziel*.

Casujojah, Casuijah, Casujoiah The angel who rules Capricorn according to the *Lemegeton*.

Cathneylyn A Monday angel in the Sloane manuscript *Book of Raziel* and the *Liber Juratus*.

Cazabriel An angel of the element water, under the planet Madin (Mars), to be invoked when working under this planet, according to the Sloane manuscript *Book of Raziel*.

Cefania, Cefanya An angel of the third lunar month according to the *Liber Juratus* and the Sloane manuscript *Book of Raziel*.

Cegnel The angel that rules the sixth degree of Aries under AIEL, according to the *Lemegeton*.

Celabel, Celabryll An angel of the day of Mars (Tuesday) in the *Liber Juratus* and the Sloane manuscript *Book of Raziel*.

Celestial Hierarchy see HIERARCHY OF ANGELS

Celidoal, Celydael In the *Liber Juratus* and the Sloane manuscript *Book of Raziel*, an angel of the thirteenth lunar month (March).

Celiel The angel that rules the first degree of Virgo under VOIL, found in the *Lemegeton*.

Ceradadyn According to the *Liber Juratus* and the Sloane manuscript *Book of Raziel* this is one of the angels with special care of Monday.

Cerviel Cerviel is said to rule the PRIN-CIPALITIES, along with HANIEL and NISROC. He is also said to be the angel who helped David when he fought and killed Goliath.

Cesiel The angel that rules the third degree of Scorpio under JOSEL, according to the *Lemegeton*.

Cetabiel, **Cetabyel** In the *Liber Juratus* and the Sloane manuscript *Book of Raziel*, an angel of the twelfth lunar month. If invoked in the relevant month, he will ensure success in your enterprise.

Cethenoylyn, **Cetennoylyn** A Tuesday angel in the *Liber Juratus* and the Sloane manuscript *Book of Raziel*.

Ceyabos, **Ceyabgos** In the *Liber Juratus* and the Sloane manuscript *Book of Raziel*, an angel of the thirteenth lunar month (March).

Ceytatynyn A Sunday angel in the Sloane manuscript *Book of Raziel* and the *Liber Juratus*.

Chabiel The angel that rules the twentieth degrees of Scorpio under JOSEL and of Sagittarius under SUIAJASEL, according to the *Lemegeton*.

Chabrion see SARANDIEL

Chabriz see TARTYS

Chadiel The angel that rules the sixteenth degree of Taurus under TUAL and the sixteenth degree of Gemini under GIEL, according to the *Lemegeton*.

Chadros see BARIEL

Chaiel The angel that rules the second degree of Libra under JAEL, according to the *Lemegeton*.

Chaioth ha-Qadesh One of the ten choirs of the Holy Angels, according to *The Key of Solomon*.

Chalkydri see PHOENIX

Chameray see IASSUARIM

Chamuel Meaning 'He who seeks God', this is one of the seven ARCHANGELS in some systems, and is also said to be the ruler of the DOMINIONS or the POWERS. Chamuel's name is also put forward as the angel that comforted Jesus in the Garden of Gethsemane, although this is more often said to be GABRIEL. As **Chamiel** he is the angel that rules the first degree of Aquarius under AUSIUL, according to the *Lemegeton*. However, there is a large degree of overlap in the forms of the name of Chamuel with those of HANIEL, CAMAEL and SIMIEL, and it not easy to distinguish where one angel ends and another begins.

Charaby see ABASDARHON

Charbiel Charbiel, whose name means 'dryness', is the angel whose task it was to dry up all the water on the earth after Noah's Flood.

Chardiel see HANIEL

Chariots The concept of a god riding a chariot is widely found in Middle Eastern religion (see further under MERKABAH). This, combined with the vision of Ezekiel (chapter 1), which has had such a profound influence on the concepts of the heavenly hosts, has led some writers to speak of Chariots or Chariots of God as a rank of angels, which should probably simply be taken as an alternative for OPHANIM. Others use the term for the SERAPHIM and CHERUBIM (who uphold God's chariot), or as a collective term for angels in general. This last view is reinforced by

Psalm 68:17, which reads, 'The Chariots of God are twenty thousand, even thousands of angels: the Lord is among them, as in Sinai, in the holy place.'

Charny see ORIEL

Charon Charon is the Greek ferryman of the underworld, who takes the souls of the dead over the river Styx (or in earlier versions the river Acheron) to Hades, the land of the dead. In Greek iconography he was usually shown as an old man, dressed as a ragged countryman, but in Etruscan iconography, Charon or, more properly for the Etruscans, **Charun**, was sometimes shown as a winged demon, who often carried a double-headed hammer. This iconography, together with that of other PSYCHOPOMPS, was a contributing factor in the development of the modern idea of the winged angel, and particularly in this case of the angel of death. The winged Charon has also been taken up by some modern fantasy illustrators, who sometimes depict him as a fully-fledged angel of death.

Charpon see SAMAEL

Charuch see SANIEL

Chasen Angel of the air and one of the angels whose name is used in the Seventh Pentacle of the Sun which, 'If any be by chance imprisoned or detained in fetters of iron, at the presence of this Pentacle, which should be engraved in Gold on the day and hour of the Sun, he will be immediately delivered and set at liberty', according to *The Key of Solomon*.

Chasmalim see HASHMALIM

Chavakiah A GUARDIAN ANGEL for those born between 13 and 17 September under the sign of Virgo, and one of the seventy-two SHEMHAM-PHORAE angels.

Chaya, Chayot, Chayoth, Chayyoth see HAYYOT

Chazael The angel that rules the nineteenth degree of Taurus under TUAL, the nineteenth degree of Gemini under GIEL and the seventeenth degree of Pisces under PASIL, according to the *Lemegeton*.

Chengiel The angel that rules the nineteenth degree of Libra under JAEL, according to the *Lemegeton*.

Chenyon, Cheryon A Saturday angel in the *Liber Juratus* and the Sloane manuscript *Book of Raziel*.

Cherasiel see ZAAZENACH

Chermel see PAMYEL

Cherubiel see KERUBIEL

Cherubim Both the origin and the meaning of the word Cherub is disputed, although many now think the name comes from Assyria, and is derived from the word *karibu* (*karibi* in the feminine) which means 'one who prays'. In Assyrian art these are guardian spirits, often shown as winged creatures with faces of either a lion or a human, and the bodies of sphinxes, eagles or bulls. In Islam, Cherubim are called the *el-karubiyan*, which is interpreted as 'those who are brought near [to Allah]'.

The Old Testament states clearly that they are 'living beings' (Ezekiel 10:4,

18–22), and so some would exclude them from the ranks of angels. Most, however, say they are the second rank of angels, after the SERAPHIM (although Billy Graham ranks them fourth). As such, their main function is to praise the Divine Being. In the words of the *Te Deum*, an integral part of morning worship in many Christian churches, quoted here in the form from the *Book of Common Prayer*: 'To Thee Cherubin and Seraphin:/continually do cry,/Holy, Holy, Holy: Lord God of Sabaoth;/Heaven and earth art full of the Majesty: of thy Glory.'

Their closeness to, and knowledge of, The Divine means that Cherubim associated with knowledge. But in early Hebrew writings they have functions as guardians, and in this role they appear as escorts of The Divine, guard the eastern gate of paradise with a flaming sword to prevent Mankind's returning to the Tree of Life (Genesis 3:24) (these are sometimes called the ever-turning swords of flames and were appointed because angels can turn themselves from one shape into another at need, says Jewish folklore), were depicted on the veil of the Temple in Jerusalem, and two solid gold Cherubim were placed on either side of the Mercy Seat on the Ark of the Covenant (Exodus 37:7). This latter role also links with the functions of the Cherubim as a vehicle of The Divine. 'And he rode upon a cherub, and did fly: and he was seen upon the wings of the wind' (2 Samuel 22). This function leads the Talmud to identify Cherubim with OPHANIM, the order of wheels, and indeed they are closely associated with wheels in Ezekiel's vision. They have a further function as keepers of the divine records, as a source of knowledge, and in medieval Jewish thought are the keepers of the fixed stars.

In appearance, Cherubim are sometimes described in terms of bright light or fire, while the coals of fire among which they live (Ezekiel 10:6) represent The Divine's purity. More often they are described as manlike in appearance, with either two, four or six wings. Several texts remark on the sound these wings make, *The Zohar* telling us, 'the melodious sound of their wings is heard in the realms above'. The evolution of the older, majestic form of the Cherubim into the pretty little cherubs (or PUTTI) of modern popular and religious art has a number of routes. Angels in general are often background supporters to events in pictures, and therefore shown small. There are popular traditions that babies who die young become angels in heaven – a belief vehemently opposed by the Roman Catholic Church. However, orthodox theology does allow a place for the innocent among the Elect, and these are conveniently depicted as baby angels. (For one of the most moving examinations of the complexities of the fate of babies who die, see the anonymous fourteenth-century English poem, *The Pearl.*) Finally, there has been a blending in popular art of the iconography of EROS and the angels.

Prominent among the Cherubim are GABRIEL, KERUBIEL (or **Cherubiel**), often cited as their leader, OPHANIEL, RAPHAEL, URIEL and ZOPHIEL (sometimes found as **Jophiel** and claimed by some as an alternative leader of Cherubim), although some of these are also called ARCHANGELS. Many believe that SATAN was also a ruling prince of the Cherubim before his fall.

The Cherubim and Seraphim are the only classes of angel in the Hebrew Bible, and they are also discussed in many other texts. *3 Enoch* has a sub-division of the class of Cherubim, called the Fast Cherub, although it does not expand on how these differ from ordinary Cherubim. It also says they stand with their wings raised beside the HAYYOT and bear the throne of God on their backs, and are bathed in the glory of its light. The *Testament of Adam* says they carry the throne of the Lord and are keepers of the divine seals. *2 Enoch* gives a detailed description of the Cherubim in action around the throne of God: 'And the cherubim and seraphim standing about the throne, the six-winged and many-eyed ones do not depart, standing before the Lord's face doing his will, and cover his whole throne, singing with gentle voice before the Lord's face: Holy, holy, holy, Lord Ruler of Sabaoth, heavens and earth are full of Your glory.' In the Sloane manuscript *Book of Raziel* and similar texts they have power over air, although Agrippa says they have power over earth. In early art they are shown either as red or, if they are to be distinguished from the fiery Seraphim, blue. In later art, Cherubim traditionally have blue wings (either six, four or two), or more rarely golden yellow, and are often shown as just wings and head. If the rest of their bodies is shown they may have shoes in contrast to the bare-footed Seraphim and are sometimes shown standing on wheels. They may carry a book. See also under HIERARCHIES OF ANGELS.

Cherudiel, **Cheduryel** An angel presiding over Thursday, the day of Jove, according to the *Liber Juratus* and the Sloane manuscript *Book of Raziel*. The name may be a form of KERUBIEL.

Chesed see SEFIRA

Chetiel The angel that rules the eighteenth degree of Virgo under VOIL, according to the *Lemegeton*.

Chieftains The collective term for the GUARDIAN ANGELS of the nations of the earth. *The Zohar* says there are seventy of these.

Childbed Angels In Jewish tradition these are angels invoked to protect mothers in childbirth and their newborn infants, to protect them from evil spirits and the depredations of Lilith, Adam's first wife who became a demon and preys on the newborn (see further under SANSANUI). The names are inscribed on various amulets and used, for example, to ease the pain of childbirth by attaching them to the woman's body. There are usually said to be seventy, and *The Book of Raziel* lists them as MICHAEL, GABRIEL, RAPHAEL, NURIEL, **Kidumiel**, MALKIEL, TZADKIEL, **Padiel, Zumiel, Chafriel,** ZURIEL, **Ramuel, Yofiel, Sturi(el),** GAZRIEL, **Udriel, Lahariel, Chaskiel, Rachmiah, Katzhiel, Schachniel, Karkiel, Ahiel**, **Lahal, Malchiel, Shebniel, Rachsiel, Rumiel, Kadmiel, Kadal, Chachmiel, Ramal, Katchiel, Aniel,** AZRIEL, **Chachmal, Kaniel, Griel, Tzartak, Ofiel,** RACHMIEL, **Sensenya, Udrgazyia, Rsassiel,** RAMIEL, **Sniel, Tahariel, Yezriel, Neriah, Ygal, Tsirya, Rigal, Tsuria, Psisya,** ORIEL, **Kenunit, Yeruel, Tatrusia, Zechriel,** VARIEL, **Diniel, Gdiel, Briel, Ahaniel.** In addition, the names of **Chaniel, Machnia** and **Samchia** appear twice in the list, which brings the number up to the full seventy.

Chisti (or **Chista**) This is a female YAZAD personifying religious wisdom. Her name probably means 'Instruction'.

An alternative title is **Razishta Chista** ('Most Upright Chista').

Chockmah see SEFIRA

Choir Choir can have two meanings when referring to angels. As one of their main functions is to sing the praises of God, it can simply refer to their singing, in the ordinary, everyday sense of the word. More specifically, it is used to mean each of the orders of angels in phrases such as 'Choirs of CHERUBIM' or 'the Choirs of DOMINIONS'.

Chokmahiel In *The Key of Solomon,* an angel whose name appears on the Third Pentacle of Mercury. He is quite possibly a misreading of the name Cochabiel, who is also a spirit of Mercury.

Choreb see ORIEL

Choriel see BERATIEL, MENDRION

Chrasiel see SABRATHAN

Chremas see SAMAEL

Chroel see OSMADIEL

Chrusiel see SERQUANICH

Chrymas see ABASDARHON

Chushel The angel that rules the first degree of Capricorn under CASUJOJAH, according to the *Lemegeton.*

Cocabiel see KOKABEL

Comadiel see VEQUANIEL

Comaguele, Cemaguyll In the *Liber Juratus* and the Sloane manuscript *Book of Raziel*, this is one of the angels of Sunday (Solis) who should be invoked to aid works started on that day.

Comary see PAMYEL

Comial see BARIEL

Confessors One of the twelve orders of angels identified by Thomas Heywood in his *Hierarchy of the Blessed Angels*. They are ruled by BARAQIEL.

Core see AEON

Coreziel see JEFISCHA

Costiryn, Costytyn An angel of the day of Mars (Tuesday) in the *Liber Juratus* and the Sloane manuscript *Book of Raziel*.

Crosiel see BARAQIEL

Cullia, Cullya One of the angels of the seventh lunar month in the *Liber Juratus* and the Sloane manuscript *Book of Raziel*.

Cunnyryel, Cumyryel An angel presiding over Thursday, the day of Jove, according to the *Liber Juratus* and the Sloane manuscript *Book of Raziel*.

Cupid see EROS

Cursiel see HANIEL

Cyoly An angel of the south of the second heaven in the Sloane manuscript *Book of Raziel*.

Cyzamanyn According to the *Liber Juratus* and the Sloane manuscript *Book of Raziel*, this is one of the angels with special care of Monday.

D

Dabriel An angel of Monday who is found in the first heaven and invoked from the north. Reference books also suggest he appears as the angel in charge of archives in *3 Enoch*, either in this form or as **Dabariel**, describing these names as variants of **Raduerial**. However, these forms are not recorded in the most up-to-date edition of the text in translation, which records **Dadweriel**, **Daryoel** and **Daryoiel** as variants of RADWERIEL. Some of this confusion must be due to different methods of transcribing non-Roman alphabets into English, and some may be due to different interpretations of what the actual Hebrew letters on the page of the different manuscripts are. Whatever the causes of the confusion, it is a useful illustration of how difficult it is to be categorical about the form of an angel's name, and how easily angels can multiply when information is transmitted in manuscript form.

Dachiel The angel that rules the sixteenth degrees of Scorpio under JOSEL and of Sagittarius under SUIAJASEL, according to the *Lemegeton*.

Dadiel, **Dadyel(l)** One of the angels of the sixth and seventh lunar months according to the *Liber Juratus* and the Sloane manuscript *Book of Raziel*, which says that if they are named 'in each thing that thou wilt do … thou shalt profit'.

Dadweriel see DABRIEL

Daemael, **Dameyel** An angel of the element fire, under the planet Cocab (Mercury), to be invoked when working under this planet, according to the Sloane manuscript *Book of Raziel*, found in the east of the fourth heaven. He would appear to be the same as **Damael**, a Tuesday angel found in the fifth heaven who must be invoked from the east, and probably also DAMIEL.

Daemon, **Dæmon**, **Daimon** This term was used in Greek and Latin to describe spiritual beings that were classified as less than gods, but who were intermediary between gods and men. It was only when the Christians sought to denigrate belief in such beings, by, among other things, suggesting that any effectiveness of prayers to statues of pagan gods was the result of daemons that inhabited the statues, that the concept of the daemon was transmogrified into that of the evil **demon**. The original daemon was neither inherently good nor bad, but could be either. A subclass of daemons were known as **eudaemons** or **calodaemons** (both meaning good or fortunate daemons – bad daemons were **kakodaemons**), and had a role very much like that of the GUARDIAN ANGELS. When Neo-Platonists were reviving interest in such things in the Renaissance, eudaemons were specifically identified by them with guardian angels. For some medieval occultists, daemons were the gate-keepers of the spheres through which the soul had to pass to the highest heaven. Probably the most famous daemon was that referred to by Socrates, who spoke of having a *daimonion* (a 'little daemon', or perhaps a personal one) who spoke to him to warn him when he was about to do something wrong, but who never told him what he should do. This concept has recently been expanded by Philip Pullman in the *His Dark Materials* trilogy, where people in some of the parallel worlds have a dæmon in the form of an animal which is an essential part of their personality. Romans also had a similar concept of a tutelary spirit of people or places called a **genius**, and the genius of the family again had a role similar to that of a guardian spirit or angel.

Daena A female YAZAD (Zoroastrian angel), presiding over the inner self and conscience and representing divinely-inspired religion. She is a co-worker with SPENTA ARMAITI. She is said to be the daughter of **Ahura Mazda** and **Armaiti**. She is also known as **Den, Dena** and **Din**.

Daevas see DEVA

Dagiel, Daghiel, Daiel The angel that rules the thirteenth degree of Pisces under PASIL, according to the *Lemegeton,* and a 'strong angel, a mighty and potent prince' who is an angel of Friday, the day of Venus, in the *Heptameron.* He is also considered the angel who rules over fish (although his ralationship to ARARIEL, who is invoked by fishermen, is not clear). The connection to fish is inherent in his name, for *dag* is the Hebrew for 'fish'. This links him to Dagon, the national deity of the ancient Philistines, who is shown with the upper parts of a man, but with the tail of a fish – in other words as a prototype of a merman. The name Dagon means 'dear little fish'.

Dagnel The angel that rules the thirteenth degree of Taurus under TUAL, according to the *Lemegeton.*

Dahariel see DARIEL

Dahiel The angel that rules the fourteenth degree of Virgo under VOIL, according to the *Lemegeton.*

Dahm YAZAD (Zoroastrian angel) honoured on the fourth day after a death.

Dahma Afriti, Dahman Afrin A powerful female YAZAD (Zoroastrian angel), who is embodiment of the power of benediction.

Daiel see DAGIEL

Daimon see DAEMON

Dajiel The angel that rules the twenty-second degree of Taurus under TUAL, according to the *Lemegeton.*

Dalia, Dalya An angel of the third lunar month in the *Liber Juratus* and the Sloane manuscript *Book of Raziel.*

Daliel, Dalyell In the *Liber Juratus* and the Sloane manuscript *Book of Raziel*, an angel of the eleventh lunar month. If invoked in the relevant month, he will ensure success in your enterprise. He is also angel of the element fire, under the planet Labana (Luna, the moon), to be invoked when working under this planet.

Dalquiel In the Kabbalah, Dalquiel is one of the three princes of the third heaven (the other two being Jabniel and Rabacyal). Together they rule over fire.

Damabiah, Damabiath As well as being one of the seventy-two SHEMHAMPHORAE, Damabiah is a patron of ship-building. As the GUARDIAN ANGEL of those born under Aquarius between 10 and 14 February, he is considered an angel of Wisdom who works against sorcery and slander and helps bring success in undertakings.

Damael, see DAEMAEL

Damar see DARDARIEL

Damasiel see SARANDIEL

Dameriel see DARDARIEL

Damery see SARANDIEL

Damiel In Wim Wenders' acclaimed 1987 film, *Wings of Desire* Damiel and CASSIEL are GUARDIAN ANGELS who watch over the people of Berlin. Damiel longs to experience the immediacy of human experience, and after an accident is able to do so, and, like the GRIGORI, falls in love with a human. The film is influenced by both Cocteau's use of angels in his films and by Rilke's ideas about angels as a transcendent reality, uniting will and capability. The name is not original, featuring as an angel in magic texts, variously described as an angel of the fifth hour or the ninth hour. See also under DAEMAEL.

Damoish Upamana YAZAD (Zoroastrian angel) personifying anathema and noted for bravery.

Dandaniel The angel of the planet Hanina (Sol, the sun) and of the element fire, to be invoked when working under this planet, according to the Sloane manuscript *Book of Raziel*.

Danel One of the GRIGORI, 'a chief of

ten', according to *1 Enoch 6*.

Dani In *The Key of Solomon*, an angel whose name is invoked when preparing materials for the practice of magic.

Daniel, **Danjal** This name means 'God is my judge', and is best known as the name of a man, a biblical visionary famous for being saved from the lions by an angel, and for his involvement with the three men saved by an angel in the fiery furnace. There is much disagreement over the function and nature of the angel named Daniel. Some say he is one of the PRINCIPALITIES, other list him as one of the seventy-two angels who bears the mystic name of God, SHEMHAMPHORAE. According to the Sloane manuscript *Book of Raziel*, he is one of the GUARDIAN ANGELS of Sunday. He also has power over the element of earth. As a guardian angel of humans born under Sagittarius between 28 November and 2 December he is described as the angel of poise, who helps to perceive the beauty and grace in every individual. He also teaches goodness and the arts of appeasement. On the other hand, in *1 Enoch* he is listed among the FALLEN ANGELS. In hell he is said to rule over lawyers.

Danjal One of the GRIGORI according to *1 Enoch*. The name is also an alternative spelling of DANIEL.

Danpi, **Danpy** An angel of the sixth lunar month according to the *Liber Juratus* and the Sloane manuscript *Book of Raziel*.

Danroc An angel of the fourth lunar month in the *Liber Juratus* and the Sloane manuscript *Book of Raziel*.

69

Danyturla see AAL

Dapsion, Dapsyon This is one of the angels presiding over Saturday in the *Liber Juratus* and the Sloane manuscript *Book of Raziel*. If invoked appropriately and in a state of purity, they will aid you.

Darbiel An angel of the south of the first heaven in the Sloane manuscript *Book of Raziel*. In some versions of the *Lemegeton* he is an angel of the tenth hour of the day, serving under ORIEL.

Darda'il An angel invoked in exorcism in Arabic tradition.

Dardariel The angel governing the eleventh hour of the night according to the *Lemegeton*. His many followers include CARDIEL, **Permon, Armiel, Nastoriel, Casmiroz, Dameriel, Furamiel, Mafriel, Hariaz, Damar, Alachuc, Emeriel, Naveroz, Alaphar, Nermas, Druchas, Carman, Elamyz, Jatroziel, Lamersy** and **Hamarytzod.**

Dargoyeyl(l) In the *Liber Juratus* and the Sloane manuscript *Book of Raziel* this is one of the GUARDIAN ANGELS of Sunday (Solis).

Dariculin According to the Sloane manuscript *Book of Raziel* this is one of the GUARDIAN ANGELS with special care of Monday (Luna). He is **Daryenyn** in the *Liber Juratus*.

Dariel, Daryel In the Sloane manuscript *Book of Raziel*, an angel of the eleventh lunar month. This is probably the same as **Dahariel**, described variously as a guard of the first or fifth heaven.

Darifiel An angel of the element fire, under the planet Cocab (Mercury), to be invoked when working under this planet, according to the Sloane manuscript *Book of Raziel*.

Dark Angel The term Dark Angel is used of SATAN and other denizens of hell, and widely found in fantasy writing and games, but has a special use in a positive sense. It is used to describe the entity – variously identified as a man, an angel or the Lord himself, with whom Jacob wrestles all night at Peniel (see Genesis 32:30). When it is identified as an angel, various names have been put forward. *The Zohar* calls him SAMAEL; Talmudic commentators MICHAEL-METATRON and others have suggested PENIEL or URIEL.

Darosiel see SAMAEL

Darquiel An angel of the south of the first heaven in the Sloane manuscript *Book of Raziel*. In the *Heptameron* he is an angel of Monday and of the first heaven, who should be invoked from the south.

Daryoel, Daryoiel see DABRIEL

Dasfripyel, Daffrypeyl An angel of Tuesday in the *Liber Juratus* and the Sloane manuscript *Book of Raziel*.

Dathiel The angel that rules the twelfth degree of Gemini under GIEL, according to the *Lemegeton*.

Datziel The angel that rules the fifteenth degree of Libra under JAEL, in the *Lemegeton*.

Debitael An angel of the element fire,

under the planet Noga (Venus), to be invoked when working under this planet, according to the Sloane manuscript *Book of Raziel*.

Dedion This is one of the angels presiding over Saturday, the day of Saturn or Sabat, according to the Sloane manuscript *Book of Raziel*. If invoked appropriately and in a state of purity, they will aid you.

Degalim The Degalim are a brigade of angels whose name simply means 'division'. As a class they are found in Qumran scrolls and in *3 Enoch*, whose author has a habit of taking general terms describing angels and turning them into a new class of angels.

Deinatz see ABASDARHON

Delgna, **Dalqua** An angel of the fourth lunar month found in the *Liber Juratus* and the Sloane manuscript *Book of Raziel*.

Demanoz see SERQUANICH

Demaor see PAMYEL

Demarac, **Demarae** see BERATIEL

Demarot see OSMADIEL

Demasor see BARIEL

Demiurge From the Greek *demiourgos*, 'craftsman' this is a word used by Plato (in his *Timaeus*) for the divine being who created the visible world. It was used by the early Greek Christian writers for God in his role as Creator. However, Gnostics and those influenced by them, used the word for a lesser

being, the inferior deity who merely made the tangible world (see IALDABOATH), as opposed to the much higher supreme God, and this led to its abandonment by orthodox Christians. Because of these varied meanings there can be some confusion about exactly what a writer means when they use it.

Den, **Dena** see DAENA

Denaryz see SARANDIEL

Denmerzym In the Sloane manuscript *Book of Raziel*, this is one of the angels of Sunday, who is not in the *Liber Juratus*.

Deparael An angel of the element fire, under the planet Noga (Venus), to be invoked when working under this planet, according to the Sloane manuscript *Book of Raziel*.

Dersam An angel of the third lunar month, whose naming brings benefits according to both the Sloane manuscript *Book of Raziel* and the *Liber Juratus*.

Destroying Angels Destroying angels are angels who act as the Sword of God in meting out deserved punishment. They are innumerable, but rarely named. They are counterbalanced by **Mediating Angels** who, like GUARDIAN ANGELS, protect the individual from the Pit.

Detriel According to the Sloane manuscript *Book of Raziel*, this is one of the GUARDIAN ANGELS of Sunday (Solis) who should be invoked to aid works started on that day. This angel also appears in the *Liber Juratus* as **Detryeyll**.

Devachiah One of the angels whose name is used in the First Pentacle of Jupiter, used in hunting for treasure in *The Key of Solomon.*

Devas, Devis, Daevas There is an enormous range of meanings that can be attached to the word 'deva'. Its origin lies in Hinduism, but even there, so varied is the religion in practice that deva can carry many different aspects of meaning. In its simplest form, the word means a god (with **devi** for goddess), but is more strictly a celestial power that is a manifestation of a natural power. It can be used to indicate a god worshipped as an aspect of the Supreme Being. It can also be used more loosely to indicate a lesser god. When these ideas were taken up in the West, particularly by the Theosophists in the later nineteenth and twentieth centuries, the concept of the Deva developed into that of a type of nature spirit. In this view they are the architects of the physical realm who hold the blueprints to all earthly creation. Everything that is manifested in the physical realm is watched over by a Deva. A Deva in the New Age movement refers to any of the spiritual forces or beings behind nature, and can include any elemental or nature spirit down to, and including, fairies. For followers of the ideas developed by the Findhorn community, the term refers to archetypal spiritual intelligences behind species; in other words the group soul of a species.

The use of the word in Zoroastianism is very different. While Zoroastrianism developed from the same religious pool of ideas as Hinduism, there the concept of Devas (or as is it usually spelt in a Persian context **Daevas**) was very different. The Daevas were a group of gods in ancient Persia who were denounced by Zoroaster as demonic and as gods of war and strife. They were the spirits that chose to follow **Ahriman** or **Angra Mainya**, the Zoroastrian devil. There are three principal Daevas, **Aka Manah, Druj**, and **Aeshma**. Zoroaster believed that one of the AHURAS (the word means 'Lord' i.e. divine being) **Ahura Mazda** (also called Ohrmazd or **Ormazd**), was the supreme god, and chose to be good, while Ahriman chose to be evil. He then created the evil things of this world (such as the Daevas) to fight against the good things Ahura Mazda created. In ancient Persian mythology Daevas are demons who cause plagues and diseases and who fight every form of religion. They are the male servants (or followers) of Ahriman. The female servants are called the **Drugs**. Together they fight Ahuru Mazda and his AMESHA SPENTAS.

Dexxeyl An angel of the day of Mars (Tuesday) in the Sloane manuscript *Book of Raziel.*

Dik This is the word for a cock in Arabic. Some say that there is an angel in the form of a gigantic cock in paradise. His place is immediately below the throne of Allah. When he crows, the sound is repeated by all the cocks in the world, and this way the hours of prayer are announced. In *3 Baruch* (second century AD) there is a similar heavenly cock whose cry alerts all the cockerels on earth to the rising on the sun, but the call to prayer is not found outside Islam.

Din see DAENA

Dirachiel A MOON ANGEL who rules the

sixth mansion of the moon in Gemini. On the plus side he helps in hunting, in the revenge of princes and those besieging cities. On the negative side, he destroys harvests and interferes with the work of doctors.

Diviel see VATHMIEL

Djibril, **Djabra'il**, **Jibril**, **Jabriel** This is the Islamic form of the angel otherwise known as GABRIEL. Many of the traditions associated with Gabriel were taken over from Judaism into Islam, but Djibril has a very important role in the Koran, where he is called 'the faithful spirit', as the constant counsellor and companion of the Prophet. It is he who brings the revelations to the Prophet. He usually appears as a very strong man, dressed in two green garments and a silk turban, but in his true form he is of vast size, and has 600 wings, every pair of which fills the space from east to west.

Djinn The difference between angels and Djinn in Islam is that angels were created from light, the djinn from smokeless fire. Most say IBLIS is a Djinn. The singular of Djinn is **Djinni**, with **genie** and **genii** being common Western forms of the word. Djinn are of various natures, some good and some bad, and are capable of salvation – on the final day some will go to paradise, some to hell. Normally they cannot be detected by humans, but if they choose they can take on bodily forms; either animal or human. As with the angels, there are different classes of Djinn including **Ghul**, IFRIT and **Silat**, although in practice the terms are often interchangeably. There is even a class of sea-djinn, with a king that some say lives in the sea off Leander's Tower on the Bosphorus. It is thought that belief in Djinn goes back to the time when they were nature spirits ('nymphs and satyrs of the desert' as one authority puts it) in pre-Islamic Arabia. However, they are fully recognised in the Koran, and allowances for their existence even worked their way into some law codes. In popular folklore they are strongly associated with magic. In the West this is best known through the *1001 Arabian Night* stories; although once these stories became widely known in the West, Djinn, or rather genii, became a mainstay of children's stories and fairy tales. In India a copy of the Koran may be put into a new house to expel any Djinn which may have taken up residence there. In Turkish folklore Djinn are divided into Muslim ones and heathen ones, which are much more difficult to control. They are often thought to be active only at night, but if you leave them alone most will not harm you, or at least only tease you. However, if you antagonise them – polluting the area in which they live is a common way of doing this – they will punish you, often with paralysis. On the other hand, they may reward the deserving. Unlike fairies, whose gold will often turn to old leaves, the Djinn may reward you with onion skin which subsequently turns to gold, or with garlic skin which turns to silver.

Dobiel see DUBIEL

Dokiel, **Doquiel and Puriuel**, **Puruel** These are two angels of Judgement found only in the *Testament of Abraham* which dates from the first to second century AD. In this work Abraham has a vision of souls being judged after their death. The souls come before a board of angels, among whom are Dokiel, a sun-like ARCHANGEL who uses a balance to weigh the soul's righteous deeds against its sins. Then Puriuel, who has command over fire, uses fire to test the works of the man. If the fire burns up his works, then he is consigned to hell, but if they pass through the fire unscathed, then the angels of righteous-ness carry the soul up to heaven. There is some debate over the origin of the name Dokiel, as to whether it comes from a Hebrew word meaning 'exactitude' (in weighing), from a word meaning 'Justice of God' or, as has recently been suggested, from the Hebrew for 'veil'. Puriuel, it has been suggested, is a corruption of the name URIEL.

Domaras see SABRATHAN

Dominions or **Dominations** In Paul's letter to the Colossians 2:16, he declares 'For by him were all things created, that are in heaven, and that are in earth, visible and invisible, whether they be thrones, or dominions, or principalities, or powers: all things were created by him, and for him.' This is the major source for Christians of a number of CHOIRS of angels. Dominions, also known as Dominations, are said by Dionysius the Areopagite in his HIERARCHY OF THE ANGELS to rank fourth. They regulate angels' duties and through them the majesty of God is manifested. Their emblems of authority are sceptres and orbs. However, Paul is not the first to have written of them. They appear, for example, among the many ranks of angels in *2 Enoch* 20: 'And those two men lifted me up thence on to the seventh heaven, and I saw

there a very great light, and fiery troops of great archangels, incorporeal forces, and dominions, orders and govern-ments, cherubim and seraphim, thrones and many-eyed ones, nine regiments … and I became afraid, and began to tremble with great terror, and those men took me, and led me after them.' The word for Dominion has also been translated as **Lords** or **Lordships**, and some have equated them with the HASHMALIM. Using the word as a proper name, Philo call Dominion the oldest angel. In art, Dominions are tradition-ally shown crowned and carrying sceptres, orbs, swords or books. They have two wings, are dressed in green with gold belts and hold the seal of Jesus Christ in their right hand and a cross on a golden staff in their left.

Domoras see SABRATHAN

Donachiel In the *Key of Solomon*, Donachiel is an angel whose name in invoked when exorcising demons.

Doquiel see DOKIEL

Doranel An angel of the north of the third heaven in the Sloane manuscript *Book of Raziel*.

Dormason see SABRATHAN

Douma see DUMA

Drabiel see ORIEL

Dracon see ZAAZENACH

Dragos In the Sloane manuscript *Book of Raziel*, an angel of the thirteenth lunar month (March). If invoked in the relevant month, he will ensure success in your enterprise. He is not in the *Liber Juratus*.

Dramaz see ZAAZENACH

Dramozyn see NARCORIEL

Drelmech see VEQUANIEL

Dromiel see SARANDIEL

Druchas see DARDARIEL, PAMYEL

Drufiel see BARAQIEL

Drvaspa Female YAZAD (Zoroastrian angel) who protects cattle, children and friendship, although the root meaning of her name suggests she was originally associated with horses, and may thus be connected with the Celtic horse goddess Epona. The fourteenth day of the month is dedicated to her.

Dubiel, **Dubbiel**, **Dobiel** A PRINCE (or ruling angel) of the Kingdom of Persia in *3 Enoch*; to others an ACCUSING ANGEL. Daily, he sits alongside SATAN and SAMAEL to write down the sins of Israel. They pass the writing tablets to the SERAPHIM to pass on to God, but the Seraphim burn them instead. In the *Lemegeton* he is a duke of the night. Some say that his name means 'bear-god' and rank him among the FALLEN ANGELS.

Dubraz see MENDRION

Duchiel An angel whose name is used for conjuration in the *Key of Solomon*.

Dufuel One of the angels of Wednesday, the day of Mercury, according to the Sloane manuscript *Book of Raziel*. It has become **Dafngel** in the *Liber Juratus*.

Duma, **Dumah**, **Douma** In Rabbinic sources Duma is the angel of the underworld. The name comes from the Hebrew or Aramaic for 'silence', probably because he guards those who are silent in death. In *The Zohar* he is said to have 10,000 angels of destruction under him, and in Jewish folklore he is an ANGEL OF DEATH. In Isaac Bashevis Singer's *Short Friday* (1964) he is described as a 'thousand-eyed angel of death, armed with a fiery rod or flaming sword'. But elsewhere he is seen in a more kindly light, and described as an angel who is the ruler of dreams, invoked to send dreams that will give advice or answer questions. The ritual for this is performed on a Sunday night, and must only be performed for really important matters. In this tradition Duma, the angel of dreams, is carefully distinguished from Dumah, the angel of the stillness of death.

Duraniel An angel of the south of the first heaven in the Sloane manuscript *Book of Raziel*.

Durba'il An angel invoked in exorcism in Arabic tradition.

E

Eazerin An angel presiding over Friday, the day of Venus, according to the Sloane manuscript *Book of Raziel*. The *Liber Juratus* has a completely different angel in this place: **Rayoryn**.

Edriel see BERATIEL

Effignax One of the angels of the sixth lunar month according to the Sloane manuscript *Book of Raziel*. In the *Liber Juratus* the name has become **Effygmato**.

Effilin, **Esfylyn** An angel presiding over Friday, the day of Venus, according to the *Liber Juratus* and the Sloane manuscript *Book of Raziel*.

Egibiel A MOON ANGEL who rules the eighteenth mansion of the moon in Scorpio. He helps in the binding and freeing of prisoners, but otherwise is destructive, causing disputes, sedition and conspiracy against those in power and helping in revenge.

Eiael, **Eyael** This is one of the seventy-two SHEMHAMPHORAE angels. He has dominion over longevity and over occult knowledge. When he is conjured the fourth verse of the thirty-second Psalm must be recited. As the GUARDIAN ANGEL of those born under Pisces between 20 and 24 February he is said to be an angel of happiness, giving a positive outlook on life. He is also said to give knowledge of philosophy and physics.

Eisheth Zenunim see AGRAT BAT MAHLAT, HARUT AND MARUT

Elamyz see DARDARIEL

Elberith see BALBERITH

Eldil C S Lewis's religious science-fiction trilogy (*Out of the Silent Planet* (1938), *Perelandra* (1943), and *That Hideous Strength* (1945)) deliberately sets out to recreate biblical figures in allegory, showing how Earth had fallen from the true path, unlike other planets. In these books **Eldila** (**Eldil** in the singular) are creatures that most of Mankind can only perceive, if they are lucky, as a vague shimmer in the air, but that more enlightened races can see and converse with. Ransome, the hero of the books, realises that they are angels. Each planet has a GUARDIAN ANGEL, called an **Oyarsa**, who embodies the planet. **Perelandra** (Venus) and **Malacandra** (Mars) ring out with praise for **Maledil** the Young (the Creator/Christ figure), but **Thulcandra** (Earth) is silent – the name means 'the silent planet' – because the Black Oyarsa of Thulcandra (Lewis's Satan figure) has fallen, along with other Black Oyarsa called **Macrobres**. The portrayal of Tinidril, the Eve that does not disobey and fall in Perelandra, is an important element behind Philip Pullman's *His Dark Materials* trilogy, in which his Eve, Lyra, redeems the world through falling. (See further on Pullman under BALTHAMOS and XAPHANIA.)

Eleleth Meaning 'sagacity', this is the name of the Great Angel who stands before the face of God, in the Gnostic text *The Hypostasis of the Archons*. He gives instructions on the nature of the ARCHONS (see also AEONS) that rule the Spheres.

Elementals This is another term for

spirit beings that varies in meaning according to who is using it and which belief system they are dealing with. At their most basic, Elementals are attuned to the four basic elements – believed in the past to be the basic components of the tangible world – earth, air, fire and water. The sixteenth-century mystic Paracelsus seems to have been the first person to formulate this basic system, and he called his elementals **Sylphs** for those of air, **Gnomes** for earth, **Salamanders** for fire and **Undines** for water. Elementals are important in magic, and can be summoned with the correct formula and made to do the summoner's bidding. Elementals are said to be ruled by angels – one system says ARIEL rules the earth Elementals, CHERUB those of air, THARSIS water, and NATHANIEL or SERAPH fire. The concept of elementals has been widely developed by different people in the last century and has also been taken up in fantasy gaming, writing and comic books.

Elemiah One of the eight SERAPHIM of the Tree of Life who also rules over travel, particularly at sea. As the GUARDIAN ANGEL of those born under Aries between 5 and 9 April he is said to be the angel of change, who supports travel, immigration and new beginnings. The *Liber Juratus* and *Aprippa* list him as one of the seventy-two angels who bear the mystic name of God, SHEMHAMPHORAE.

Eliel, **Elieyl** According to the Sloane manuscript *Book of Raziel* this is one of the GUARDIAN ANGELS of Sunday. Elsewhere, he is simply described as an angel invoked for magic, while the *Lemegeton* describes him as an angel of the night serving under **Maseriel**.

Elim A class of angels in *3 Enoch*. The name comes from Exodus 15:11 'Who is like unto thee, O Lord, among the gods [*elim* in Hebrew]?' It is also found as the proper name of an angel, and as a divine name associated with the moon.

Eliphamasai The *Lemegeton* says that this is an angel that can be invoked to control the loss or gain of wealth. When conjured it appears as a child or small woman, dressed in green and silver, with a wreath of bay leaves decorated with white and green flowers, and leaves a sweet smell behind.

Elisafan, **Elysafan** An angel of the fourth lunar month according to the *Liber Juratus* and the Sloane manuscript *Book of Raziel*.

Elisuaig An angel of the eighth lunar month according to the Sloane manuscript *Book of Raziel*, which says that if they are named 'in each thing that thou wilt do … thou shalt profit'.

Ellalyel An angel of the element fire, under the planet Hanina (Sol, the sun), to be invoked when working under this planet, according to the Sloane manuscript *Book of Raziel*.

Elmia One of the angels of Wednesday, the day of Mercury, according to the Sloane manuscript *Book of Raziel*.

Elmoym see HANIEL

Elohim This term can mean either God, the angels in general, or a specific class of angels, depending on which text it is found in. Modern angelologists have identified them as the seven great angels who are also the Lords of Karma.

They are one of the ten CHOIRS of the Holy Angels, according to the *Key of Solomon, The Zohar* and Moses Maimonides. The singular form, **Eloha** is invoked as an angel in kabbalistic rites. See also under HIERARCHY OF THE ANGELS, BENE ELOHIM, MELCHIZEDEK.

Elomnia The *Lemegeton* says that this is an angel that can be invoked to control the loss or gain of wealth. When conjured it appears as a child or small woman, dressed in green and silver, wearing a wreath of bay leaves decorated with white and green flowers, and leaves a sweet smell behind.

Elynzy An angel of the ninth lunar month according to the *Liber Juratus* and the Sloane manuscript *Book of Raziel.*

Emalon see SABRATHAN

Emarfiel see VATHMIEL

Emarion see SARANDIEL

Emaryel, Ematyel see TARTYS

Emarziel see IASSUARIM

Emcodeneyl A Tuesday angel in the Sloane manuscript *Book of Raziel.* The name is **Lyncodoneyl** in the *Liber Juratus.*

Emeriel see DARDARIEL

Emim see NEPHILIM

Emyel An angel of the element water, under the planet Noga (Venus), to be invoked when working under this planet, according to the Sloane manuscript *Book of Raziel.*

Enariel see ZAAZENACH

Enatriel see JEFISCHA

Enediel A MOON ANGEL who rules the second mansion of the moon in Aries. He helps you to find treasure, and supports planting of seeds. He helps keep prisoners secure, but impedes the function of purging medicine.

Enoch see GREEN MAN, METATRON

Enplyn An angel of the day of Mars (Tuesday) in the Sloane manuscript *Book of Raziel.*

Eralyn An angel of the day of Mars (Tuesday) found in the Sloane manuscript *Book of Raziel.* He is also an angel of Tuesday in the *Liber Juratus.*

Erelim, Erellim A class of angels found in *3 Enoch* and other texts. The name derives from a passage in Isaiah 33:7: 'Behold, their valiant ones [*erellim*] shall cry without: the ambassadors of peace shall weep bitterly.' They are one of the ten orders of angels listed by Maimonides. They are sometimes equated with THRONES, BENE ELOHIM or ISSIM. In the form **Aralim** they are listed as one of the ten CHOIRS of the Holy Angels in the *Key of Solomon,* and they are also called **Arelim**. They are said to be made of white fire and to be very numerous, to be ruled by either MICHAEL or RAZIEL, to live in the fourth or fifth heaven, and to rule over vegetation. An alternative view is that they are of the angelic order of BINAH (Intelligence), the third sephira of the Kabbalistic Tree of Life under the rule of TZAPHKIEL.

Eremiel see REMIEL

Erethe Female YAZAD (Zoroastrian angel) personifying truth.

Ergediel A MOON ANGEL who rules the fourteenth mansion of the moon in Virgo. He encourages love between married people and cures the sick. He helps those travelling by sea, but hinders those on land.

Ermaziel see HANIEL

Ermiel see OSMADIEL

Eros In the earliest Greek theological writing Eros is simply an abstract concept of sexual passion, but he was soon transformed into a beautiful youth, often shown with wings. There are various stories of his origins. Some describe him as the first of the gods, hatched from the world egg; but he is most often seen as the son of Aphrodite, the goddess of love and passion, fathered by Hermes, who is a phallic god as well as a PSYCHOPOMP, or by Ares, god of war, symbolising the close connection between sex and violence or even by her own father Zeus, king of the gods. The many illustrations of Eros and his Roman equivalent **Cupid**, as a winged child or youth, have had a profound influence on the popular depiction of angels. It is worth noting that the famous statue in Piccadilly Circus, popularly known as Eros, is actually meant to be of Christian Charity, showing just how blurred the borders are in iconography. **Erotes**, the plural form of Eros, appear in Greek myth as aspects of love. They are depicted as winged youths which are often indistinguishable from angels. The

Erotes are: **Anteros**, god of mutual love; Eros; **Hedylogos**, the god of sweet talk and flattery; **Hermaphroditos**, whose body took on aspects of both male and female after the nymph, Salmakis, prayed they would never be parted; **Himeros**, sexual desire; **Hymenaios**, the god of the wedding ceremony, and **Pothos**, the god of passionate longing. These are sometimes shown flocking round Aphrodite, in much the same way as angels are shown around the throne of God. Cupid gets his name from *cupido*, the Latin for 'I desire', and was seen by the Romans not only as a god of life but also as a symbol of life after death. Cupid figures are given the role of conducting the souls of the dead, thus linking them with Hermes. Because of this they are often found on sarcophagi and funerary monuments, again reinforcing the associations with angels.

Esiel An earth angel under Sabaday (Saturn), to be invoked when working under this planet, according to the Sloane manuscript *Book of Raziel*. He is probably the same as **Eschiel** or **Eshiel**, one of the four angels whose names are inscribed on the First Pentacle of the planet Mars in magic rites.

Esmaadyn According to the *Liber Juratus* and the Sloane manuscript *Book of Raziel,* this is one of the angels of Sunday (Solis), who should be invoked to aid works started on that day. He also appears in the *Liber Juratus* as an angel of Sunday.

Espandarmaz, **Esphand** see SPENTA ARMAITI

Essaf An angel of the fifth lunar month

according to the *Liber Juratus* and the Sloane manuscript *Book of Raziel*.

Eudaemon see DAEMON

Evadar see SANIEL

Evandiel see PAMYEL

Evanuel see SERQUANICH

Evarym see BARAQIEL

Exousiai The Greek term for a CHOIR of angels equated variously with AUTHORITIES, DOMINIONS, POWERS or VIRTUES.

Expaoniel An angel of the element water, under the planet Noga (Venus), to be invoked when working under this planet, according to the Sloane manuscript *Book of Raziel*.

Expion This is one of the angels presiding over Saturday in the Sloane manuscript *Book of Raziel*.

Eyael see EIAEL

Eyzad see YAZAD

Ezekeel, **Ezeqeel** One of the GRIGORI who taught Mankind augury from the clouds according to *1 Enoch* 6.

Ezuiah, **Eznyah** In the *Liber Juratus* and the Sloane manuscript *Book of Raziel* this is a Sunday angel.

F

Faceyeyl In the *Liber Juratus* and the Sloane manuscript *Book of Raziel*, this is one of the GUARDIAN ANGELS of Sunday.

Falafon In the Sloane manuscript *Book of Raziel*, an angel of the twelfth lunar month. The name appears as **Falason** in the *Liber Juratus*, a not surprising form as an old-fashioned long 's' (effectively an 'f' without the cross-bar) and an 'f' are easily confused.

Falha According to the Sloane manuscript *Book of Raziel*, this is one of the GUARDIAN ANGELS of Sunday (Solis) who should be invoked to aid works started on that day.

Fall of the Angels see ANGELS, FALL OF THE

Fallen Angels A general term used for those angels who have fallen from grace and are now confined to either one of the punishment levels of heaven, to earth or to hell, depending on which version is being told, although popular belief generally puts them in hell as demons. There are two main groups, the GRIGORI, or WATCHERS, who were so attracted by Mankind (and particularly womankind) that they came to earth to join with and instruct them; and those who rebelled with SATAN or one of his analogues. In addition, there are various other stories of individual or smaller groups of angels being cast out of heaven. While images of demons in hell are too familiar to need elaboration, the punishment of angels in the heavens is less familiar. One such description is found at *2 Enoch* 7: 'And those men picked me up and brought me up to the second heaven. And they showed me, and I saw a darkness greater than earthly darkness. And there I perceived prisoners under guard, hanging up, waiting for the measureless judgement. And those angels have the appearance of darkness itself, more than earthly darkness. And unceasingly they made weeping, all the day long. And I said to the men who were with me, "Why are these ones being tormented unceasingly?" Those men answered me, "These are those who turned away from the Lord, who did not obey the Lord's commandments, but of their own will plotted together and turned away with their prince and with those who are under restraint in the fifth heaven." And I felt very sorry for them: and those angels bowed down to me and said to me, "Man of God, pray for us to the Lord!"' The number of named fallen angels is vast, but most of them have been omitted from this book, as not belonging here, unless there has been a good reason to put them in.

Falling Angels, City of A name for Venice, used as the title of a 2005 book by John Berendt. In the early 1970s, when Venice seemed to be crumbling, this was the wording of a sign on the steps of the Salute church.

Faly An angel of the west of the fifth heaven in the Sloane manuscript *Book of Raziel*.

Famaras see BERATIEL

Famoriel see TARTYS

Faniel, Fanyel In the Sloane manuscript *Book of Raziel* an angel of the twelfth lunar month. If invoked in the relevant month, he will ensure success in your enterprise. He serves a similar function on Thursdays, the day of Jupiter. The name may be a form of PHANAEL, who is also found as **Fanuel**.

Farabyn An angel of the day of Mars (Tuesday) in the *Liber Juratus* and the Sloane manuscript *Book of Raziel*.

Farbiel An angel of the east of the fifth heaven in the Sloane manuscript *Book of Raziel*.

Farielin According to the Sloane manuscript *Book of Raziel* this is one of the angels with special care of Monday (Luna) who should be invoked to aid works started on that day.

Farionon One of the angels of Wednesday, the day of Mercury, found in the Sloane manuscript *Book of Raziel*.

Farmos see BARAQIEL

Farnnial, Faranyeal One of the angels of Wednesday, the day of Mercury, according to the *Liber Juratus* and the Sloane manuscript *Book of Raziel*.

Farohars see FRAVASHIS

Farrah see KHWARENAH

Felyypon, Selyypon This is one of the Saturday angels in the *Liber Juratus* and the Sloane manuscript *Book of Raziel*.

Fenadros see PAMYEL

Feniturla, Fenyturla One of the angels of Wednesday, the day of Mercury, according to the *Liber Juratus* and the Sloane manuscript *Book of Raziel*.

Fenosiel see BERATIEL

Feyn One of the angels of Wednesday, the day of Mercury, according to the Sloane manuscript *Book of Raziel*. **Feynon** in the *Liber Juratus* is presumably the same.

Fimarson see BERATIEL

Flatoniel An angel of the element air, under the planet Madin (Mars), to be invoked when working under this planet, according to the Sloane manuscript *Book of Raziel*.

Foniel An angel of the element fire, under the planet Zedek (Jupiter), to be invoked when working under this planet, found in the Sloane manuscript *Book of Raziel*.

Forces An order of angels identified by John of Damascus, who ranked them fourth in the hierarchy, and said their domain was earthly affairs. They are sometimes equated with POWERS.

Foylylon This is one of the angels presiding over Saturday, the day of Saturn or Sabat, according to Sloane manuscript *Book of Raziel* and the *Liber Juratus*.

Framion see OSMADIEL

Framoth see MENDRION

Franedac see SABRATHAN

Fravashis, **Arda Fravash** or **Farohars** The Zoroastrian equivalents of GUARDIAN ANGELS. Each person is said to be accompanied by a Fravashi through their life to act as a guide, although, like Socrates' DAEMON, the Fravashi will not actually interfere with the person's decisions. However, it will act as a conscience, to guide the person away from spiritual danger, while still leaving them with free will. They are considered manifestations of the energy of God, and the Creator, **Ahura Mazda**, is said to have created the Fravashis before he created the universe. At one time they were guardians of the ramparts of heaven, but volunteered to descend to earth to be guardians of men instead. They preserve order in creation and if it were not for their guardianship animals and people could not have continued to exist, because the wicked Druj or Drug ('lies, falsehood' – see under DAEVAS) would have destroyed them all. Humans should try to emulate the Fravashis, and hope after death to be united with them. The earth, sun, moon, stars, trees and human beings all have their Fravashis, and the duty of the Fravashis is to watch over the orderly growth of the world and to make it prosper. The Fravashis of the dead expect to be remembered by the living and are invoked by a dead person's descendants: in return they will bless the living, and there is a feeling that each family has its own protective Fravashi. Fravashis are depicted as human figures riding on a winged disc with hooked streamers below the disc. This is a pre-Zoroastrian design, from a time when the spirits of departed heroes were believed to be powerful winged beings and were invoked by the living for protection and help. These figures are known as **Fravahar** and are common on ancient Persian ruins, particularly those from the times of Darius and Xerxes, who are thought to have adopted this winged symbol to indicate that they had received glory and sovereignty from Ahura Mazda. The iconography of the **Fravahar** is firmly fixed with a detailed interpretation. The figure as a whole signifies divinity; the three layers of feathers in the tail depict good thoughts, good words and good deeds. The five layers of feathers in the wings represent the five periods of the day and the two hooks that hang below the spread wings depict the two opposing forces of good and evil that exist in this universe. The raised hand depicts the truth and the central ring, the power of righteousness. This iconography goes back to the earliest Mesopotamian carvings of angel-type spiritual beings, and has distinct similarities with Jewish concepts of spiritual beings, including the MERKABAH.

Fremiel see JEFISCHA

Fromezyn see TARTYS

Fronyzon see SERQUANICH

Fuheylyn A Tuesday angel in the *Liber Juratus* and the Sloane manuscript *Book of Raziel*.

Fulitiel A water angel under Sabaday (Saturn), to be invoked when working under this planet, according to the Sloane manuscript *Book of Raziel*.

Furamiel see DARDARIEL

Furiel see VEQUANIEL

G

Gabal One of the angels of Wednesday, the day of Mercury, according to the *Liber Juratus* and the Sloane manuscript *Book of Raziel*.

Gabamiah, **Jabamiah** Gabamiah is subordinate to URIEL, and can be conjured using his name. He is also considered a GUARDIAN ANGEL of those born under Pisces between 6 and 10 March and in this role is an angel of power who assists in the pursuit of one's ambitions. He is also one of the SHEMHAMPHORAE.

Gabanael In the *Liber Juratus* and the Sloane manuscript *Book of Raziel*, an angel of the thirteenth lunar month (March). If invoked in the relevant month, he will ensure success in your enterprise.

Gabgel In the Sloane manuscript *Book of Raziel*, an angel of the thirteenth lunar month (March). If invoked in the relevant month, he will ensure success in your enterprise.

Gabiel The angel that rules the thirteenth degree of Aries under AIEL, according to the *Lemegeton*.

Gabion This is one of the angels presiding over Saturday, the day of Saturn or Sabat, according to the Sloane manuscript *Book of Raziel*. If invoked appropriately and in a state of purity, they will aid you. **Gabmion**, found there as an angel of the second lunar month, may be the same angel.

Gabriel Gabriel means 'Man of God', although some interpret it as 'God is my strength'. Of his many roles, Gabriel's most important is to be God's messenger. His most famous message is the Annunciation to Mary, when he is sent to tell her that she is to give birth to Jesus. He is one of only two angels mentioned by name in the main body of the Bible, and he holds the rank of ARCHANGEL. He appears in the Bible in the Book of Daniel in the shape of a man, sent to Daniel by God to explain his vision. Some identify him with the 'man clothed with linen' in Ezekiel 9. In Jewish tradition he is governor of paradise, controls serpents and rules the CHERUBIM. He stands before the face of God or on the left side of the Lord, and dominates all the forces of heaven. *3 Enoch* calls him the angel of fire, a role also given to NURIEL, MICHAEL and others, and he is also called an ANGEL OF MERCY. He is also said to be an angel of prayer, light, and an ANGEL OF PARADISE. In *2 Enoch* it is Gabriel who takes Enoch up to heaven. With Michael, he is said by some to be the GUARDIAN ANGEL of the Jews, but others say that after the destruction of the Tower of Babel the seventy angels that attend the throne of God cast lots for the guardianship of the newly formed nations, with the nation of Israel falling to God's lot. He is called archangel of the moon. He is a saint of the Catholic Church, with a feast day on 24 March, and is patron of those who relate to his functions as messenger – telecommunication workers, broadcasters, messengers, postal workers (and the stamp collectors dependent on them), clerics and diplomats. For those influenced by the Kabbalah, he commands the spiritual wisdom of

SOPHIA and is the angel to call on for assistance with our hopes, dreams, aspirations and the birth of new projects, all things to do with motherhood, physical birth, babies and children and those aspects of spirituality which are associated with Divine Mother, and for strength to overcome fear.

There are numerous legends about Gabriel. During the creation of Mankind, Gabriel is sent by God to gather dust from the earth to be used to form Man, but the Earth refuses to co-operate, unless God himself gathers the dust. When Mankind was created not all the angels thought it was a good idea. The band of angels under Gabriel objected, and as a result, were all consumed by fire. When the new-born Abraham was abandoned in a cave, it was Gabriel who caused milk to flow from his right little finger, so that by sucking it Abraham was fed, and Gabriel later instructed him in religion and protected him from danger. By tradition it was Gabriel who was in charge of the destruction of Sodom and Gomorrah. Gabriel is also sent by God to destroy the NEPHILIM in *1 Enoch*.

He is important in books of conjuration: the *Lemegeton* says Gabriel rules in the north, with SAMAEL, MADIEL and MAEL under him, and is to be addressed when dealing with the watery signs of the zodiac (Cancer, Scorpio and Pisces). It also states that he is an angel who is invoked for fertility in animals, plants and women. In the Sloane manuscript of *The Book of Raziel,* as well as being ANGEL OF THE MOON (although the same work elsewhere gives this job to ANAEL), he is angel of the element fire, and of the east and the eleventh lunar month. He also has power over air. He is said to reside in the east of the first heaven, although *3 Enoch* says Gabriel is in charge of the sixth heaven, Makon. Gabriel is said by some to be the angel who rules the fifth mansion of the moon in Taurus, helping scholars, giving health and goodwill and helping those travelling home, but others say this is CABRIEL. Gabriel is sometimes said to wear green and have a golden horn held to his lips, but can be identified in pictures by the lily he holds in his hand, particularly in pictures of the Annunciation. In earlier painting this may be a sceptre topped by a fleur-de-lis. Wound round this there may be a scroll with the words *Ave Maria* ('Hail Mary') or *Ave gratia plena Dominus tecum* ('Greetings most favoured one. The Lord is with you') taken from Luke 1:28. For his role in Islam see under DJIBRIL.

Gabrinoz see TARTYS

Gabrynyn An angel of the day of Mars (Tuesday) in the *Liber Juratus* and the Sloane manuscript *Book of Raziel*.

Gabuthelon One of the nine 'angels who are over the consummation' (interpreted as meaning the end of the world) in the Greek *Apocalypse of Ezra,* about which nothing more is known.

Gadaf An angel of the fifth lunar month according to the Sloane manuscript *Book of Raziel*, who if invoked brings benefits. He appears as **Gadeff** in the *Liber Juratus*.

Gadiel An angel of the south of the fourth heaven in the Sloane manuscript *Book of Raziel*. In *The Key of Solomon*, an angel whose name is invoked when preparing materials for the practice of magic. According to the *Lemegeton,* the

angel that rules the fifteenth degree of Aries under AIEL. Elsewhere he is a guardian of the gates of the South Wind, and invoked for protection against evil.

Gadreel A leader of the GRIGORI who showed Mankind how to use weapons and defensive arms, so that war has been the lot of man ever since, according to *1 Enoch*. In some traditions he is said to have seduced Eve. As **Gadriel** he is considered to be an angel, while keeping his associations, for he is said to be in charge of wars among nations. In *The Zohar* it says that when a prayer rises up to the fifth heaven **Gadriel** crowns it and takes it on to the sixth heaven. Since ANPIEL resides in the sixth heaven and is also involved in the transmission of prayer, they would appear to work as a team.

Gael An air angel under Sabaday (Saturn), to be invoked when working under this planet, according to the Sloane manuscript *Book of Raziel*. He is to be found in the east of the fourth heaven.

Galbiet An angel presiding over Thursday, the day of Jove, according to the Sloane manuscript *Book of Raziel*. He appears as **Galbyel** in the *Liber Juratus*, so at some point someone has forgotten to cross a 't' or inadvertently crossed an 'l'.

Galgaliel, Galgalli'el The angel of the course of the sun in *3 Enoch*. With the aid of ninety-six other angels, his job is to see that the sun runs its daily course. He is also chief of the GALGALLIM, the connection between his different roles being the wheel of the sun. **Galgall,** an angel of the fourth lunar month according to the Sloane manuscript *Book of Raziel,* is likely to be the same. The name is spelt **Galgal** in the *Liber Juratus.*

Galgallim A class of angels whose name means 'wheels'. They are derived from the description of the wheels in the vision of Ezekiel (Ezekiel 10:13). These are usually called OPHANIM, but in some texts, such as *3 Enoch,* Galgallim are a separate class.

Galliel In the Sloane manuscript *Book of Raziel* an angel with power over water. Elsewhere **Galiel** is the angel of the twenty-third hour of Thursday as well as being one of the many names of METATRON.

Gallisur YHWH A mighty Prince in *3 Enoch* 'who reveals all the secrets of the Torah'. The name also appears as **Galizur**, and he is sometimes identified with the angel RAZIEL, and said to be the angel who gave the *Book of Raziel* to Adam. He is also said to be found in the second heaven and to spread his wings over the HAYYOT to prevent their fiery breath consuming the ministering angels.

Galms An angel of the second lunar month according to the Sloane manuscript *Book of Raziel* with the power to grant your wishes. He appears as **Galmus** in the *Liber Juratus.*

Galnel An angel of the ninth lunar month according to the *Liber Juratus* and the Sloane manuscript *Book of Raziel,* which says that if they are named 'in each thing that thou wilt do … thou shalt profit'.

Galuf An angel of the fourth lunar month according to the *Liber Juratus* and the Sloane manuscript *Book of Raziel*, who if invoked brings benefits. **Galus**, an angel of the second lunar month according to the Sloane manuscript *Book of Raziel* with the power to grant wishes, may be an alternative form of the name, with the old long 's' form and an 'f' being confused.

Gamaliel In Gnostic texts Gamaliel is a great AEON, among whose roles is taking the elect to heaven. However, others see him as an evil spirit who serves the spirit of debauchery, Lilith.

Gamidoi In *The Key of Solomon*, an angel whose name is invoked when preparing materials for the practice of magic.

Gamiel, **Gamyel** An angel of the ninth lunar month according to the Sloane manuscript *Book of Raziel*. As Gamyel, he is a follower of SANIEL, angel of the sixth hour in the *Lemegeton* although elsewhere he is said to rule the first hour of the night.

Gamsiel see NARCORIEL

Gandalf There has been some debate as to whether Gandalf in Tolkien's *Lord of the Rings* trilogy should be regarded as an angel or not. T A Shippey in *The Road to Middle Earth* doubts it was more than something Tolkien said to cope with pressure from fans, and points out that as a philologist Tolkien would be quite comfortable using angel in its original sense of 'messenger'. David Colbert, on the other hand, takes a diametrically opposite view in his *Magical Worlds of the Lord of the Rings*.

There he states, 'As Tolkien explained in letters to readers, Gandalf is actually an angel, sent to Middle Earth on a mission. The **Valar** want to help the creatures of Middle Earth resist Sauron, so they send spirits to Middle Earth to do some gentle prodding. Gandalf and some other angels, together called **Istari**, share that task.' Some of the confusions arise because of the vast amount of material that was published after Tolkien's death which has many inconsistencies, because it represents different drafts of his ideas that he never worked up into a unified whole. What cannot be doubted is that Tolkien was a deeply devout Christian, and that his work is imbued with Christian imagery.

Garasyn In the *Liber Juratus* and the Sloane manuscript *Book of Raziel*, an angel of the thirteenth lunar month (March). If invoked in the relevant month, he will ensure success in your enterprise.

Gasca In the Sloane manuscript *Book of Raziel*, an angel of the tenth lunar month. If invoked in rites his name will ensure good results.

Gasoryn According to the Sloane manuscript *Book of Raziel* this is one of the GUARDIAN ANGELS with special care of Monday (Luna). He is also a Monday angel in the *Liber Juratus*.

Gaw YAZAD (Zoroastrian angel) personifying cattle.

Gazriel, **Gazril** In the Sloane manuscript *Book of Raziel*, an angel of the eleventh lunar month. If invoked in the relevant month, he will ensure

success in your enterprise. It also describes him as having power over fire and flame. This may be the same angel as **Gazardiel**, who according to *The Zohar* is supervisor of the east and is an angel who kisses prayers and takes them up to heaven. He is also said to oversee the rising and setting of the sun.

Gebarbayea According to the Sloane manuscript *Book of Raziel* this is one of the angels of Sunday (Solis) who should be invoked to aid works started on that day. He also appears as an angel of Sunday in the *Liber Juratus*.

Gebiel The angel that rules the twelfth degree of Pisces under PASIL, according to the *Lemegeton*.

Geburah In the *Key of Solomon* identified as one of the angels who preside over the ten SEFIROTH. Elsewhere he is described as the fifth of the Sefiroth, and a SERAPH who is the upholder of the left hand of God.

Geburatiel YHWH, **Geburathiel** One of the greatest angels in heaven, according to *3 Enoch*. He represents divine strength and power and is chief steward of the fourth hall of the seventh heaven.

Gebyn One of the angels of Wednesday, the day of Mercury, found in the Sloane manuscript *Book of Raziel* and the *Liber Juratus*.

Geciel The angel that rules the nineteenth degree of Aries under AIEL, according to the *Lemegeton*.

Gediel The angel that rules the thirteenth degree of Virgo under VOIL, in the *Lemegeton*. In the *Book of Raziel* he features as an angel whose name can be used in CHILDBED amulets.

Gedobonai The *Lemegeton* says that this is an angel that can be invoked to control the loss or gain of wealth. When conjured it appears as a child or small woman, dressed in green and silver, wearing a wreath of bay leaves decorated with white and green flowers, and leaves a sweet smell behind. He appears as an angel who can be invoked in magic in other works as well.

Gedudim An obscure class of angel found in **Hekalot** (a pre-Kabbalah form of Jewish mysticism) literature. The name simply means 'band, legion' and as a vocabulary word is found in the Bible used of both angels and humans. Their leader is TAGAS.

Gedulah In the *Key of Solomon* identified as one of the angels who preside over the ten SEFIROTH. **Gedulin**, an angel presiding over Friday, the day of Venus, according to Sloane manuscript *Book of Raziel* and the *Liber Juratus*, is probably the same.

Geliel A MOON ANGEL who rules the twenty-second mansion of the moon in Capricorn. He helps prisoners to escape and in curing illness.

Gelomiros The *Lemegeton* says that this is an angel that can be invoked to control the loss or gain of wealth. When conjured it appears as a child or small woman, dressed in green and silver, wearing a wreath of bay leaves decorated with white and green flowers, and leaves a sweet smell behind.

Gemary see ABASDARHON and VEQUANIEL

Gematzod see ZAAZENACH

Gemezin see JEFISCHA

Gemraorin According to the Sloane manuscript *Book of Raziel* this is one of the angels with special care of Monday (Luna) who should be invoked to aid works started on that day

Genarytz see MENDRION

Genie, Genii see DJINN

Geniel A MOON ANGEL who rules the first mansion of the moon in Aries. He supports successful journeys and medicine, particularly laxatives, but causes dissent.

Geniniturla One of the angels of Wednesday according to Sloane manuscript *Book of Raziel*.

Genius see DAEMON, GUARDIAN ANGELS

Gepheel The angel that rules the fourteenth degree of Libra under JAEL, according to the *Lemegeton*.

Geriel The angel that rules the eleventh degree of Gemini under GIEL, according to the *Lemegeton*.

Gerthiel see SARANDIEL

Gesiel The angel that rules the second degree of Aries under AIEL, according to the *Lemegeton*.

Gethiel The angel that rules the twelfth degree of Taurus under TUAL according to the *Lemegeton*. **Getiel**, who rules the twenty-first degree, looks as if he is the same angel.

Geush Urvan Meaning 'the soul of the cow' this is the YAZAD (Zoroastrian angel) who is the personification of animal life. The name also appears as **Gosh** and **Goshorun**. He assists the AMESHA SPENTA, VOHU MANO. He gives his name to the fourteenth day of the month in the Zoroastrian religious calendar.

Geziel The angel that rules the fifteenth degree of Scorpio under JOSEL and the fifteenth degree of Sagittarius under SUIAJASEL, according to the *Lemegeton*.

Ghedoriah In *The Key of Solomon*, an angel whose name appears on the Third Pentacle of Mercury.

Ghul see DJINN, IFRIT

Gibborim see NEPHILIM

Gibryl According to the Sloane manuscript *Book of Raziel* this is one of the GUARDIAN ANGELS of Sunday (Solis) who should be invoked to aid works started on that day.

Giel The angel who rules Gemini according to the *Lemegeton*. Confusingly, he also appears there as the angel that rules the twenty-first degree of Aries under AIEL.

Gimon One of the angels of the ninth lunar month according to the Sloane manuscript *Book of Raziel*, which says that if they are named 'in each thing that thou wilt do … thou shalt profit'. The name appears in the same role in the *Liber Juratus*.

Gnabriza One of the angels of the seventh lunar month found in the Sloane manuscript *Book of Raziel*.

Gnachiel The angel that rules the sixth degree of Libra under JAEL, according to the *Lemegeton*.

Gnadiel The angel that rules the thirteenth degree of Scorpio under JOSEL, according to the *Lemegeton*.

Gnaheel The angel that rules the thirteenth degree of Sagittarius under SUIAJASEL, according to the *Lemegeton*.

Gnakiel The angel that rules the tenth degree of Taurus under TUAL, the sixth degree of Scorpio under JOSEL and the sixth degree of Sagittarius under SUIAJASEL, according to the *Lemegeton*.

Gnaliel The angel that rules the fourth degree of Gemini under GIEL and the sixth degree of Taurus under TUAL, according to the *Lemegeton*.

Gnamiel The angel that rules the eighth and fourteenth degrees of Capricorn under CASUJOJAH and the eleventh degree of Libra under JAEL, in the *Lemegeton*.

Gnaphiel The angel that rules the fifth degree of Virgo under VOIL, according to the *Lemegeton*.

Gnashiel The angel that rules the eighth and fourteenth degrees of Aquarius under AUSIUL, according to the *Lemegeton*.

Gnasiel The angel that rules the fourth degree of Aquarius under PASIL and the eleventh degree of Virgo under VOIL, in the *Lemegeton*.

Gnathiel The angel that rules the tenth degree of Pisces under PASIL, according to the *Lemegeton*.

Gneliel The angel that rules the fourth degree of Taurus under TUAL, according to the *Lemegeton*.

Gnethiel The angel that rules the thirteenth degree of Leo under OL, in the *Lemegeton*.

Gnetiel The angel that rules the ninth degree of Gemini under GIEL, according to the *Lemegeton*.

Golid An angel of the sixth lunar month in the Sloane manuscript *Book of Raziel*.

Gosh, **Goshorun** see GEUSH URVAN

Govad, **Gowad** see VAYU

Governments A class of angels found in various visionary texts including *2 Enoch* 20, where they are part of a list of CHOIRS of angels which include 'fiery troops of great ARCHANGELS, incorporeal forces, and dominions, orders and governments, cherubim and seraphim, thrones and many-eyed ones'.

Granozyn see TARTYS

Granyel see HANIEL

Green Man, The, or **The Green One**
Al-Khidr, 'the Green One', is an important figure in Islamic folklore and particularly in Sufi mysticism. He is variously described as one of the Prophets, as a saint or guide, and as a sort of GUARDIAN ANGEL. Green is a significant colour in Islam. In the case of Al-Khidr (the name is also found as **Khidr, al-Khadir, Khezr** and **Khizr**), it symbolises the fact that the knowledge he has to impart is drawn from the living sources of Allah's own knowledge, as well as the wild green countryside in which he is most often to be encountered (thus linking him to the Green Man found in Western European churches), but above all his immortality, for he is said to have drunk from the Waters of Life, and to be undying. His roots go back to pre-Islamic tradition, but in Islamic traditions he is said to be one of the four Prophets who are still alive; the others being **Idris** (Enoch), **Ilyas** (Elias or Elijah) and **Isa** (Jesus). Some, however, would identify him with Elias, while others have made connections between al-Khidr and St George, who may be the patron saint of England, but whose origins lie in the Middle East. Still others say he is **Enoch**.

There are innumerable traditions and stories about al-Khidr, which can be found from Turkey to India. He is said to be met by those wandering in the wilderness, and the fortunate may find enlightenment with his help. As a result, he is a very important figure in Sufi mysticism, and there are a number of orders that claim him as a founder. Sometimes he takes the role of protector, acting as a GUARDIAN ANGEL to those in danger, particularly if God has a purpose for them. He is said to have travelled the River of Life on the back of a fish and is often shown in art in this way, and to have witnessed the return to life of a salted fish when it was placed in the Waters of Life. Although he is sometimes described as a man dressed in white, more usually he is said to be dressed in green, his robes sometimes said to resemble green fire.

Grigori One of the most detailed accounts of the Grigori is found in *2 Enoch* 18: 'And those men took me up on their wings and placed me on the fifth heaven. And I saw there many innumerable armies called Grigori. And their appearance was like the appearance of a human being, and their size was larger than that of large giants. And their faces were dejected, and the silence of their mouths was perpetual. And there was no liturgy in the fifth heaven. And I said to the men who were with me, "What is the explanation that these ones are so very dejected, and their faces miserable, and their mouths silent? And why is there no liturgy in this heaven?" And those men answered me, "There are the Grigori, who turned aside from the Lord, 200 myriads, together with their prince Satanail. And similar to them are those who went down as prisoners in their train, who are in the second heaven, imprisoned in great darkness.

"'And three of them descended to the earth from the Lord's Throne onto the place Ermon. And they broke the promise on the shoulder of Mount Ermon. And they saw the daughters of men, how beautiful they were: and they took wives for themselves, and the earth was defiled by their deeds.

"'...[They] acted lawlessly and practised miscegenation and gave birth to giants and great monsters and great enmity. And that is why God has judged them with a great judgement; and they mourn their brothers, and they will be outraged on the great day of the Lord". And I said to the Grigori, "I have seen your brothers and their deeds and their torments and their great prayers; and I have prayed for them. But the Lord has sentenced them under the earth until

heaven and earth are ended forever." And I said "Why are you waiting for your brothers? And why don't you perform the liturgy before the face of the Lord? Start up your liturgy ..." And they responded to my recommendation, and they stood in four regiments in this heaven. And behold, while I was standing with those men, four trumpets trumpeted in unison with a great sound, and the Grigori burst into singing in unison. And their voice rose in front of the face of the Lord, piteously and touchingly.' In *1 Enoch* 6 we get a different version of this story. 'In those days, when the children of man had multiplied, it happened that there were born unto them handsome and beautiful daughters. And the angels, the children of heaven, saw them and desired them; and they said to one another, "Come, let us choose wives for ourselves from among the daughters of man and beget us children." And Semyaz, being their leader, said unto them, "I fear that perhaps you will not consent that this deed should be done, and I alone will become responsible for this great sin." But they all responded to him, "Let us swear an oath and bind everyone among us by a curse not to abandon this suggestion but to do the deed."' The text continues to tell us that 200 of them descend to Mount Hermon, take wives and proceed to instruct Mankind in many technological skills – from metalwork to make-up via magic. The offspring of the union between the angels and women, as described in Genesis, are the monstrous and insatiable NEPHILIM. Despite Semyaz being the leader, it is AZAZEL who is cast in the role of chief villain in this version. These angels are called WATCHERS (the meaning of 'grigori'), rather than Grigori, and their sin is not only sexual, but also the passing on of knowledge that was not meant to be revealed. Ginzberg calls SEMYAZA **Shemhazai** (others call him **Salamiel**), and adds further traditional material to the account, saying, 'the lovely sister of Tubal-cain, led the angels astray with her beauty, and from her union with SHAMDON sprang the devil Asmodeus. She was as shameless as all the other descendants of Cain, and as prone to bestial indulgences. Cainite women and Cainite men alike were in the habit of walking abroad naked, and they gave themselves up to every conceivable manner of lewd practices. Of such were the women whose beauty and sensual charms tempted the angels from the path of virtue. The angels, on the other hand, no sooner had they rebelled against God and descended to earth than they lost their transcendental qualities, and were invested with sublunary bodies, so that a union with the daughters of men became possible.' There is some suggestion that not all the Grigori fell.

Gromeyl An angel of the day of Mars (Tuesday) in the Sloane manuscript *Book of Raziel*. The angel appears as **Gronyeyll** in the same role in the *Liber Juratus*.

Guadriel In the Sloane manuscript *Book of Raziel*, an angel of the eleventh lunar month. If invoked in the relevant month, he will ensure success in your enterprise.

Guanrinasuch In the Sloane manuscript *Book of Raziel*, an angel of the tenth lunar month.

Guardian Angels The idea of a personal, guardian spirit is widely found in different religions, and is a major role of angels and angel analogues. Thus, as well as the Guardian Angels of Christianity and Judaeism, there are the FRAVASHIS in Zoroastrianism, the DAEMON of the ancient Greeks, the equivalent **Genius** for the Romans. Followers of various New Age theologies have found a wide variety of other guardian spirits. In Islam it is said that there are four different angels that guard each of us, two in the day and two at night, to protect from the assaults of **Shaitan** (SATAN). You should be on your guard at dusk, as that is the time when the pairs of angels switch positions as guardians, and their protective barrier is at its weakest. The second-century Christian writer Tertullian wrote that one of the roles of the Guardian Angel was to assist their ward in prayer, and St Augustin himself wrote, 'Every visible thing in this world is put under the charge of an angel.'

As well as there being Guardian Angels for individuals, whose chief role is the salvation of the soul, (although some people believe their angels are involved in more detailed aspects of their daily life), there are Guardian Angels of nations – seventy according to early sources. Some would multiply the number of things with guardians many times to include everything in this world. The Catholic Church regards the role of guardian angels as one duty of the order of ANGELS. In the Kabbalah they are an order, with four ruling princes – URIEL, RAPHAEL, GABRIEL and MICHAEL.

Modern angelologists have identified the following angels as the Guardian Angels related to birth date, each of which is discussed under its own heading: **Capricorn** 1–5 January – NEMAMIAH, 6–10 January – IEILAEL or Yeialel, 11–15 January – HARAEL or Harahel, 16–24 January – MITZRAEL; **Aquarius** 21–25 January – UMABEL, 26–30 January – IAHHEL, 31 January–4 February – ANAUEL, 5–9 February – MEHIEL, 10–14 February – DAMABIAH, 15–19 February – MANAKEL; **Pisces** 20–24 February – EIAEL or Eyael, 25–28/9 February – HABUHIAH, or Habuiah, 1–5 March – ROCHEL, 6–10 March – GABAMIAH, JABAMIAH, 11–15 March – HAIAIEL, 16–20 March – MUMIAH; **Aries** 21–25 March – VEHUIAH, 26–30 March – JELIEL, 1–4 April – SITAEL, 5–9 April – ELEMIAH, 10–14 April – MAHASIAH, 15–20 April – LELAHEL; **Taurus** 21–25 April – ACHAIAH, 26–30 April – CAHATEL, 1–5 May – HAZIEL, 6–10 May – ALADIAH, 11–15 May – LAUVIAH, 16–20 May – HAHAIAH; **Gemini** 21–25 May – IEZALEL, 26–31 May – MEBAHEL, 1–5 June – HARIEL, 6–10 June – HAKAMIAH, 11–15 June –LAUVIAH, 16–21 June – CALIEL; **Cancer** 22–26 June – LEUVIAH, 27 June–1 July – PAHALIAH, 2–6 July – NELCHAEL, 7–11 July – IEIAEIL or Yeiayel, 12–16 July – MELAHEL, 17–22 July – HAHUIAH; **Leo** 23–27 July – NITH-HAIAH, 28 July–1 August – HAAIAH, 2–6 August – TERATHEL, 7–12 August – SEHEIAH, 13–17 August – REIIEL or Reiyel, 18–22 August – OMAEL; **Virgo** 23–28 August – LECABEL, 29 August–2 September – VASARIAH, VASAIRIAH, 3–7 September – YEHUDIAH, 8–12 September – LEHAHIAH, 13–17 September – CHAVAKIAH, 18–23 September – MENADEL; **Libra** 24–28 September – **Aniel** (see HANIEL), 29 September–3 October – HAAMIAH, 4–8 October – REHAEL, 9–13 October – Ieiazel or IHIAZEL, 14–18 October – Hahahel or HAHAEL, 19–23 October – MIKAEL; **Scorpio** 24–28 October – VEUALIAH, 29 October—2 November – IELAHIAH or Iela(h)iah, 3–7 November – **Sehaliah** or SEELIAH, 8–12 November – ARIEL, 13–17 November – ASALIAH, 18–22 November – MIHAEL; **Sagittarius** 23–27 November – VAHUEL or Vehuel, 28 November–2 December– DANIEL, 3–7 December – HAHASIAH or Hahaziah, 8–12 December – IMAMIAH, 13–16 December – NANAEL, 17–21 December – NITHAEL; **Capricorn** 22–26 December – MEBAHIAH, 27–31 December – Poyelor or POIEL.

Gunfiel An angel presiding over Thursday, the day of Jove, according to the Sloane manuscript *Book of Raziel*.

Guracap In the Sloane manuscript *Book of Raziel*, an angel of the thirteenth lunar month (March). If invoked in the relevant month, he will ensure success in your enterprise.

Guriel In the Sloane manuscript *Book of Raziel*, an angel of the eleventh and twelfth lunar month. If invoked in the relevant month, he will ensure success in your enterprise. Davidson describes him as a ruler of Leo and says the name means 'whelp of God'.

H

Haaiah One of the DOMINIONS, Haaiah rules diplomacy and ambassadors, and is one of the seventy-two angels bearing the mystic name of God, SHEMHAM-PHORAE. As a GUARDIAN ANGEL he is said to care for those born under Leo between 28 July and 1 August. He propagates light, civilisation and liberty. He supports justice and defends against injustice and brings success in law, as well as helping in social settings.

Haamiah One of the POWERS, he rules religious cults and protects those who seek the truth. The *Liber Juratus* calls him **Hammiab** (the 'b' is undoubtedly a slip of the pen or misreading) or CHAAMIAH, and lists him among the seventy-two SHEMHAMPHORAE angels. As the GUARDIAN ANGEL of those born under Libra between 29 September and 3 October he is considered an angel of love who grants love and happiness, particularly in lasting relationships. He also grants spirituality and enhanced powers in the fields of the arts and aesthetics.

Haayn A Tuesday angel in the Sloane manuscript *Book of Raziel* and the *Liber Juratus*.

Habalon see ABASDARHON

Habiel The angel that rules the twenty-third degree of Aries under AIEL, according to the *Lemegeton*. In the *Heptameron*, however, he is listed among 'the Angels of the first heaven, ruling on Monday, which ought to be called from the four parts of the world'

as one of the angels to be addressed from the west.

Habuhiah, **Habuiah** This is an angel who presides over agriculture and fertility, as well as being one of the seventy-two who bear the sacred name of God, SHEMHAMPHORAE. He is also considered the GUARDIAN ANGEL of those born under Pisces between 25 February and 28 or 29 February. In this form he is considered an angel of advantages whose role in promoting abundance is extended to work and life in general. Some manuscripts of the *Liber Juratus* call him **Chabuiah**.

Hac see SALOR

Hachael The angel that rules the twenty-fourth degree of Taurus under TUAL, according to the *Lemegeton*. **Hachashel**, one of the seventy-two angels of the zodiac, may be the same.

Hacoylyn According to the *Liber Juratus* and the Sloane manuscript *Book of Raziel* this is one of the angels with special care of Monday (Luna) who should be invoked to aid works started on that day.

Hadiel The angel that rules the fourteenth degree of Pisces under PASIL, according to the *Lemegeton*.

Hadraniel, **Hadriel** see ADRIEL

Hadzbeyeyl According to the Sloane manuscript *Book of Raziel*, this is one of the angels of Sunday (Solis) who should be invoked to aid works started on that day.

Hael The angel that rules the second

degree of Aries under AIEL, according to the *Lemegeton*. He is also invoked in the *Liber Juratus* and the *Grimorium Verum*.

Hafaza Angels In Islam, a class of angels that keep a record of each and every good or bad deed performed in a person's life.

Hagith An OLYMPIC SPIRIT who rules 21 of the 196 provinces and ruled the events of the world between 1411 and 1900.

Hahael, **Hahahel** One of the VIRTUES who is the protector of Christian missionaries and of faithful Christians in general. In the *Liber Juratus* he is listed as one of the seventy-two who bear the mystic name SHEMHAMPHORAE. He is held to be the GUARDIAN ANGEL of those born under Libra between 14 and 18 October. As such his dominant characteristic is to supervise the pursuit of the essential, and of good causes. He helps the recovery of the sick.

Hahaiah One of the CHERUBIM, who influences thoughts and reveals hidden mysteries to mortals. As GUARDIAN ANGEL of those born under Taurus between 16 and 20 May he is considered an inspirational angel of protection. In this role he gives peace and protection to those who feel persecuted or desperate. In the *Liber Juratus* he is listed as one of the seventy-two who bear the mystic name SHEMHAMPHORAE.

Hahasiah, **Hahaziah** One of the seventy-two angels bearing the mystic name of God, SHEMHAMPHORAE, and the GUARDIAN ANGEL of those born under Sagittarius between 3 and 7

December. In this role he is considered an angel of providence who contributes towards the acquisition of higher knowledge, particularly in the mysteries of nature, and in healing.

Hahon In the Sloane manuscript *Book of Raziel*, an angel of the tenth lunar month.

Hahuiah, **Haheuiah** One of the seventy-two angels bearing the mystic name of God, SHEMHAMPHORAE. As GUARDIAN ANGEL of those born under the sign of Cancer between 17 and 22 July he is considered an angel of health, both giving and restoring it.

Haiaiel One of the seventy-two angels of the zodiac, and one of the same number who bear the mystic name of God, SHEMHAMPHORAE. Also the GUARDIAN ANGEL of those born under Pisces between 11 and 15 March. As such he is an angel of lucidity, helping people to see clearly and quickly, both physically and mentally. He also offers protection to those in the military.

Hakamiah, **Hekamiah** One of the CHERUBIM, who is both the GUARDIAN ANGEL of France and invoked against traitors. As an individual guardian angel of those born under Gemini between 6 and 10 June he is held to be an angel of evolution who offers the chance to improve one's lot in life.

Halilin An angel presiding over Friday, the day of Venus, according to the Sloane manuscript *Book of Raziel*.

Hamarytzod see DARDARIEL

Hamayz see JEFISCHA

Hameriel see ABASDARHON

Hamon In *3 Enoch* Hamon is a mighty angel whose voice, when he summons the angels to sing 'Holy, Holy, Holy' before the throne of God, makes the angels tremble.

Hananel One of the GRIGORI according to *1 Enoch*.

Haniel, **Hanyel**, **Anael**, **Anapael**, **Amael**, **Anapiel YHWH**, **Anafiel**, **Anapel**, **Anaphiel**, **Aniel**, **Aniy(y)el** While this is undoubtedly a very important angel, he seems to have as many aspects as there are variant forms of his name, and it is quite clear that at times the different forms of his name get split up into different angels. He is generally accepted to be an ARCHANGEL, and one of the holy SEFIROTH. He rules Venus and December, and has been said to be the angel of the signs of Capricorn, Libra and Taurus. He is invoked for love, compassion, harmony, beauty and wisdom, and is said to be the guardian of innocents. He is called ruler of the PRINCIPALITIES and VIRTUES. He is a prince of angels who takes Enoch up to heaven in a fiery chariot in *3 Enoch*. He also holds the keys to the palaces of heaven. The name is similar to the Hebrew word *anap*, 'bough', and *3 Enoch* explains that this is because his splendour overshadows the palaces like the shadow cast by a bough. Some manuscripts of *3 Enoch* give the name in the form **Aniyyel**. This name occurs elsewhere. For example, the Sloane manuscript *Book of Raziel* gives **Aniyel** as the name of an angel of the tenth lunar month. In the *Key of Solomon* Aniel is the angel that governs the second hour of the day with many angels under him, the chief of whom are **Menarchos**, **Archiel**, **Chardiel**, **Orphiel**, **Cursiel**, **Elmoym**, **Quosiel**, **Ermaziel** and **Granyel**. He is also an angel whose name is used in conjuration. He is the angel that rules the sixth degree of Cancer under CAEL and the sixth degree of Leo under OL, according to the *Lemegeton*. In the Sloane manuscript *Book of Raziel*, Anael is an angel of the tenth lunar month. He is also described as the angel of the moon itself, although elsewhere the work gives this title to GABRIEL. He resides in the south of the first heaven. The same work identifies Amael (merely another form of the name) as the angel of the planet Venus, found in the east of the third heaven, thus linking the name firmly to Haniel. The *Key of Solomon* lists Anael among the names of God. The name can also appear as **Anapiel**. There is a legend that when God wished to punish METATRON, Anapiel, as chief angel of the MERKABAH, is the angel who was ordered to give him sixty lashes of fire.

Hanin An angel of the south of the first heaven in the Sloane manuscript *Book of Raziel*. This is probably the same angel as **Hanun** or **Hanum**, a Monday angel of the first heaven who, the *Heptameron* says, should be invoked from the south, although others say it should be from the north.

Hanyel An angel of the sixth lunar month according to the Sloane manuscript *Book of Raziel*. He is found in the north of the fifth heaven. He is probably the same in origin as HANIEL.

Haoma A YAZAD (Zoroastrian angel) who rules over all medicinal herbs and grants immortality. He is associated with the purification of fire, and believed to have the power to provide husbands for unmarried women. He gets his name from a plant, the sap of which is drunk in Zoroastrian rituals. This plant exists not only on a mythological level, where it is said to grow from the 'World Tree' or in paradise, the juice of which confers immortality, but also on a real level. Although there has been much debate as to whether the same plant has always been used or not, the plant used today is a variety of ephedra, which grows in a limited area of the Middle East, the sap of which produces a variety of ephedrine. This acts as a stimulant, variously described as intoxicating or anaesthetic. Haoma is also known as **Hom**, and the word comes from the same Indo-European root as the Soma of Hindu tradition.

Haphekiel, Haphkiel see MAHPEKIEL AND HAPHEKIEL

Haptoring, Haptoiringa A star YAZAD (Zoroastrian angel), associated with Ursa Major (The Great Bear) and the planet Warharan (Mars). He has the title of Chieftain of the north. See further under TISHTRYA.

Harahel, Haroel, Harahel, Harael The protector of libraries, archives, schools and universities. In the *Liber Juratus* Harahel or **Harachel** is among the seventy-two angels who bear the holy name SHEMHAMPHORAE. As the GUARDIAN ANGEL of those born under Capricorn between 11 and 15 January, he grants intelligence and the ability to learn and succeed in any examination or competitive exams. He reinforces skills and intellectual capacity.

Harbonah An angel of confusion, often listed among the DESTROYING ANGELS. Ginzberg lists him among the angels sent to bring about Ahasuerus's downfall for defiling the vessels of the temple by using them in his drunken, lascivious feasts, saying God 'sent down seven Angels of Confusion to put an end to Ahasuerus's pleasure. They were named: **Mehuman**, Confusion; **Biztha**, Destruction of the House; **Harbonah**, Annihilation; **Bigtha** and **Abagtha**, the Pressers of the Winepress, for God had resolved to crush the court of Ahasuerus as one presses the juice from grapes in a press; **Zetha**, Observer of Immorality; and **Carcas**, Knocker.' Ahasuerus, in his drunkenness, orders his wife Vashti to appear naked in front of the assembled princes. When she refuses he has her executed and loses half his realm in the subsequent revolt.

Hardiel see SARANDIEL

Hareryn An angel presiding over Friday, the day of Venus, according to the Sloane manuscript *Book of Raziel* and the *Liber Juratus.*

Hariaz see DARDARIEL

Hariel A cherub with dominion over the arts and sciences and with dominion over wild and domesticated beasts. On top of all this he is also invoked against impieties. He is said to be GUARDIAN ANGEL of those born under Gemini between 1 and 5 June. As such he is an angel of clarity, bestowing intelligence and the appreciation of morality and beauty. The *Liber Juratus* lists him among the seventy-two angels who bear the mystic name of God, SHEMHAMPHORAE.

Harmary see BERATIEL

Harmiel see BARAQIEL

Haron see KEZEF

Harut and Marut, Haroot and Maroot Harut and Marut take much the same role in Islamic tradition as UZZAH and AZZAH and SEMYAZA do in Jewish tradition, and have obvious parallels with the GRIGORI. The story goes that when the angels in heaven observe the sinful behaviour of man, they start to make derogatory remarks. God responds by challenging the angels to do better when exposed to the same conditions. Harut and Marut are chosen to represent the angels in the test. As soon as they arrive on earth they are captivated by a beautiful woman and try to seduce her. They then proceed to kill a man who witnesses their misbehaviour. The angels in heaven have been set by God to watch what happens, and seeing Harut and Marut's conduct, they have to admit their original judgement was wrong. The two offending angels are punished by being hung by the feet down a well in Babylon. Some traditions say there they teach sorcery. A further story, also told of Semyaza and other Grigori, says that on earth the two angels lost the use of the ineffable Name of God, which would have allowed them to return to heaven. Before they lost it, they had confided it to the woman they lusted after. She used it to escape from them to heaven where God rewarded her virtue by turning her into a star. In Muslim tradition she is **Anahid, Bidukht** or **Zahra**, all of which names associate her with the planet Venus. In Jewish tradition this woman is called **Naamah**, and her fate was very

different. In Kabbalistic lore she is listed as one of four angels of prostitution, although angel seems a rather odd term for her. Along with Lilith, another of the four, the others being AGRAT BAT MAHLAT and **Eisheth Zenunim**, she causes epilepsy in children, when she is not busy seducing both men and spirits. She is said to be the mother of the great demon Asmodeus. The origin of the names of Harut and Marut is obscure, but they seem to have links with two of the 'archangels' (AMESHA SPENTAS) of Zoroastrianism, HAURVATAT, 'integrity' and AMERATAT, 'immortality'.

Has(h)malim, Has(h)mallim, Chasmalim Derived from a Hebrew word meaning either 'Those of bronze' or 'Those of electrum', these are one of many classes of angels which come from the description of the Chariot of the Lord (see MERKABA) in Ezekiel. Maimonides lists them as fourth in rank in the HIERARCHY OF THE ANGELS, while *The Zohar* makes them sixth. They are often identified with the HAYYOT, although others call them CHERUBIM, SERAPHIM, POWERS or DOMINIONS. Their leader is **Hashmal** (although this role has also been given to ZADKIEL and ZACHARAEL), who is said to speak with fire. There is a story that the fiery river of the heavens was created from the sweat of the Hashmalim as they carry the throne of God.

Hasasisgafon In the Sloane manuscript *Book of Raziel* an angel of the tenth lunar month. If invoked in rites his name will ensure good results. He appears in the same role as **Hasasylgason** in the *Liber Juratus*, part of the difference being the easy confusion in manuscripts between an 'f' and an old-fashioned long 's'.

Hasmed This is an angel of annihilation and one of the ANGELS OF PUNISHMENT seen by Moses in heaven.

Hasneyeyl and Hatheylin Angels presiding over Friday, the day of Venus, according to the Sloane manuscript *Book of Raziel*.

Hasruel In Diana Wynne Jones's novel *Castles in the Air* (1990), the sequel to her *Howl's Moving Castle*, she draws on Arabic legends to put an amusing twist on the world of the Arabian Nights. The great djinn Hasruel has been stealing princesses – despite the fact that he is numbered among the good djinns and attended by 200 angels. He explains that his behaviour is because he has a detachable life, which has passed out of his control. As Hasruel explains, 'Know that my mother, the Great Spirit Dazrah, in a moment of oversight allowed herself to be ravished by a djinn of the Host of Evil some twenty years ago. She then gave birth to my brother Dalzel who – since Good and Evil do not breed well together – proved weak and white and undersized. My mother could not tolerate Dalzel and gave him to me to bring up. I lavished every care upon him as he grew. So you can imagine my horror and sorrow when he proved to inherit the nature of his Evil Sire. His first act, when he came of age, was to steal my life and hide it, thereby making me his slave.'

Haurvatat, **Haurevetat** Called **Hordad** in the Middle Persian Pahlavi language and **Khordad** or **Hordad** in modern Persian, this AMESHA SPENTA or ARCHANGEL of the Zoroastrians presides over water. The name means 'Perfection, Health, Wholeness', and she embodies these qualities. She is also associated with life after death. Her eternal opponent is the archdemon **Tawrich**, the DAEVA who is the personification of hunger and, like Haurvatat, feminine. Haurvatat and AMERETAT (Immortality) are the last two of the seven Amesha Spentas, the emanations of God which Zoroastrians call the 'Bounteous Immortals'. They are the virtues and gifts of the future, things devoutly to be hoped for, the signs of the Renewal at the End of Time. TISHTRYA and VAYU are associated with her. See also HARUT AND MARUT.

Hawan, **Havani**, **Havni**, A YAZAD (Zoroastrian angel) presiding over the second watch of each day (sunrise to midday), but particularly associated with noon. See also under RAPITHWIN.

Hayel An angel of the north of the fifth heaven in the Sloane manuscript *Book of Raziel*.

Hayliel YHWH *3 Enoch* derives this name from the Hebrew *hayyah* 'creature' (see HAYYOT), and says that it is his task to whip the creatures with lashes of fire. However, the name is more correctly derived from *hayil* 'an army', a term often used for angels in general. So great is he that he could swallow the whole world in one gulp.

Haylon see SERQUANICH

Haynynael An angel of the north of the fourth heaven in the Sloane manuscript *Book of Raziel*.

Hayyot, Hayyoth, Chaya, Chayot, Chayoth, Chayyoth Meaning 'living creatures', these are the creatures who support the divine chariot, the MERKABAH. They are described as composite beings with four faces – a human, a lion, a bull and an eagle – four wings, calf's feet, and human hands under their wings. In *3 Enoch* we get a more detailed description 'There are four creatures facing the four winds. Each single creature would fill the whole world. Each of them has four faces, and every single face looks like the sunrise. Each creature has four wings and every single wing would cover the world. Each of them has faces within faces and wings within wings.' In appearance they bear distinct resemblances to creatures found in other Near Eastern religions, such as those of the Canaanites and the Babylonian tradition. The ideas about the Hayyot come from the visions in Ezekiel 1 and 10. The Hayyot are sometimes identified with the CHERUBIM, although Western Cherubim now have a very different iconography. The leader of the Hayyot is HAYLIEL YHWH. Moses Maimonides lists them as the highest rank of angels, while *The Zohar* puts them in fourth place (see HIERARCHY OF THE ANGELS). While Ezekiel only writes of four Hayyot, *The Zohar* says there are thirty-six and that they hold up the universe.

Hayzoym see SABRATHAN

Hazaniel see IASSUARIM

Haziel Haziel's name means 'vision of God' and he is invoked to obtain God's pity. He is a cherub and also one of the seventy-two SHEMHAMPHORAE. He is considered the GUARDIAN ANGEL of those born under Taurus between 1 and 5 May, and as such accounted an angel of providence. He helps settle conflicts and establish harmony both between people and within the individual. Some, however, count him among the FALLEN ANGELS.

Hechaloth see MERKABAH

Hegnel The angel that rules the thirteenth degree of Gemini under GIEL, according to the *Lemegeton*.

Hehudael An angel of the ninth lunar month according to the Sloane manuscript *Book of Raziel*.

Hekalot, Hekhalot see MERKABAH

Hekamiah see HAKAMIAH

Hekiel The angel that rules the sixteenth degree of Libra under JAEL, according to the *Lemegeton*.

Helemmelek In *1 Enoch* 82, Helemmelek is named as the angel of the second season of the year, the ninety-one days when there is 'glowing heat and dryness, and the trees ripen their fruits and produce all their fruits ripe and ready, and the sheep pair and become pregnant, and all the fruits of the earth are gathered in, and everything that is in the fields, and the winepress: these things take place in the days of his dominion.' Under him serve **Gidaljal**, **Keel**, and **Heel**, headed by **Asfael**.

Hellison According to the *Lemegeton*, this is an angel who is invoked for fertility in animals, plants and women.

Helmas see BARIEL

Hemah A DESTROYING ANGEL representing the divine attribute of Wrath (the meaning of the name). He is often linked with APH, 'anger', and like him was forged out of chains of black and red fire. He has dominion over the death of domestic animals. According to the legend in which Aph and Hemah attack Moses (described under APH), Moses kills Hemah in revenge. In *The Zohar*, Hemah is one of the three angels of Gehenna (hell) who punish sinners who have committed incest, idolatry and murder. The other two are Aph again and **Mashit**. See also under KEZEF.

Heman According to *The Zohar*, during the morning he leads the hosts of angels who sing hymns to God (ASAPH leads the night chants and JEDUTHUN the evening ones).

Hephiel The angel that rules the seventeenth degrees of Scorpio under JOSEL and of Sagittarius under SUIAJASEL, according to the *Lemegeton*.

Hermes The Greek god Hermes belongs in a dictionary of angels on three counts. First, as messenger of the gods he acts in the classic angel role of intermediary between the divine and man. Secondly, one of his roles as messenger is that of PSYCHOPOMP – conductor of souls, taking the spirit of the dead to its reward – another classic angel role. Thirdly, he is a winged figure. Traditionally, Hermes' speed as a messenger, and his ability to go anywhere – another angelic attribute – is indicated in representations of him by his winged boots. He is also sometimes shown with a winged hat and with wings on his messenger's staff. Occasionally he is shown with full angelic wings.

Hermiel see VATHMIEL

Herphatz see ABASDARHON

Hevael The angel that rules the fifteenth degree of Virgo under VOIL, according to the *Lemegeton*.

Hezael The angel that rules the eighteenth degree of Aries under AIEL, according to the *Lemegeton*.

Hiaeyel An angel of the north of the first heaven in the Sloane manuscript *Book of Raziel*. He is **Hyeyll**, a Sunday angel in the *Liber Juratus*.

Hierarchy of the Angels The Celestial Hierarchy has many different forms according to different writers, and over time the number of different ranks of angels has multiplied almost infinitely. However, there is one version which has become the standard version, with others considered variants. This is *The Celestial Hierarchy* established by Dionysius (or Denys) the Areopagite who died about AD 500. (This writer is also known as Dionysius the Pseudo-Areopagite or even Pseudo-Dionysius. This is because the author was traditionally thought to be the Dionysius the judge of the Areopagus in Athens who, as related in Acts 17:34, was converted to Christianity by the preaching of St Paul. Later on it was realised from material in his texts that the author could not possibly have lived this early.) His views were the basis on which later Catholic writers on angels, such as Peter Lombard, Albertus Magnus,

Bonaventure, Duns Scotus and, most influential of all, Thomas Aquinas, based their work. This hierarchy divides nine CHOIRS of celestial beings into three hierarchies of three ranks. His rankings put SERAPHIM at the top, followed by CHERUBIM and THRONES; in the second hierarchy are **Dominations** or DOMINIONS, VIRTUES and POWERS; in the third, PRINCIPALITIES, ARCHANGELS and, finally, the lowest rank, and those who are the main contact between the celestials and man, come ANGELS. This is the Christian tradition; the traditions in Judaism and in other belief systems can be very different. There are two main Jewish hierarchies. That proposed by Moses Maimonides (1135–1203) list the ranks as: 1 HAYYOT; 2 OPHANIM; 3 ERELIM; 4 HASHMALIM; 5 SERAPHIM; 6 MALAKHIM; 7 ELOHIM; 8 BENE ELOHIM; 9 CHERUBIM; 10 ISHIM. *The Zohar*, which took its current form around 1275, lists them as: 1 MALAKHIM; 2 ERELIM; 3 SERAPHIM; 4 HAYYOT; 5 OPHANIM; 6 HASHMALIM; 7 ELIM; 8 ELOHIM; 9 BENE ELOHIM; 10 ISHIM. Islam does not seem to have gone in for such orderings of angels. See individual entries for more information on each rank.

Hifaliel An angel of the east of the third heaven in the Sloane manuscript *Book of Raziel*.

Himeilin An angel presiding over Friday, the day of Venus, according to the Sloane manuscript *Book of Raziel*. He appears as the Friday angel **Hymeylyn** in the *Liber Juratus*.

Hobraiym see NARCORIEL

Hod see SEFIRA

Hofniel Hofniel is ruler of the BENE ELOHIM according to *The Zohar*. His name means 'fighter for God'.

Hom see HAOMA

Homycabel An angel of the element earth, under the planet Hanina (Sol, the sun), to be invoked when working under this planet, according to the Sloane manuscript *Book of Raziel*. **Hometibymal** or **Hometibimal**, who is invoked in the *Liber Juratus*, looks as if it was originally the same, for 'c' and 't' can often be confused in fifteenth-century handwriting.

Hoquiel A water angel under Sabaday (Saturn), to be invoked when working under this planet, in the Sloane manuscript *Book of Raziel*.

Horaeus, Horaios, Oreus, Oraios One of the seven great ARCHONS of Ophitic Gnosticism. He governs the moon.

Hordad see HAURVATAT

Horrion, Horryon One of the angels presiding over Saturday in the Sloane manuscript *Book of Raziel* and the *Liber Juratus*.

Hosael An angel of the south of the fourth heaven in the Sloane manuscript *Book of Raziel*. It may be the same as **Hosel**, a divine name, in the *Liber Juratus*.

How many angels can dance on the point of a pin? This question (often, nowadays, found in the form '… on the head of a pin') is well known as an example of useless debate, but behind it lies a serious purpose. In the thirteenth century the scholastic philosophers were trying to develop concepts of time, space, the nature of matter and the universe, and of similar problems. These are now matters for theoretical physics, but the discipline did not then exist. There was only theology and philosophy. Debates on the nature of angels acted as vehicles for such discussions. One big debate was on the nature of angels; what, if anything, was their substance, and were they limited in time and space. The debates and conclusions were complex, and depend very much on how you interpret the technical Latin in which they were written; but put simply, were this: if angels are tied by time and space, can they be limited to only one place or point (the Latin can be translated either way)? This is the origin of the mocking point of a pin. The great Thomas Aquinas argues that you can tell the presence of an angel by its effects – hence, if it has an effect on a person or place, it can be tied to a point in time and space. But that means only one angel can be on the point of a pin, as the knowledge of the angel and its presence at one point is known by its effect. But others, such as Duns Scotus, argued that it is ridiculous to posit the existence of something from its effect – existence must come before effect – and anyway, where is the angel when it is inactive? (Hence the need for the angel(s) to be actively dancing on the pin.) Scotus would argue that an angel can probably be tied, by its nature, to a point in time and space, but that there is probably no limit to numbers. All this may sound trivial and obscure, but represents an important step in Mankind's intellectual development towards scientific method and an understanding of the universe, and does it really differ that much from the modern quantum physicist discussing particles with charge and no mass, or which can change state from particle to wave?

Hubayel An angel of the south of the first heaven in the Sloane manuscript *Book of Raziel*.

Hufrbria An angel of the east of the third heaven in the Sloane manuscript *Book of Raziel*.

Hujael The angel that rules the second degree of Taurus under TUAL, according to the *Lemegeton*.

Hula'il An angel invoked in exorcism in Arabic tradition.

Humaziel see ZAAZENACH

Hutriel An ANGEL OF PUNISHMENT who is to be found in the fifth camp of hell involved in the punishment of nations. The name means 'rod of God'.

Hvare-Khshaeta Meaning 'the shining sun', this is the YAZAD presiding over the Sun. The name also appears as **Khwarshed** and **Khorshed**. In the form **Khursan** he appears among the Russians and eastern Slavs as one of several solar spirits. In the late 900s he was one of the gods worshipped officially in Kievan Rus.

Hyeyl A Sunday angel in the *Liber Juratus* and the Sloane manuscript *Book of Raziel*.

Hypnos see THANATOS

Hyzy An angel of the ninth lunar month according to the *Liber Juratus* and the Sloane manuscript *Book of Raziel*, which says that if he is named 'in each thing that thou wilt do … thou shalt profit'.

I

Iabynx One of the angels of the eighth lunar month in the Sloane manuscript *Book of Raziel*.

Iachadiel This angel appears in *The Key of Solomon* as the angel of the Fifth Pentacle of the Moon. We are told, 'Iachadiel serveth unto destruction and loss, as well as unto the destruction of enemies.'

Iahhel One of the seventy-two SHEMHAMPHORAE angels. In the Kabbalah he is an ARCHANGEL, who looks after philosophers and those who wish to withdraw from the world. He also inspires meditation. As a GUARDIAN ANGEL of those born under Aquarius between 26 and 30 January he is an angel of peace, love and tenderness.

Ialdaboath, Iadalboath, Jaldaboath Ialdaboath is one of the most prominent ARCHONS in Gnosticism, and also features in Jewish mysticism. Depending on which system of Gnosticism is followed, he is the DEMIURGE – not the supreme God, but the creator God, who makes the world and Mankind – or merely one of the most prominent of the archons. In the main versions, he is the son of SOPHIA, engendered by her own desire for knowledge. In *1 Enoch* and elsewhere Ialdaboath is identified with the FALLEN ANGEL SAMAEL.

Iameth An angel in *The Testament of Solomon* who can thwart the demon Kunopegos, a demon with the front half of a horse and the tail of a fish, who destroys ships. The name seems to come from the word *Yah*, for God and *iaomai*, the Greek for 'I heal'.

Iao, Jao Ioa is one of the ARCHONS in Gnosticism. Although Iao and Jao look very different to the modern eye, in medieval manuscripts the letters I and J are identical. Because of the confusion, it is not clear if the name is derived from the Hebrew name for God, Jehovah/Yaweh, a suitable source for an archon who rules the planet Jupiter, named for the king of the gods, or from the Greek cry of *iao*, the paean raised in religious rites, including the mysteries. In some systems of Gnostic belief he is the DEMIURGE and the master of the seven heavens. In others this role belongs to IALDABOATH. In the form **Little Iao** the name is listed among the titles of METATRON in *3 Enoch*.

Iaoel In the *Apocalypse of Abraham,* the simple 'vision' that Abraham has in Genesis 15 is turned into an angel, Iaoel, whose main task is to guide Abraham from Mesopotamia to the Promised Land, while instructing him in the way of true religion. This text also tells us that he controls the Leviathans and every reptile. His actions show that he can also be an avenging angel. AOL and AEL, in the Sloane manuscript *Book of Raziel* and the *Liber Juratus*, may be other forms of the name.

Iaoth An angel found in magical papyri and Gnostic texts. In the *Testament of Solomon* he imprisons Kourtael, a demon who causes colics.

Iassuarim The angel of the tenth hour of the night in the *Lemegeton*, whose main followers include **Lapheriel,**

Emarziel, Nameroyz, Chameray, Hazaniel, and **Uraniel.**

Iazeriel see JAZERIEL

Ibajah The angel that rules the first degree of Libra under JAEL, according to the *Lemegeton.*

Iblis Iblis, in Islam, takes the role played by the devil in Judeo-Christian myth. Indeed, the name appears to be a contraction of the Greek word *diabolos*, which is also the origin of devil; although some have argued it comes from Arabic, and that he is so called because 'he has nothing to expect (*ublisa*) from the mercy of God'. He is also known as 'the Enemy' or SATAN (*al-shaytan*). When Man is created and God orders all the angels to bow down to Adam, Iblis proudly refuses to bow down to a mere mortal made from clay. For this he is cursed until the Day of Doom, but at his own request his punishment is deferred until the Day of Judgement, and in the meanwhile he is empowered to lead astray all who are not faithful servants of God. This means he is able to tempt Adam and Eve to eat the forbidden fruit. When the Day of Judgement comes, Iblis and all his followers will be thrown into the fires of hell. Iblis's refusal to bow down to Adam has caused debate. The Koran teaches that angels are, by nature, obedient to God's will. This had led to much debate about how Iblis could, then, refuse to obey God. One solution is to say that Iblis is one of the DJINN, and that when the Koran says that God ordered the angels to bow down, the word 'angel' is being used as a collective term for the angels and djinn. One tradition tells a story that the djinn inhabited the earth before the creation of Man, and were fighting among themselves. Iblis was then a young djinni, and when God sent the angels to restore order he was captured by them and taken up to heaven. There he was given the title of *al-Hakam*, The Arbitrator, and was set to settle debates among the djinn. He held this post for 1,000 years, but then, through pride, fomented trouble among the djinn. When God destroyed the troublesome djinn with fire, Iblis took refuge in heaven, where he remained a faithful servant of God until the creation of Adam. While pride and disobedience are Iblis's obvious sins, some put a kinder interpretation on his behaviour. It is said that when ordered to bow down to Adam he replied, 'No, I shall worship only Thee,' and that he thought he was being tested as to his obedience to the rule of absolute monotheism. But others say he willingly chose to disobey God. Some traditions say that Iblis was originally called AZAZIL, or **al-Harith**.

Idecidaniach In *The Key of Solomon*, an angel whose name is invoked when the master is putting on the white linen vestments of powers before practising magic.

Ieiaiel, Yeiayel This angel shares with TEIAIEL dominion over the future and is also one of the seventy-two angels bearing the mystic name SHEMHAM-PHORAE. As the GUARDIAN ANGEL of those born under Cancer between 7 and 11 July he is considered an angel of fortune who favours success in business.

Ieiazell see IHIAZEL

Ieilael, Yeialel One of the seventy-two

SHEMHAMPHORAE angels. As a GUARDIAN ANGEL of those born under Capricorn between 6 and 10 January he is considered an angel of understanding who grants intelligence and the skills needed to succeed in activities that need accurate attention to detail.

Ielahiah, Yela(h)iah As well as being one of the seventy-two angels who bear the mystic name of God, SHEMHAM-PHORAE, and an angel of the zodiac, this is an angel who protects magistrates and oversees decisions in legal cases. As the GUARDIAN ANGEL of those born under Scorpio between 29 October and 2 November he is considered an angel of evolution who helps the development of useful projects and contributes to the development of society.

Ierathel see TERATHEL

Iezalel A zodiac angel who is also a GUARDIAN ANGEL of those born under Gemini between 21 and 25 May. As such he is an angel of union who aids in human communication and socialisation as well as the establishment of families.

Ifrit, Afrit, Afarit The name Ifrit comes from the Arabic word for 'rebellious', and describes the nature of the **Afarit** (the plural of Ifrit). There is much confusion between the Ifrit, **Marid**, **Ghul** and DJINN. One writer on the subject, al-Djahiz, explains the difference as 'the shaytan is a renegade djinni who sows discord and does evil; one who is strong enough to perform difficult tasks, carry heavy burdens and overhear what passes in the upper regions is a marid; one who is more powerful still is an ifrit', yet in some stories of the *1001 Nights* the relationship between Ifrit and Marid is reversed.

In popular tales the Ifrit is basically just smoke – hence its ability to fit into a bottle (when it is usually called a genie in the West). It traditionally has wings and, like the djinn, lives in ruins or underground. Afarit have a busy social life. They have kings, who may go to war with each other and marry either humans or each other (the feminine form is called an **Ifrita**, and can be stronger than the male). Afarit are not necessarily evil spirits, although some can be. They can be believers and carry out God's purpose.

Ihiazel, **Ieiazel** As well as being one of the seventy-two angels who bear the mystic name of God, SHEMHAMPHORAE, this angel is held to be the GUARDIAN ANGEL of those born under Libra between 9 and 13 October. As such he is an angel of awakening who aids communication and boosts self-confidence.

Imamiah Once one of the seventy-two PRINCIPALITIES that bore the mystic name of God, SHEMHAMPHORAE, Imamiah fell, and now resides in hell where he supervises and controls voyages and, either at whim or when invoked, destroys and humiliates enemies. Nevertheless, Imamiah is considered a GUARDIAN ANGEL of those born under Sagittarius between 8 and 12 December and as such an angel of deliverance who can bring freedom from a negative state, or liberation. He also brings social success.

Impuryn An angel of the day of Mars (Tuesday) in the Sloane manuscript *Book of Raziel*.

Indam In the Sloane manuscript *Book of Raziel*, an angel with power over fire and flame.

Insquen In the Sloane manuscript *Book of Raziel*, an angel of the tenth lunar month. If invoked in rites his name will ensure good results.

Intelligences Intelligences is a term widely used in discussing spiritual beings, and particularly found in Neo-Platonism, used for the equivalent of Judeo-Christian angels.

Iofiel One of the seven ARCHANGELS, and the equal of METATRON. Iofiel is also a prince of the law, and the ruler of Saturn and Jupiter.

Irmanotzod see SARANDIEL

Irrin see QADDISIN

Ishim, **Issim** One of the ten CHOIRS of angels, according to the *Key of Solomon*. Both Maimonides and *The Zohar* rank them as the tenth and lowest of the choirs in the HIERARCHY OF THE ANGELS. Others rank them higher or lower. There are contradictory accounts of their nature – some say they are beings of snow and ice; others call them 'Flaming Ones' and 'Souls of Fire' and equate them with the passage in Psalm 104: 'who makest the winds their messengers, fire and flame thy ministers'. In the Kabbalah they are sometimes described as the souls of just men, but *The Zohar* equates them with the BENE ELOHIM or THRONES and says **Zephania(h)** is their chief, although others say AZAZEL is their leader. There seems to be agreement that their chief function is to praise God.

Islington In Neil Gaiman's cult work *Neverwhere* (published in book form and dramatised as a serial by the BBC, both in 1996), Islington is the name of a FALLEN ANGEL incarcerated under London. He had been the GUARDIAN ANGEL of Atlantis, but had lost his temper and drowned it. Being locked under London is his punishment. The book is a dark fantasy based on the geography of London, particularly the underground railway stations, and the point here is that The Angel is an area and an underground station to the south of Islington. In reality, The Angel gets its name from a local pub.

Isma'il An angel invoked in exorcism in Arabic tradition.

Israel A THRONE, or one of the HAYYOT depending on which source you use, although these terms can be inter-changeable. In the *Sepher Raziel* Israel ranks sixth among the Thrones. Elsewhere he is said to be an ARCHANGEL, and to be an aspect of URIEL, who visited earth in the form of the biblical Jacob-Israel (Jacob got his name Israel 'he who strives with God' after fighting all night with a 'man' – variously interpreted as an angel, said by some to be CAMAEL, PENIEL, URIEL or the DARK ANGEL, or even to have been God) and has now returned to his proper role. In the Sloane manuscript *Book of Raziel*, he is an angel of the eleventh lunar month. If invoked in the relevant month, he will ensure success in your enterprise.

Israfil, **Israfel**, **Asrafil** In Islam, the ARCHANGEL who is to blow the last trump. The name (also found as **Sarafil**, **Sarafin**) is probably connected with the name of the SERAPHIM. Add an 'A' or 'I' in front of the alternative names and the connection becomes clear. He is tradi-tionally called Lord of the Trumpet from his role on the Day of Resurrection. Indeed, some say he holds his trumpet to his mouth at all times, so that he can blow it the instant God commands him to blow the last trump; others that he will be the first to rise on that day, and that he will go to the holy rock in Jerusalem to give the signal for man to leave the grave. Once the righteous have entered paradise, they will be refreshed by the music he makes. Israfil has other functions in addition to his main one. For three years he was the companion to the Prophet, until God's messenger DJIBRIL (GABRIEL) replaced him. Three times each day and three times each night he looks into hell, and earth is watered by the tears he weeps for what he sees there. In his true form he is vast, covered with hair, mouths and tongues (as are many Middle Eastern angels – the tongues to praise God with). He has four wings; one in the west, one in the east, one to cover his body and one to protect him from the majesty of God when he stands before him. Modern angelologists have focused on him as the angel of music, and see him as attended by subordinate angels of music. Israfil's name, which is said to mean 'burning one' does not appear in the Koran, but he is generally accepted as one of the four archangels of Islam. The form Israfel is particularly associated with the American poet Edgar Allan Poe, for he published a poem by that name in 1831, which opens with the lines: 'In Heaven a spirit doth dwell/'Whose heart-strings are a lute;'/None sing so wildly well/As the angel Israfel,/And the giddy stars (so legends tell),/Ceasing their hymns, attend the spell/Of his voice, all mute.' Poe claimed the line in quotations comes from the Koran, but he was mistaken. Israfel was used as the title of an important 1926 biography of Poe by the novelist Anthony Allen.

Istari see GANDALF

Itael The angel that rules the eighth degree of Aries under AIEL, according to the *Lemegeton*.

Ithoth Ithoth is a telling illustration of how dependent the study of angels can be on the quality of translation of very difficult texts, unless the student has absolute mastery of a number of challenging ancient languages. Davidson lists Ithoth among the angels mentioned in Conybeare's 1898 translation of an earlier edition of the Greek text of the *Testament of Solomon*. Conybeare's translation reads: 'The twelfth [demon] said: "I am called Saphathoraél, and I inspire partisanship in men, and delight in causing them to stumble. If any one will write on paper these names of angels, Iacô, Iealô, Iôelet, Sabaôth, Ithoth, Bae, and having folded it up, wear it round his neck or against his ear, I at once retreat and dissipate the drunken fit."' Alas, this angel disappears in the translation in Charlesworth, based on a more modern edition of the work. This now reads 'I am called Saphthrael. I put dissensions into the minds of men and I delight when I cause them to stumble. If anyone writes down these words, "Iae, Ieo, sons of Sabaoth," and wears them around his neck, I retreat immediately.'

Ithuriel see MALKIEL

Ivvim see NEPHILIM

Izamiel The angel that rules the tenth degree of Aquarius under AUSIUL, according to the *Lemegeton*.

Izashiel The angel that rules the tenth degree of Capricorn under CASUJOJAH, according to the *Lemegeton*. He appears as **Izachel** in the *Greater Key of Solomon* as an angel invoked through prayer in ritual magic.

Izrail, **Azrael**, **Azrail** Izrail is the Islamic angel of death, and some say that it is he, rather than ISRAFIL who sounds the last trump. He is one of the four ARCHANGELS of Islam, along with ISRAFIL, MIKAIL and DJIBRIL. He is of vast size. It is said that if all the water of the world were to be poured on his head, not a drop of it would reach the earth. There are varying accounts of his appearance. Some say he has 70,000 feet, but others only 2. Again, some say he has 4 faces, but it is generally agreed that he has 4,000 wings and that his body is made up of eyes and tongues – one for each of the living. He sits on a throne of light in either the fourth or the seventh heaven.

There is a story that explains how he came to be the angel of death. When God decided to create Man He sent Djibril to fetch the clay from which he was to be formed. But Earth objected and resisted having some of her clay taken. Some say that it was IBLIS who advised her to do this. So Djibril took pity and returned without the clay. Mikhail and Israfil were each sent in turn with the same results. But Izrail was unmoved and returned with the clay. Because of his pitilessness Allah made him angel of death with a host of subordinate angels under him. But he is not death itself; rather the master of death.

As the angel of death he keeps a scroll on which are the names of Mankind. On this scroll the names of the blessed are surrounded by a bright circle, but the names of the damned are marked with a dark circle. When the time of a man's death draws near Allah causes a leaf bearing that man's name to drop from the tree that stands beneath his throne. Izrail reads the name on the leaf, and will separate the body and soul within forty days.

J

Jaajah The angel that rules the third degree of Capricorn under CASUJOJAH, according to the *Lemegeton*.

Jaajeh The angel that rules the third degree of Aquarius under AUSIUL, according to the *Lemegeton*.

Jabamiah see GABAMIAH

Jabniel see DALQUIEL

Jabriel, Jibril see DJIBRIL

Jachoroz see PAMYEL

Jael, Joel A cherub who, with his twin ZARALL, guards the Ark of the Covenant. He is also the angel who rules Libra, according to the *Lemegeton*. Jael is also recorded as one of the names of God. Joel is cited as an angel with power over the west in the Sloane manuscript *Book of Raziel*.

Jahoel, Jehoel, Jaoel Jahoel is an ANGEL OF THE PRESENCE who is said by some to be chief of the SERAPHIM, although others say this is SERAPIEL. He is also the choir-master of the angels. In the *Apocalypse of Abraham* it is Jahoel who guides and instructs Abraham. There he is described as robed in purple and wearing a turban of rainbow; his hair is white and his body like sapphire. He is also known as Metatron-YAHOEL. When Judgement Day comes, says one Jewish legend, the monster Leviathan will swallow the souls of sinners. Until then, Jahoel has the job of holding Leviathan in check.

Jaldaboath see IALDABOATH

Jamedroz see NARCORIEL

Janael An angel of the east of the first heaven in the Sloane manuscript *Book of Raziel* and *The Heptameron*.

Janiel The angel that rules the second degree of Sagittarius under SUIAJASEL, according to the *Lemegeton*. In *The Heptameron,* an angel of the south of the fifth heaven. This may be the same angel as JANAEL above.

Jannes and Jambres see ABEZETHIBOU

Janofiel see OSMADIEL

Janothyel see SERQUANICH

Jao see IAO

Jaoel see JAHOEL, YAHOEL

Japhael The angel that rules the seventh degree of Aries under AIEL, according to the *Lemegeton*.

Japuriel see JEFISCHA

Jarael An angel of the north of the second heaven in the Sloane manuscript *Book of Raziel,* and in *The Heptameron* in the form **Jariahel**.

Jasphiel see JEFISCHA

Jastrion see NARCORIEL

Jasyozyn According to the Sloane manuscript *Book of Raziel* this is one of the GUARDIAN ANGELS with special care of Monday (Luna) who should be invoked to aid works started on that day.

Jatael The angel that rules the nineteenth degree of Pisces under PASIL, according to the *Lemegeton*.

Jatroziel see DARDARIEL

Javiel The angel that rules the eighteenth degree of Taurus under TUAL and the eighteenth degree of Gemini under GIEL, according to the *Lemegeton*. As **Jauiel** ('u' and 'v' are identical in some manuscripts), an angel presiding over Thursday, the day of Jove, in the Sloane manuscript *Book of Raziel*.

Jazeriel, Iazeriel A MOON ANGEL who rules the thirteenth mansion of the moon in Virgo. He is generally a benevolent angel, aiding the escape of prisoners, good feeling, harvests, journeys and profit.

Jebiel The angel that rules the tenth degree of Sagittarius under SUIAJASEL, according to the *Lemegeton*.

Jebrayel An angel presiding over Thursday, the day of Jove, according to Sloane manuscript *Book of Raziel*.

Jechiel The angel that rules the twentieth degree of Virgo under VOIL, according to the *Lemegeton*.

Jeduthun According to *The Zohar*, during the evening he leads the hosts of angels who sing hymns to God (ASAPH leads the night chants and HEMAN the morning ones). The name seems to have arisen from the annotations to Psalms 39, 62 and 77 which read: 'To the chief Musician, even Jeduthun'. This is believed to have referred originally to one of the directors of music at the Temple of Jerusalem, but by the Middle

Ages Jeduthun had come to be seen as an angel.

Jefischa The angel of the fourth hour of the night according to the *Lemegeton*. The most important of his many attendant angels are **Armosiel, Nedruan, Maneyloz, Ormael, Phorsiel, Rimezyn, Rayziel, Gemezin, Fremiel, Hamayz, Japuriel, Jasphiel, Lamediel, Adroziel, Zodiel, Bramiel, Coreziel** and **Enatriel.**

Jehoel see JAEOL

Jehudiel Considered by some to be one of the seven ARCHANGELS. He rules the movement of the heavenly bodies.

Jeliel This is a seraph who is one of the eight SERAPHIM of the Tree of Life, according to the Kabbalah, residing in the world of Yetsirah (Formation). He gives victory to those who are unjustly attacked and controls the destiny of kings and other powerful people. He is the GUARDIAN ANGEL of Turkey. He is also an angel with an especial interest in the family, inspiring passion between the sexes and faithfulness within marriage. As the guardian angel of those born under Aries between 26 and 30 March he is an angel of solutions who resolves conflict.

Jenaziel see TARTYS

Jeniel The angel that rules the second degree of Scorpio under JOSEL, according to the *Lemegeton*.

Jenotriel see SANIEL

Jeqon One of the GRIGORI who was, so it says in *1 Enoch*, 'the one who led astray [all] the sons of God, and brought them down to the earth, and led them astray through the daughters of men.' The name means 'inciter'. It is AZAZEL, however, who reaps the greatest opprobrium in *1 Enoch*, while SEMYAZA is another of the leaders.

Jeremiel see REMIEL

Jermiel see VATHMIEL

Jetrel One of the GRIGORI according to *1 Enoch*.

Jezisiel The angel that rules the sixth degree of Taurus under TUAL, according to the *Lemegeton*.

Jibril see DJIBRIL

Jmonyel see MENDRION

Joel see JAEL

Johiel One of the ANGELS OF PARADISE and ANGELS OF THE PRESENCE, to be identified with JAHOEL.

Jomjael, Yomyael One of the GRIGORI, 'a chief of ten', according to *1 Enoch* 6. The name means 'day of God' and is to be identified with **Yomiel**, the angel of the day (see under SHAMSIEL). The Thursday angel **Jumyel**, found in the *Liber Juratus*, is probably the same name, as is **Juniel**, the angel presiding over Thursday in the Sloane manuscript *Book of Raziel*.

Jonadriel see MENDRION

Josel, Sosol The angel who rules Scorpio according to the *Lemegeton*.

Jumyel, Juniel see JOMJAEL

K

Kabriel see CABRIEL, SARANDIEL

Kabshiel A name well-used on amulets, and an angel said, if well disposed to the petitioner, to confer grace and power. As **Kachiel** he is the angel that rules the ninth degree of Libra under JAEL, according to the *Lemegeton*. The form **Kabchiel** is said to be the name of an angel among the Gnostic Mandeans.

Kafziel In *The Zohar* **Kafziel is an aide to** GABRIEL **in his role as** WARRIOR ANGEL. Elsewhere, he is seen as the angel who governs the death of kings and who is one of the seven archangels of Saturn. As Qaphsiel or Qafseil he is ruler of the moon. There is an ancient Hebrew charm for getting rid of an enemy which involves invoking Qaphsiel, writing the words of the charm in bird blood, then tying it to the leg of a dove. If the bird flies away, so too will the enemy. All these names are aspects of the name CASSIEL.

Kakabel see KOKABEL

Kakodaemons see DAEMONS

Kalkail An angel invoked in exorcism in Arabic tradition.

Kalkydras see PHOENIX

Kanorsiel see NARCORIEL

Karael In the *Testament of Solomon*, an angel who should be invoked to imprison Belbel, a demon who perverts the hearts and minds of men. **Kariel** is a form used in invocation in the *Liber Juratus*.

Karason An angel of the element air, under the planet Hanina (Sol, the sun), to be invoked when working under this planet, according to the Sloane manuscript *Book of Raziel*.

Karbiel An angel of the eighth lunar month according to the Sloane manuscript *Book of Raziel*, which says that if named 'in each thing that thou wilt do … thou shalt profit'.

Karin This is an Arabic word meaning 'companion', but in pre-Islamic Arabic it had the implied sense of 'spirit-companion', and this is the sense that it is usually used in the Koran. However, although the Prophet had the angels DJIBRIL or ISRAFIL as guides, Karin is not always used in a good sense, for Shaytan (SATAN) is described as a Karin (4.42/38) and the plural form **Kurana** is used of tempting spirits (42.24/5).

By tradition, every human has two Kurana at his side; one of them a shaytan whose role is to tempt him to evil (although this is sometimes identified as a DJINN), the other angelic. These are to be distinguished from the traditional Recording Angels, for it is said that at Judgement Day the shaytans will be thrown into the fires along with those who have listened to them. It is said that even the Prophet had a shaytan Karin, but that he converted his to Islam. In pre-Islamic days the term Karin was more widely used than now, and could be used, for example, of the djinn who brought his verses to a poet.

Kasbeel An angel called **Biqa** tried to get from MICHAEL the secret name of

God so that he could use it in an oath and so have power over other angels. As a result Biqa, meaning 'good person', was renamed Kasbeel, which means 'sorcery'. He is listed among the leaders of the GRIGORI in *1 Enoch*.

Kasdeja, Kesdeya, Kesdaye A leader of the GRIGORI, who introduced demonic practices to Man, including the art of abortion, according to *1 Enoch*.

Kasiel An angel of the element fire, under the planet Madin (Mars), to be invoked when working under this planet, according to the Sloane manuscript *Book of Raziel*.

Kathos see BARAQIEL

Kawkabel see KOKABEL

Keballa Keballa is an angel in the Samaritan tradition who resides in the holy place of the temple and who cannot be looked upon without the promise of death.

Keialin An angel presiding over Friday, the day of Venus, according to the Sloane manuscript *Book of Raziel*. **Kelfeielyn** is another Friday angel.

Kemerion One of the angels of Wednesday, the day of Mercury, according to the Sloane manuscript *Book of Raziel*.

Kemuel see CAMAEL

Kerubiel YHWH, Cherubiel This is the lord of the CHERUBIM in *3 Enoch*, although *1 Enoch* says gabriel has this role. 'His body is full of burning coals … The opening of his mouth blazes like a fiery torch, and his tongue is a consuming fire. His eyelashes are as the splendour of lightning, his eyes like brilliant sparks and his face looks like a blazing fire.' The angel Kerub 'who was made the Guardian of the Terrestrial Paradise, with a Sword of Flame', whose name is used for conjuration in the *Key of Solomon*, may be identical, or it may simply be a form of the word Cherub taken as a proper name.

Kery An angel of the ninth lunar month according to the *Liber Juratus* and the Sloane manuscript *Book of Raziel*, which says that if named 'in each thing that thou wilt do … thou shalt profit'.

Kesdaye, Kesdeya see KASDEJA

Kether In the *Key of Solomon* identified as one of the angels who preside over the ten SEFIROTH.

Kezef One of the five ANGELS OF DESTRUCTION. According to Ginzberg there is a legend that Moses had particular trouble with him. Moses had been carried up to heaven, and when he was to be sent back to guide his people, 'The angels, hearing that God meant to send him from His presence, wanted to kill him, and only by clinging to the Throne of God, who covered him with His mantle, did he escape from the hands of the angels, that they might do him no harm. He had particularly hard struggle with the five Angels of Destruction: Kezef, **Af** [see under APH], HEMAH, **Mashit**, and **Haron**, whom God had sent to annihilate Israel.' In the role of angel of death Kezef was imprisoned by Aaron in the Tabernacle.

Khamael see CAMAEL

Kharuara'il An angel invoked in exorcism in Arabic tradition.

Kheel The angel that rules the sixteenth degree of Aries under AIEL, according to the *Lemegeton*.

Khezr, Khidr, Khizr see GREEN MAN

Khordad see HAURVATAT

Khorshed see HVARE-KHSHAETA

Khshathra Vairya The name of a Zoroastrian archangel (AMESHA SPENTA) whose name translates as 'Desirable Country' or 'Righteous Power'. His realms are the sky, stones and metals, and he protects both warriors and the poor. He symbolises self-control from sensual indulgence, as well as bringing prosperity and the Kingdom of God. The modern form of the name is **Shahrewar** and in this form he gives his name to the fourth day of the month according to the Zoroastrian religious calendar, and to the sixth month, which runs from 23 August to 22 September.

Khursan, Khwarshed see HVARE-KHSHAETA

Khwarenah YAZAD (Zoroastrian angel) presiding over Divine Grace or Fortune. The name is also found as **Khwarrah** and **Farrah**.

Kingael The angel that rules the seventh degree of Taurus under TUAL, and the seventh degree of Gemini under GIEL according to the *Lemegeton*.

Kipod see NASARGIEL

Kiriel see KYRIEL

Kmiel The angel that rules the eleventh degree of Capricorn under CASUJOJAH, according to the *Lemegeton*.

Kokabel, Kokabiel, Kakabel, Kawkabel, Cocabiel The angel responsible for all the stars. So many are there that he needs the help of 365,000 myriad angels to keep them in their course. His name means 'star of God'. However, *1 Enoch* 6 says he fell with the GRIGORI and thereafter taught Mankind the knowledge of the constellations. **Kokaviel**, in *The Key of Solomon* an angel whose name appears on the Third Pentacle of Mercury, looks to be the same angel. In the form **Cocabiel** he is found in Agrippa, as one of seven princes who stand before God and in the Kabbalah as a spirit of the planet Mercury. See also under ARAKIEL

Kolazonta One of THE ANGELS OF DESTRUCTION. The name appears to come from the Greek meaning 'the chastiser'.

Kosmokratores see ANGEL OF DEATH

Kphiel The angel that rules the seventh degree of Pisces under PASIL, according to the *Lemegeton*.

Kralym see ABASDARHON

Kranoti see ORIEL

Kriel The angel that rules the eighth degree of Virgo under VOIL, according to the *Lemegeton*.

Kshiel The angel that rules the eleventh degree of Aquarius under AUSIUL, according to the *Lemegeton*. It may be a shortened form of **Kushiel**, 'rigid one of God', who is an ANGEL OF PUNISHMENT.

Kurana see KARIN

Kutiel An angel who is invoked when using divining rods.

Kyriel, **Kiriel** A MOON ANGEL who rules the twentieth mansion of the moon in Sagittarius. He can be used to force a person to go to a preordained place, he strengthens prisons, helps tame wild animals, but destroys the wealth of societies.

L

Laabiel see LABIEL

Labbiel see LABIEL, RAPHAEL

Labelas According to the *Liber Juratus* and the Sloane manuscript *Book of Raziel*, this is one of the GUARDIAN ANGELS with special care of Monday (Luna) who should be invoked to aid works started on that day.

Labiel, **Laabiel** In the Sloane manuscript *Book of Raziel*, both forms are given as the name of an angel of the twelfth lunar month. If invoked in the relevant month, he will ensure success in your enterprise. He is also listed as one of the angels presiding over Thursday, the day of Jove. He appears in the same role in the *Liber Juratus* as **Labyel**. However, in the more usual spelling **Labbiel**, this is the name of the archangel RAPHAEL, before God changes his name.

Lacana An angel of the west of the fourth heaven in the Sloane manuscript *Book of Raziel*.

Laccudonyn According to the Sloane manuscript *Book of Raziel*, this is one of the angels with special care of Monday.

Lachiel The angel that rules the first degree of Pisces under PASIL, according to the *Lemegeton*. **Lacyel**, the angel with power over the thirteenth lunar month in the *Liber Juratus,* may be the same.

Ladrotzod see SARANDIEL

Lafaqnael An angel of the element earth, under the planet Labana (Luna, the moon), to be invoked when working under this planet, according to the Sloane manuscript *Book of Raziel*.

Lafiel An angel presiding over Thursday, the day of Jove, according to the Sloane manuscript *Book of Raziel*. The same angel appears as a Thursday angel by the name of **Lafyel** and as an angel of the fourth month as **Lafayel** in the *Liber Juratus*.

Lahabiel An assistant to RAPHAEL in his role as ruler of the first day. His name also appears on amulets.

Lahash Moses' greatest desire, before he died, was to reach the Promised Land, but he knew his death was at hand before he could do this. When he knew his prayer had been rejected, he asked the Israelites to pray for him. Ginzberg tells the following legend of this time: 'When the people and their leaders heard these words of Moses, they broke out into mournful weeping, and in the Tabernacle with bitter tears they entreated God to answer Moses' prayer, so that their cries rose even to the Throne of Glory. But then one hundred and eighty four myriads of angels under the leadership of the great angels **Zakun** and Lahash descended and snatched away the words of the supplicants, that they might not reach God. The angel Lahash indeed tried to restore to their place the words which the other angels had snatched away, so that they might reach God, but when SAMAEL learned of this, he fettered Lahash with chains of fire and brought him before God, where he received sixty blows of fire and was expelled from the inner chamber of God because, contrary to God's wish, he had attempted to aid Moses in the fulfilment of his desire. When Israel now saw how the angels dealt with their prayers, they went to Moses and said, "The angels will not let us pray for thee."'

Lahtiel and the Lehatim Derived from the Hebrew name for the flame of the whirling sword that guards the Tree of Light, Lahtiel is described in early Jewish mystic material as the leader of a rank of angels called the Lehatim. He is said to keep the gates of death. This idea of flame-angels fits in with other concepts current in the Middle East at the time. For example, flame-like messengers are found in the Baal cycle of Ugarit.

Lailah, **Leliel**, **Lailiel**, **Laylah** As well as being the angel of the night, according to Jewish tradition, Lailah has a vital role in uniting the soul and body at conception. When a woman conceives, it is Lailah who carries the sperm before God. God then decrees what sex the child will be, what they will look like, their character and their lot in life. Piety and wickedness alone are left to the determination of Man himself. The angel in charge of souls then brings the appropriate soul from paradise to enter the sperm, and Lailah, guarded by two angels to make sure she does not drop it, carries the sperm back to the womb of the mother. Lailah was also the angel who fought for Abraham in his victory against the forces of Nimrod.

Lamachiel In the *Testament of Solomon* Lamachiel is identified as the angel who thwarts the members of the group of seven evil stars known as Deception, who plot deception and devise heresies.

Lamajah The angel that rules the fifth degree of Capricorn under CASUJOJAH, according to the *Lemegeton*.

Lamediel see JEFISCHA

Lamerotzod see ZAAZENACH

Lamersy see DARDARIEL

Lamiel see BARIEL

Langael The angel that rules the fourth degree of Sagittarius under SUIAJASEL, according to the *Lemegeton*.

Langhasin According to the Sloane manuscript *Book of Raziel* this is one of the GUARDIAN ANGELS with special care of Monday (Luna) who should be invoked to aid works started on that day.

Lanifiel, **Lanyfiel** An angel of the east of the fifth heaven in the Sloane manuscript *Book of Raziel*. In the *Lemegeton* Lanifiel is one of the servant angels of BARIEL, the angel governing the eleventh hour of the day.

Lanoziel see ZAAZENACH

Lantiel In the Sloane manuscript *Book of Raziel*, an angel of the thirteenth lunar month (March).

Lantrhots see OSMADIEL

Lapheriel see IASSUARIM

Larfuty see OSMADIEL

Lariagathyn According to the Sloane manuscript *Book of Raziel*, this is one of the angels of Monday.

Lariel An earth angel under Sabaday (Saturn), to be invoked when working under this planet, according to the Sloane manuscript *Book of Raziel*. The angel that rules the tenth degree of Aries under AIEL, according to the *Lemegeton*.

Larmich see VATHMIEL

Lashiel The angel that rules the fifth degree of Aquarius under AUSIUL, according to the *Lemegeton*.

Latebayfanysyn A Monday angel in the Sloane manuscript *Book of Raziel*.

Latgriel In the Sloane manuscript *Book of Raziel*, an elemental angel with power over the earth.

Latiel The angel that rules both the first degree of Taurus under TUAL, and the first degree of Gemini under GIEL, according to the *Lemegeton*.

Laudulin An angel presiding over Friday, the day of Venus, in the Sloane manuscript *Book of Raziel*.

Lauviah, **Lauiah** Lauviah is variously described as belonging to the order of THRONES or CHERUBIM although some say he is a FALLEN ANGEL. His power is over scholars and the elite. As the GUARDIAN ANGEL of both those born under Taurus between 11 and 15 May and those born under Gemini between 11 and 15 June, he is accounted as an angel of joy who unites thought with action, and controls emotive impulses.

Lawidh When the devout Muslim Abu

Yazid visited heaven, it is said he was greeted by the angel Lawidh. When Lawidh offered him an earthly kingdom Abu Yazid rejected it, realising that this was a test of his faith. Lawidh is also known as **Naya'il**.

Laylah see LAILAH

Layzaiosyn According to the Sloane manuscript *Book of Raziel*, this is one of the angels with special care of Monday. **Layralosyn** in the *Liber Juratus* – also a Monday angel – would seem to be the same name.

Leal One of the angels of Wednesday, the day of Mercury, in the Sloane manuscript *Book of Raziel*.

Lebes According to the *Lemegeton*, this is an angel who is invoked for fertility in animals, plants and women.

Lebraieil An angel presiding over Friday, the day of Venus, according to the Sloane manuscript *Book of Raziel*. **Lebrachiel**, angel of the eleventh month in the *Liber Juratus,* may be the same.

Lecabel This is an angel in charge of agriculture and the growth of vegetation. He is also one of the seventy-two angels bearing the mystic name of God, SHEMHAMPHORAE. As GUARDIAN ANGEL of those born under Virgo between 23 and 28 August he is an angel of gifts, overseeing talent and financial success, the solutions of problems and the communication of ideas.

Lehahiah GUARDIAN ANGEL of those born under Virgo between 8 and 12 September. He is a SHEMHAMPHORAE

angel and a protector of rulers.

Lehatim see LAHATIEL

Lelahel An angel of the zodiac with power over love, art, science and good fortune. One of the eight SERAPHIM of the Kabbalah. Listed in the *Liber Juratus* among the seventy-two angels bearing the mystic name of God, SHEMHAMPHORAE, but not always in the lists found elsewhere. As the GUARDIAN ANGEL of those born under Aries between 15 and 20 April he is an angel of achievement, giving good health and energy in enterprises leading to success in life and careers.

Lelalion This is one of the angels presiding over Saturday, the day of Saturn or Sabat, according to the *Liber Juratus* and the Sloane manuscript *Book of Raziel*. If invoked appropriately and in a state of purity, these angels will aid you.

Leliel see LAILAH

Lemaron see SERQUANICH

Lemozar see NARCORIEL

Lemur see ORIEL

Lengael The angel that rules the fourth degree of Scorpio under JOSEL, according to the *Lemegeton*.

Lepiron This is one of the angels presiding over Saturday in the Sloane manuscript *Book of Raziel*.

Letityelyn An angel of the day of Mars (Tuesday) in the Sloane manuscript *Book of Raziel*. The *Liber Juratus* gives the name an even more exuberant form, **Letytyeylyn**.

Leuainon This is one of the angels presiding over Saturday in the Sloane manuscript *Book of Raziel*.

Leuviah, **Leuuiah**, **Leviah** One of the seventy-two angels bearing the mystic name of God, SHEMHAMPORAE. As the GUARDIAN ANGEL of those born under Cancer between 22 and 26 June he is regarded as an angel of profusion who helps to see targets clearly and to achieve them successfully.

Leviel The angel that rules the seventeenth degree of Aries under AIEL, according to the *Lemegeton*.

Lezaidi An angel of the fourth lunar month according to the *Liber Juratus* and the Sloane manuscript *Book of Raziel*, who if invoked brings benefits.

Libiel A fire angel under Sabaday (Saturn), to be invoked when working under this planet, according to the Sloane manuscript *Book of Raziel*. In the *Lemegeton* he is a duke of the night serving under Malgaras, who rules in the west (See under MALGAS). We are told that these spirits are 'all very courteous and will appear willingly to do your will'.

Libral In the Sloane manuscript *Book of Raziel*, an angel of the eleventh lunar month. If invoked in the relevant month, he will ensure success in your enterprise.

Lilith see AGRAT BAT MAHLAT, CHILDBED ANGELS, GAMALIEL, HARUT AND MARUT, SANSANUI

Living Creatures see HAYYOT

Locariel An angel of the element earth, under the planet Hanina (Sol, the sun), to be invoked when working under this planet, according to the Sloane manuscript *Book of Raziel*.

Loch An angel of the fifth lunar month in the Sloane manuscript *Book of Raziel*.

Loriqniel An angel of the element air, under the planet Cocab (Mercury), to be invoked when working under this planet, according to the Sloane manuscript *Book of Raziel*.

Lucifel An angel of the element earth, under the planet Hanina (Sol, the sun) found in the Sloane manuscript *Book of Raziel*.

Lucifer Lucifer is a Latin name, meaning 'light bringer'. How then has such a one been equated with SATAN? Lucifer is a translation of the Hebrew *Helel ben Sahar*, 'Bright Son of the Morning', and was a term applied to the planet Venus in its appearance as the morning star. In Isaiah 14:12, Isaiah exclaims, 'How art thou fallen, Lucifer son of the morning!' This passage was originally an attack on Nebuchadnessar, king of Babylon, one of the great villains of the Old Testament, who had captured Jerusalem and led the Jews into exile. Isaiah is prophesying his downfall. However, the references to Babylon, still used as a term for a place of sin, were interpreted by Christian writers to be metaphorical, and Lucifer taken to be a FALLEN ANGEL. This was no doubt helped by the way in which St John writes of falling stars in Revelation (see under ABADON) and the way that angels and stars are so widely associated. Lucifer soon came to be associated with the greatest of the fallen angels, SAMAEL or Satan. Lucifer raising rebellion against heaven through pride had become established in English by the Middle Ages, and was given its most memorable form in Milton's *Paradise Lost*.

Luel In the Sloane manuscript *Book of Raziel*, an angel of the eleventh lunar month. If invoked in the relevant month, he will ensure success in your enterprise. Elsewhere, he is found as an angel invoked in magic using divining rods.

Luliaraf An angel of the fourth lunar month in the Sloane manuscript *Book of Raziel*.

Luma'il An Arabic GUARDIAN ANGEL who is also invoked in exorcism.

Lustifion see NARCORIEL

Lyenyel An angel of the south of the third heaven in the Sloane manuscript *Book of Raziel*.

M

Maachin An angel of the east of the second heaven in the Sloane manuscript *Book of Raziel*.

Maadon An angel of the fourth lunar month according to the *Liber Juratus* and the Sloane manuscript *Book of Raziel*.

Maaliel An angel of the eighth lunar month according to the *Liber Juratus* and the Sloane manuscript *Book of Raziel*. **Maarim** is a companion angel.

Maasiel An angel of the third lunar month in the *Liber Juratus* and the Sloane manuscript *Book of Raziel*.

Maasim Derived from a Hebrew word meaning either 'creatures' or 'structures', these are one of many classes of angels derived from the description of the Chariot of the Lord (see MERKABAH) in Ezekiel.

Mabareylyn An angel of the day of Mars (Tuesday) in the Sloane manuscript *Book of Raziel* and found in the same role in the *Liber Juratus*.

Mabsuf An angel of the third lunar month according to the Sloane manuscript *Book of Raziel*.

Macareton An angel of the west of the second heaven in the Sloane manuscript *Book of Raziel*.

Maccafor An angel of the third lunar month according to the Sloane manuscript *Book of Raziel*. The name is

Maccasor in the *Liber Juratus,* in a typical confusion between old forms of 'f' and 's'.

Macgron This is a Saturday angel in the Sloane manuscript *Book of Raziel.*

Machatan, Machator According to the *Heptameron,* a great and powerful angel of Saturday, serving under CASSIEL. He is counted by some as a spirit of the air.

Machidiel Angel of March and Aries. He is also used in love magic, invoked to send the lover the maiden of his desires. As **Melchulael** he is an angelic personification of the SEFIRA **Malkuth,** alongside SANDALPHON, Messiah and Emanuel.

Machmag see MENDRION

Macracif, Macratif An angel of the sixth lunar month according to the *Liber Juratus* and the Sloane manuscript *Book of Raziel.*

Macria An angel of the fifth lunar month according to the *Liber Juratus* and the Sloane manuscript *Book of Raziel,* who if invoked brings benefits.

Macrobres see ELDIL

Madan The angel who rules Mercury, according to Heywood's *Hierarchy of the Blessed Angels.*

Madarilyn In the Sloane manuscript *Book of Raziel* this is one of the angels with special care of Monday (Luna) who should be invoked to aid works started on that day.

Maday An angel of the fourth lunar month according to the *Liber Juratus* and the Sloane manuscript *Book of Raziel.*

Madiel The angel that rules the seventeenth degree of Cancer under CAEL, according to the *Lemegeton,* which also says he shares the rule of the north with GABRIEL. In the *Heptameron* he is one of the angels of the first heaven, ruling Monday, who should be invoked from the east.

Madrat An angel of the fifth lunar month according to the *Liber Juratus* and the Sloane manuscript *Book of Raziel.*

Maduch see NADUCH

Mael The *Lemegeton* says GABRIEL rules in the north, with SAMAEL, MADIEL and Mael under him. The *Heptameron* describes Mael as an angel of the first heaven, ruling Monday, who should be invoked from the north. Still others say he is an ARCHANGEL of water who is one of the intelligences of the planet Saturn.

Mafatyn According to the *Liber Juratus* and the Sloane manuscript *Book of Raziel,* this is one of the angels with special care of Monday.

Mafriel see DARDARIEL

Magdiel An angel of the eighth lunar month according to the Sloane manuscript *Book of Raziel.*

Magel In the Sloane manuscript *Book of Raziel,* an angel of the thirteenth lunar month (March).

Magiel The angel that rules the sixteenth degree of Leo under OL, according to the *Lemegeton*. He is also invoked in the *Liber Juratus*.

Magnael The angel that rules the eighth and the fourteenth degrees of Cancer under CAEL, according to the *Lemegeton*.

Magnyny, **Magnia** The angel with power over the sixth lunar month according to the Sloane manuscript *Book of Raziel*. In the *Liber Juratus* the name appears as the rather more dignified **Magnyuya** ('n' and 'u' are easily confused in manuscripts) and as **Manyny**.

Magossangos In the Sloane manuscript *Book of Raziel*, an angel of the thirteenth lunar month (March). In the *Liber Juratus* the name appears in the same role rather more convincingly as two separate angels, **Magos** and **Sangos**.

Mah see MAONGHAH

Mahamel An angel of the south of the fourth heaven in the Sloane manuscript *Book of Raziel*.

Mahasiah One of the seventy-two angels bearing the mystic name of God, SHEMHAMPHORAE. When regarded as the GUARDIAN ANGEL of those born under Aries between 10 and 14 April he is said to be an angel of harmony, bringing happiness and improvement and a productive blending of knowledge and intuition.

Mahpekiel and Haphekiel or **Haphkiel** This pair of angels are recorded on a Jewish Aramaic magic bowl found in Babylon and in a papyrus found in Egypt. The bowl states they 'turn around the heavens and the earth,

the stars and the constellations'. Haphekiel gets his name from an Aramaic root which means 'to turn, change, overturn'.

Mahraspand see MANTHRA SPENTA

Maiel The angel that rules the twenty-third degree of Gemini under GIEL, according to the *Lemegeton*.

Maimas see ZADKIEL

Maint In the Sloane manuscript *Book of Raziel*, an angel of the tenth lunar month.

Makael The angel that rules the eleventh degree of Cancer under CAEL, according to the *Lemegeton*.

Malacandra see ELDIL

Malak, **Malaika** Malaika are Islamic angels. Just as the word angel comes from the Greek for 'messenger', so Malak comes from the Arabic root with the same meaning. By tradition, angels were created from light, as opposed to DJINN who were created from fire. Malaika are guardians of Mankind, and also recorders, who write down what Man does. As with Judeo-Christian angels, there are various classes of angels such as *al-mukarrubun*, angels that have been 'brought near' to Allah, and who praise Him day and night without ceasing, and the *malak al mawt*, an ANGEL OF DEATH who is keeper of hell. This angel is helped by nineteen guards called *al-Zabaniyya*, a rather obscure title which seems to mean 'violent thrusters'. These are distinct from the devils of hell, for we are told that these angels will enter heaven on the final day.

Malakhim A class of angels, often equated with VIRTUES. They are ranked sixth in the hierarchy by Maimonides and first by *The Zohar*. In the *Key of Solomon* the **Malachim** are described as one of the ten choirs of Holy Angels. They are associated with metals.

Malak Ta'us Malak Ta'us or The **Peacock Angel** is the prime angel in the belief system of the Yezidis of Kurdistan. They see him as the chief ARCHANGEL, who bestows responsibilities and good and bad fortune as he sees fit. Outsiders have identified Malak Ta'us with SATAN and accused the Yezidis of devil worship, but the Yezidis believe that God and Satan were reconciled after Satan's repentance, and that he was restored to his original position in heaven.

Malaquiran An angel of the first lunar month, according to the Sloane manuscript *Book of Raziel*. He appears as a mighty angel of the first month in the slightly different form of Malquiram in the *Liber Juratus*.

Maledil see ELDIL

Malgas An angel of the first lunar month according to the Sloane manuscript *Book of Raziel* He may be the same as **Malgaras**, of whom the *Lemegeton* says, 'The ninth spirit in order, but the first under the Emperor of the West is called Malgaras – he Rulleth as king in the Dominion of the West, and hath 30 Dukes under him to attend him, in the day, and as many for the night, and several under them againe.'

Malgel An angel of the sixth lunar month in the Sloane manuscript *Book of Raziel*. The same name appears to be found as an aerial spirit, **Malguel**, who serves as a duke under **Asyriel** in the *Lemegeton*.

Malik In Islamic folklore, the chief angel of hell.

Malisan In the Sloane manuscript *Book of Raziel*, an angel of the tenth lunar month.

Malkiel, **Malkhiel**, **Malquiel**, **Malquyel** In Kabbalah, Malkiel is one of three angelic princes – the other two being **Ithuriel** and **Nashriel** – who serve under Sephurion, the lowest ranking of the ten SEFIROTH. Malkhiel is one of the angels whose names are used in the Second Pentacle of the Sun which 'serveth to repress the pride and arrogance of the Solar Spirits, which are altogether proud and arrogant by their nature,' in *The Key of Solomon*. In the Sloane manuscript *Book of Raziel*, Malquiel is an angel of the twelfth lunar month. If invoked in the relevant month, he will ensure success in your enterprise. He is also said there to have power over fire and flame. In the *Liber Juratus* Malquyel(l) appears as an angel of both the thirteenth and ninth months.

Malkuth In *The Key of Solomon* identified as one of the angels who preside over the ten SEPHIROTH.

Malquiel, **Malquyel** see MALKIEL

Mamael, **Mamiel**, **Mamyel** Mamael is the angel of the planet Mars (or Madin) according to the Sloane manuscript of *The Book of Raziel*. In this work and the *Liber Juratus* Mamiel or Mamyel is an angel of the eleventh lunar month. He is found in the north of the fifth heaven. Since these are attributes given elsewhere to SAMAEL (also known as CAMAEL) this angel may have originated as a slip of the pen, with an 'M' appearing in the place of a 'C' or 'S'. Elsewhere, Mamiel is said to be one of the chief angel-officers of the seventh hour of the day, who serves under **Barginiel**.

Mamiazicaras An angel of the third lunar month according to the Sloane manuscript *Book of Raziel*. In the *Liber Juratus* **Mamiah** appears as one of the seventy-two angels bearing the mystic name of God, SHEMHAMPHORAE, so Mamiazicaras may be another case of two angel names being run together in this manuscript.

Mamiel, Mamyel see MAMAEL

Mamirot An angel of the fifth lunar month according to the Sloane manuscript *Book of Raziel*, who if invoked brings benefits.

Mammon Although Mammon is generally considered to be an embodiment of the sin of greed or of the corrupting influence of money, in some Christian texts he actually appears as an angel, albeit now a fallen one. De Plancy's *Dictionnaire Infernal* (1825–6) is said to claim Mammon is hell's ambassador to England, but this may have more to do with the French nationality of the author than with ancient tradition.

Manakel A GUARDIAN ANGEL of those born between 15 and 19 February under Aquarius. He has special care of the sea and sealife.

Mandielm, Mandyel An angel of the ninth lunar month according to the *Liber Juratus* and the Sloane manuscript *Book of Raziel*.

Maneyloz see JEFISCHA

Manistiorar An angel of the eighth lunar month according to the Sloane manuscript *Book of Raziel*, which says that when named 'in each thing that thou wilt do … thou shalt profit'.

Manit An angel of the second lunar month according to the *Liber Juratus* and the Sloane manuscript *Book of Raziel*, with the power to grant wishes.

Manthra Spenta, Mahraspand The YAZAD (Zoroastrian angel) who embodies the Holy Word (the meaning of the name). The twenty-ninth day of the month in the Zoroastrian religious calendar is named after him.

Manuel see BARAQIEL

Many-eyed Ones An alternative name for the OPHANIM. Some rabbinical writings claim that the patriarchs became Many-Eyed Ones on entering heaven.

Maonghah, Mah YAZAD (Zoroastrian angel) presiding over the moon.

Marachy see SARANDIEL

Marchiel see MENDRION

Marcuel An angel of the eighth lunar month in the Sloane manuscript *Book of Raziel*.

Mardiel see SABRATHAN

Marfiel see VATHMIEL

Margabiel An angel of the north of the fifth heaven in the Sloane manuscript *Book of Raziel*. **Margiviel**, a prince of the face and one of the angelic guards of the fourth heaven, seems to be the same name, as the same sound can be transcribed as either 'b' or 'v'.

Marhil, **Marhyll** According to the *Liber Juratus* and the Sloane manuscript *Book of Raziel* this is one of the angels of Sunday.

Marhum One of the angels of the seventh lunar month in the Sloane manuscript *Book of Raziel*. In the *Liber Juratus* it is spelt **Marham**.

Marid see DJINN, IFRIT

Mariel An angel of the ninth lunar month according to the Sloane manuscript *Book of Raziel*. The *Lemegeton* lists Mariel as one of the attendant angels of OSMADIEL, angel of the eighth hour of the day. In a Syriac charm this is one of a list of angels conjured in a charm which ends, 'By these holy names, I bind, ban, stop the mouth and tongues of evil men, jealous and wicked judges, emirs, satraps, governors, men in authority, rulers and chiefs, executioners, prefects, the foreigner, the gentile, the infidel. I bind the mouths of all wicked judges, and all the sons of Adam and Eve, evil ones, men, women, and children; I bind their tongues and lips, their minds and thoughts, those of wicked ones, rebels, judges, court-officials, and prefects; and the lips of the emir, prefects, executioners, satraps, and rulers. I bind the tongues and mouths of these wicked ones by that Word which our Lord spake to his disciples: Whatever you shall bind on earth, shall be bound in heaven. I bind them from off him who carries this charm!'

Marifiel see NARCORIEL

Marilin An angel presiding over Friday, the day of Venus, according to Sloane manuscript *Book of Raziel*.

Marinoc An angel of the second lunar month in the Sloane manuscript *Book of Raziel*.

Mariuk see ARIUK

Marmanyn An angel of the day of Mars (Tuesday) in the Sloane manuscript *Book of Raziel*. It takes the form **Marmaryn** in the *Liber Juratus*.

Marmaroth In the *Testament of Solomon* the evil star of Fate, which causes Man to fight on when defeated rather than make peace, can be thwarted through the power of the angel Marmaroth. This may be the same as **Marmarao**, an angel invoked in magic to cure bladder trouble caused by the demon Anoster.

Marmoc In the Sloane manuscript *Book of Raziel*, an angel of the tenth lunar month.

Marneyelin In the Sloane manuscript *Book of Raziel* this is one of the angels with special care of Monday (Luna). It is **Macnayelyn** in the *Liber Juratus*.

Marut see HARUT

Maseriel see ELIEL

Mashit see HEMAH, KEZEF

Masiel see MAZIEL

Mastema The spirit of evil (SATAN) in *Jubilees* and related texts. In *Jubilees* it is Mastema, and not God, who tempted Abraham to kill Isaac; who caused the Egyptians to persue the Israelites, and who tried to kill Moses to prevent him confronting Pharaoh and demanding the release of his people. When God responds to Noah's prayers to save his sons from being led astray by demons, Mastema demands that one tenth of the demons be left at liberty so that he can perform his proper functions, and God agrees. The author of *Jubilees*, who identifies Mastema with the fallen WATCHERS or GRIGORI, always gives him the title of 'Prince Mastema'. In some of the Dead Sea Scrolls the name is found as **Mastemot**, and this later developed into the name of an order of angels. A Qumran scroll speaks of *mal'ak mastema*, 'Angels of the Animosities', which are linked with Belial. The name seems to come from the Hebrew word meaning 'to bear a grudge, be hostile to', and thus has a similar meaning to Satan.

Masulaef One of the angels of the seventh lunar month according to the *Liber Juratus* and the Sloane manuscript *Book of Raziel*.

Matariel see MATRIEL

Matiel An angel of the north of the fourth heaven in the Sloane manuscript *Book of Raziel* and an attendant angel of PAMYEL, angel of the ninth hour of the night in the *Lemegeton*. **Mathiel** is an angel of the fifth heaven in the *Heptameron*.

Matmoniel An angel used for conjuration of a magic carpet in *The Key of Solomon*.

Matriel, **Matariel** The angel of the rain in *3 Enoch*. In the Sloane manuscript *Book of Raziel* **Mattriel** is given as the name of the angel of the sixth lunar month.

Mazica An angel of the fourth lunar month according to the *Liber Juratus* and the Sloane manuscript *Book of Raziel*.

Maziel, **Masiel** An angel presiding over Thursday, the day of Jove, according to the Sloane manuscript *Book of Raziel*, as well as over the twelfth lunar month. He is also described as the aerial spirit that rules the seventh degree of Leo under OL and the twentieth degree of Cancer under CAEL, in the *Lemegeton*. In the *Liber Juratus*, where he appears in a long list of angels petitioned for help he is Maziel in some manuscripts, but takes the exotic forms **Guarmaziel** or even **Gnamazihel** in others.

Mebahel GUARDIAN ANGEL of those born under under Gemini between 26 and 31 May. He is one of the SHEMHAMPHORAE angels.

Mebehiah He is one of the seventy-two SHEMHAMPHORAE angels, and also GUARDIAN ANGEL of those born 22 and 26 December. He is a guardian of morals and religion and helps those wanting children.

Mechiel The angel that rules the first and fourth degrees of Leo under OL, according to the *Lemegeton*. Elsewhere, a zodiac angel.

Mediating Angels see DESTROYING ANGELS

Medusiel see SANIEL

Mefathiel An angel whose name means 'opener of doors'. He is an angel invoked by thieves.

Mefeniel An angel presiding over Thursday, the day of Jove, according to the Sloane manuscript *Book of Raziel*; a subordinate Thursday angel in the *Liber Juratus.*

Mehiel In the Kabbalah, an angel who protects scholars, writers and orators. GUARDIAN ANGEL of those born under Aquarius between 5 and 9 February.

Mehil In the Sloane manuscript *Book of Raziel*, this is one of the angels of Sunday (Solis) who should be invoked to aid works started on that day. He may be the same as MEHIEL, above.

Mehr see MITHRA

Mehuman see HARBONAH

Melahel GUARDIAN ANGEL of those born under Cancer, between 12 and 16 July. He is one of the seventy-two SHEMHAMPHORAE angels.

Melanas see SARANDIEL

Melchizedek In the Bible (Genesis 14) Melchizedek is described as both a king and a high priest, but in one of the Qumran Dead Sea Scroll fragments he is exalted over all the angels, presides over the heavenly assize and, with the help of other angels, can punish. There are obvious parallels here to the roles

ascribed to both MICHAEL and METATRON. This idea was taken up by early Christian writers. Origen considers him an angel and Tertullian calls him a 'celestial virtue of great grace who does for heavenly angels and virtues what Christ does for man', and certain heretics claimed he was 'a great power named Melchizedek who was greater than Christ'. In origin Melchizedek may be a Phoenician divinity, for a shortened form of his name, **Sydik**, is found in their mythology as the father of the seven ELOHIM or ANGELS OF THE PRESENCE, and in Philo as the husband of the goddess Ashtarte.

Melejal Angel of the third quarter of the year, according to *1 Enoch* 82 in Charles's old translation. The name is **Milayul** in the modern translation in Charlesworth.

Melifon This is one of the angels presiding over Saturday in the Sloane manuscript *Book of Raziel*. It appears as **Melyson** in the *Liber Juratus* with the familiar confusion between the old long 's' and 'f'.

Melkejal, **Melkayal** see MILKIEL

Mellyfiel An angel of the element water, under the planet Cocab (Mercury), to be invoked when working under this planet, according to the Sloane manuscript *Book of Raziel*.

Melrotz see SERQUANICH

Memiel, **Memyiel** An angel presiding over Thursday, the day of Jove, in the Sloane manuscript *Book of Raziel* and of the element water, under the planet Labana (Luna, the moon). In the *Liber*

Juratus he appears only as a Thursday angel, but appears twice in the same list, once as **Memyel** and once as **Memyell**.

Memitilon This is one of the angels presiding over Saturday in the Sloane manuscript *Book of Raziel*.

Memolyn An angel of the day of Mars (Tuesday) in the Sloane manuscript *Book of Raziel*.

Memunnim An order of angels found in *3 Enoch*. Their name means 'overseers', although this is often interpreted to mean 'appointed ones'. They developed in the Middle Ages into the workers among the GUARDIAN ANGELS, looking after the minutiae of the world and people's life. It has been said that it is through them that the universe operates. Their role is very like the Greek DAEMONS or the Roman Genius – each man is said to have a guiding star with a Memuneh (the singular form) in charge of it. This Memuneh is responsible for the person, and when the man dies, must show he is not responsible for his death. There are also Memunnim for each place, and care must be taken not to offend them when changes are made. Memunnim are much used in magic, and so some call them demons, although others strongly deny it. In this and their attachment to places they resemble DJINN.

Menadel One of the POWERS who is also one of the seventy-two SHEMHAMPHORAE angels. He is GUARDIAN ANGEL of those born under Virgo between 18 and 23 September. He keeps exiles loyal to their native land.

Menafiel see BARIEL

Menarchos see HANIEL

Menarym see SERQUANICH

Menasiel see BARIEL

Mendrion The angel of the seventh hour of the night according to the *Lemegeton*, whose main followers are **Ammiel, Choriel, Genarytz, Pandroz, Menesiel, Sameriel, Ventariel,** ZACHARIEL, **Dubraz, Marchiel, Jonadriel, Pemoniel, Rayziel, Tarmytz, Anapion, Jmonyel, Framoth** and **Machmag.**

Menesiel see MENDRION

Meniel see ABASDARHON, SHEMHAMPHORAE

Menoriel see ZAAZENACH

Meon An angel of the element water, under the planet Zedek (Jupiter), to be invoked when working under this planet, according to the Sloane manuscript *Book of Raziel*.

Mercoph see TARTYS

Meresyn see SAMAEL

Merigal, Merygall and Meriol, Meryel Angels of Wednesday, the day of Mercury, according to the *Liber Juratus* and the Sloane manuscript *Book of Raziel*. **Meriel**, an attendant angel of SARANDIEL, would be the same angel as Meryel.

Merkabah, Merkavah The Merkabah or Chariot, in Jewish lore, is the divine throne complex which is supported by composite, winged, divine 'living creatures' call HAYYOT. Visions of the Merkabah are a key element in much early Jewish visionary writings (starting in the Graeco-Roman period), particularly those that list many of the angels featured in this book, such as the three Books of Enoch. This type of writing is sometimes called Merkabah literature, but also **Hekalot**, **Hechaloth** or **Hekhalot**, from the Hebrew word for 'palaces, temples' which also feature prominently in the vision, as the heavenly mansions through which the visionary passes. The key source for the Merkabah is in the vision of Ezekiel, particularly chapters one and ten, from which much angel lore also developed. This iconography goes back to the general background material current in the Middle East in the past. The Canaanites described their god Baal as riding on a chariot of clouds (compare the description in Psalm 68:18) and astral cults saw the orb of the sun as being the wheel of a celestial chariot. In the sixth century BC a representation of a sun chariot was installed in the Temple in Jerusalem, a move condemned by the prophets. The gods of the Persian Empire are shown riding in winged chariots or on winged sun discs, and this image is still found in Zoroastrianism (see further under FRAVASHIS). A heavenly chariot, with Helios the classical sun god steering it, even appeared in Jewish synagogue art. According to the Talmud, a mighty angel, **Sandalfon** (see SANDALPHON), stands behind the Merkabah chariot at all times, and METATRON stands beneath its wheels in some accounts. The relationship between the chariot of God and his Throne is not always clear in these visions.

Merod In *The Key of Solomon*, an angel whose name is invoked when preparing materials for the practice of magic.

Mesial see OSMADIEL

Mesriel see ORIEL

Metatron 'The sixth heaven is an uncanny spot; there originate most of the trials and visitations ordained for the earth and its inhabitants. Snow lies heaped up there and hail; there are lofts full of noxious dew, magazines stocked with storms, and cellars holding reserves of smoke. Doors of fire separate these celestial chambers, which are under the supervision of the archangel Metatron. Their pernicious contents defiled the heavens until David's time. The pious king prayed God to purge His exalted dwelling of whatever was pregnant with evil; it was not becoming that such things should exist near the Merciful One. Only then they were removed to the earth.' (Ginzberg.) Not the least uncanny thing about the sixth heaven is Metatron himself. For not only is Metatron the greatest of all the angels by most accounts, but he is also the youngest, hence his heavenly nickname of 'Youth'. For Metatron was not created with the other angels, but is the patriarch and visionary Enoch, who was carried up to heaven in a chariot. Once there, he was transformed. To quote Ginzberg again: 'Enoch received, besides, many thousand blessings from God, and his height and his breadth became equal to the height and the breadth of the world, and thirty-six wings were attached to his body, to the right and to the left, each as large as the world, and three hundred and sixty-five thousand eyes were bestowed upon him, each brilliant as the sun. A magnificent throne was erected for him beside the gates of the seventh celestial palace, and a herald proclaimed throughout the heavens concerning him, who was henceforth to be called Metatron in the celestial regions: "I have appointed My servant Metatron as prince and chief over all the princes in My realm, with the exception only of the eight august and exalted princes that bear My name. Whatever angel has a request to prefer to Me, shall appear before Metatron, and what he will command at My bidding, ye must observe and do, for the prince of wisdom and the prince of understanding are at his service, and they will reveal unto him the sciences of the celestials and the terrestrials, the knowledge of the present order of the world and the knowledge of the future order of the world. Furthermore, I have made him the guardian of the treasures of the palaces in the heaven Arabot, and of the treasures of life that are in the highest heaven." God dressed Enoch in a magnificent robe and crowned him with a diadem with forty-nine jewels, the splendour of which pierced to all parts of the seven heavens and to the four corners of the earth. As he crowned him, God called him "little Lord" or "**Lesser Yahweh**". This crown also bears the letters by means of which heaven and earth were created, and seas and rivers, mountains and valleys, planets and constellations, lightning and thunder, snow and hail, storm and whirlwind – these and also all things needed in the world, and the mysteries of creation. Even the princes of the heavens, when they see Metatron, tremble before him, and prostrate themselves; his magnificence and majesty, the splendor and beauty

radiating from him overwhelm them.' Some say his body was transformed into celestial fire. This vision of God on his throne and Metatron as his deputy was very much influenced by the Jews' experiences in the Babylonian exile. Commentators have pointed out that in texts where God is depicted as a sort of emperor, surrounded by his court, Metatron takes the role of grand vizier, with the angels in the role of the slaves and freedmen who formed both the imperial family and the civil service in the ancient world – indeed there are Byzantine mosaics which show angels in the dress of court officials. In *3 Enoch* Metatron is a Prince of the Divine Presence and God's vice-regent who, like God himself, sits on a throne and presides over a heavenly court of law. There are times when texts which follow this tradition come close to dualism.

There are numerous theories as to the origin and meaning of the name Metatron. Some see it as from Latin *metator*, originally a term for an officer who travelled ahead of an army to prepare its camp, but which was later used to mean anyone who prepares a way. This word was borrowed into Hebrew. Others suggest the Greek *metaturannos*, which could be interpreted as 'the one enthroned with (God)'; or else the Greek *(ho) meta thronon*, '(the throne) next to the (divine) throne', 'the second throne' or, of course, it may have no meaning at all.

Innumerable roles and functions have been ascribed to Metatron. In the Tree of Life in Kabbalah he stands at the top as the angel of Yahweh and is also credited with giving the wisdom of the Kabbalah to Mankind; he is charged with the sustaining of Mankind and seen as the link between the human and divine; he is credited with revealing the Enochian alphabet, an angelic language so powerful that careless use by the uninitiated can lead to total annihilation; Indeed, there is hardly a major angelic role that has not been ascribed to him. Since he was once a man himself, he is considered the angel of Mankind. Metatron is also described as 'the Great Prince', as serving in the heavenly sanctuary, as being the GUARDIAN ANGEL of Israel, all of which are also said of MICHAEL. It is possible that Metatron was originally a secret title of Michael, and that with time this connection was lost. The identification of Enoch with Metatron is probably a late development. Metatron himself has many names. In *3 Enoch* he says, 'I have seventy names, corresponding to the seventy nations of the world, and all of them are based on the name of the King of the kings of kings; however, my King calls me "Youth".' (This is because as Enoch, son of Jared, he is younger than the angels). The name YAHOEL is also given to Metatron, although this is also attested as a separate angel. There are many variants of the seventy (or seventy-two) names that Metatron is said to have, differing with almost every manuscript. The most authoritative modern edition of *3 Enoch* lists the following, which even though the text says seventy, actually amount to ninety-three:- Yahoel Yah; Ypooiel; Apapel; Margayel; Geyorel; Tanduel; Tatnadiel; Tatriel; Tabtabiel; Ozahyah; Zahzahyah; Ebed; Zebuliel; Sapsapiel; Sopriel; Paspasiel; Senigron; Sarpupirin; Mitatron; Sigron; Adrigon; Astas; Saqpas; Saqpus; Mikon; Miton; Ruah Pisqonit; Atatyah; Asasyah; Zagzagyah; Paspasyah; Mesamyah; Masmasyah; Absannis; Mebargas; Bardas; Mekarkar;

Maspad; Tasgas; Tasbas; Metarpitas; Paspisahu; Besihi; Itmon; Pisqon; Sapsapyah; Zerah Zerahyah; Ababyah; Habhabyah; Pepatpalyah; Rakrakyah; Hashasyah; Taptapyah; Tamtamyah; Sahsahyah; Araryah; Alalyah; Zazruyah; Aramyah; Sebar Suhasyah; Razrazyah; Tahsanyah; Sasrasyah; Sabsebibyah; Qeliqalyah; Hahhahyah; Warwahyah; Zakzakyah; Titrisyah; Sewiryah; Zehapnuryah; Zazayah; Galrazyah; Melakmelapyah; Attaryah; Perisyah; Amqaqyah; Salsalyah; Sabsabyah; Geit Zeityah; Geityah; Perisperisyah; Sepat Sepatyah; Hasamyah; Sar Saryah; Gebir Geburyah; Gurtaryah; Ziwa Rabba; Naar Neeman; Lesser YHWH; Rabrakiel; Neamiel and Seganzagel, Prince of Wisdom. These extraordinary and obscure lists have generated a whole library of commentary and mystic explanation. In addition his everyday name is recorded as **Methratton** in the *Key of Solomon*.

Metatron has appeared frequently in fiction, particularly in his role as the Voice of God. Recently, in the *His Dark Materials* trilogy published 1995–2000, Philip Pullman has developed the ideas of Metatron's human origin to depict him as still, like the GRIGORI, susceptible to the allures of the flesh, and also turned his vizier-like role into that of the traditional, trecherous vizier trying to stage a takeover of power.

Metiel The angel that rules the second degree of Gemini under GIEL, according to the *Lemegeton*.

Metorilin, **Metorylyn** One of the angels of Wednesday, the day of Mercury, according to Sloane manuscript *Book of Raziel* and the *Liber Juratus*.

Metrator In *The Key of Solomon*, an angel whose name is invoked when preparing materials for the practice of magic.

Metziel The angel that rules the tenth degree of Leo under OL, according to the *Lemegeton*.

Miaga One of the angels of Wednesday in the Sloane manuscript *Book of Raziel*. In the *Magical Treatise of Solomon* **Miaga** is more specifically the angel (or demon, the text does not distinguish) of the ninth hour of Wednesday.

Michael This ARCHANGEL is leader of the angel hosts, hence his title of ARCHISTRATEGOS, which comes from the Greek for 'general'. Although Michael as archistrategos is found in early Jewish writings, the importance of Michael as warrior prince of angels for Christians comes from the passage in Revelation 12: 'And there was war in heaven: Michael and his angels fought against the dragon; and the dragon fought and his angels, and prevailed not; neither was their place found any more in heaven. And the great dragon was cast out, that old serpent, called the Devil, and Satan, which deceiveth the whole world: he was cast out into the earth, and his angels were cast out with him.' Traditionally, he is the GUARDIAN ANGEL of the people of Israel (a role he sometimes shared with GABRIEL), and as such protects them from the kings of Persia and Greece. Some say Michael is PRINCE of the World, with authority over the Princes of Kingdoms, whose job is to plead for the world when the heavenly court sits in judgement. In *1 Enoch* he is 'set over the best part of Mankind and over chaos' and in *2 Enoch*

he is Enoch's guide to the heavens and his intercessor. Elsewhere, he is the High Priest of the Temple in the celestial Jerusalem (found in the fourth heaven), where he offers the souls of the pious as sacrifices; although *3 Enoch* says Michael is in charge of the seventh heaven, Arabot. According to the first-century AD *Life of Adam and Eve* it is Michael who orders SATAN and the other angels to bow down to Adam and Eve when they are created, but a more widely known tale says that when Mankind was created the band of angels under Michael objected, and, as a result, were all consumed by fire. When Satan refused to bow down to the newly-created Adam, Michael reproved him and was the first to do homage to Adam and set a good example to the other angels. At the birth of Cain (see further under SATAN) Michael helped Eve in the absence of Adam, and later taught the young man the arts of agriculture. Although he is not named in the biblical account, it is said to have been Michael who was the angel who told Sarah that she would have a son, despite her advanced years, and who stayed the knife when Abraham was about to sacrifice him. Michael continued to guard Abraham's descendants. For example, when Esau and Jacob fought, Michael aided Jacob against Esau, who had SAMAEL's support. It was Michael, according to some commentators, disguised as a shepherd, who was the angel that Jacob wrestled with (Genesis 32), while RAPHAEL healed the injury he had been given.

One of Michael's duties is to conduct the soul of the righteous to paradise, where, according to some, they are transformed into angels, although others deny that the souls of the virtuous become angels. In the *Testament of Abraham* Michael and multitudes of angels carry Abraham's soul to paradise on his death. In the *Apocalypse of Abraham* the tears that Michael shed over the death of Abraham fall into a bowl and turn into jewels. In *3 Baruch* Michael holds the keys to heaven. In his role as archistrategos Ginzberg tells us: 'This angel bears another name besides, **Palit**, the escaped, because when God threw Samael and his host from their holy place in heaven, the rebellious leader held on to Michael and tried to drag him along downward, and Michael escaped falling from heaven only through the help of God.' He has further functions in the more magical texts. Some say he is ruler of the sun, who should be invoked for strength, spiritual protection, revelation, truth and enlightenment, although several other angels have been called ANGELS OF THE SUN. In the *Testament of Solomon* it is Michael who brings Solomon the seal ring with which he can control demons. Michael is the angel of the planet Mercury (or Cocab) according to the Sloane manuscript of *The Book of Raziel*; also of Wednesday (the day of Mercury), and under the domain of the sun as an astrological planet of the element water. The same text says Michael has power over fire and flame, along with 'RAFAEL, RASOIEL, ACDIEL, ROQNIEL, MYRIEL, INDAM, Malquiel (see MALKIEL), GAZRIEL, AMYNYEL, CARIEL, YAFRAEL. And these thou shalt name evermore when thou doest any thing in the fyer.' He is also said to have power over air. The *Lemegeton* describes Michael as an angel of the south, governing those signs of the zodiac which are fiery (Aries, Leo,

Sagittarius). He is also classed as an angel of prayer, helper of the penitent, and is called an ANGEL OF PARADISE.

Michael is a popular subject in art, where he is usually shown dressed in plate armour or chain mail with a shield and sword or spear, his foot planted on Satan in the form of either a devil or a dragon. Alternatively, he may be found in his role of the weigher of souls, holding a balance, and weighing a soul against a feather – an image which goes back to ancient Egypt.

There is often considerable overlap between what is said of Michael, and what is said of METATRON. See also MIKAL.

Micraton In the Sloane manuscript *Book of Raziel*, an angel with power over air. Also one of the angels presiding over Saturday.

Midael Described as one of the Chiefs and Captains of the Celestial Army in *The Key of Solomon*.

Miel see RAPHAEL

Mihael One of the VIRTUES whose domain is fertility and marital fidelity. He is GUARDIAN ANGEL of those born under Scorpio between 18 and 22 November. In this role he encourages happy relationships and the enjoyment of the simple pleasures of life.

Mihel The angel that rules the fifth degree of Gemini under GIEL, according to the *Lemegeton*.

Mihr see MITHRA

Mikael In the Kabbalah Mikael is regarded as an angel who influences the decisions made by rulers and those in power and helps them uncover conspiracies against the state. As the GUARDIAN ANGEL of those born under Libra between 19 and 23 October he is an angel of prosperity and brings about loyalty and a sense of what is important in life. The name can also be a form of that of the angel MICHAEL/MIKAL.

Mikal, **Mikhail**, **Mikail**, **Mikaill** Mikal is the Islamic equivalent of the Judeo-Christian ARCHANGEL MICHAEL. He is only named once in the Koran (2.92), in a slightly puzzling passage which translates: 'Whosoever is an enemy of God, or his angels, or his apostles, or to Gabriel or to Michael, verily God is the enemy of the unbelievers.' Two stories have been developed to explain this statement. The first says that some sceptical Jews challenged Mohammed to say who had brought his message to him. He replied that the messenger was DJIBRIL (GABRIEL). The Jews then declared that Gabriel was their enemy and the angel of destruction and penury. Michael, they said, was their protector and angel of fertility and salvation. The second version of this story says that Umar, a prominent follower of the Prophet who became second Caliph, questions some Jews about the two angels. He is told a similar story to the one above. Then Umar asked, 'What is the position of these two angels with God?' He is told 'Gabriel is to His right hand and Michael to his left hand and there is enmity between the two'. Umar responds that if they had such a position with God, then there can be no enmity between them, for absolute obedience to God's will is an essential part of angelic nature in Islam. Needless to say, there is no such tradition of Gabriel's hostility to the Jews, or of hostility between the two angels in Judaism. Islam has no tradition of Michael fighting the dragon, but some say that Mikal has never laughed since the creation of hell.

Milayul see MELEJAL

Milkiel, **Melkejal**, **Melkayal** Milkiel is an angel who rules the first ninety-one days of the year, according to *1 Enoch* 82. He is also known as **Tamaini** or **Tamaano**, which means 'my kingdom is God'. **Berkael**, **Zelebsel** and **Hilujaseph** are under him.

Minael An angel of the ninth lunar month according to the Sloane manuscript *Book of Raziel*.

Ministering Angels Ginzberg locates ministering angels in the seventh heaven, which 'contains naught but what is good and beautiful: right, justice, and mercy, the storehouses of life, peace, and blessing, the souls of the pious, the souls and spirits of unborn generations, the dew with which God will revive the dead on the resurrection day, and, above all, the Divine Throne, surrounded by the SERAPHIM, the OPHANIM, the holy HAYYOT, and the ministering angels'. In this case, 'ministering angels' refers to some of the highest angels who minister to God himself. But the term can also be used of some of the lowest ranking angels, who look after the everyday affairs of the world, and are thus similar to GUARDIAN ANGELS or MEMUNNIM. In the *Sefer Yetzirah* (the founding text of Kabbalah) we are told that the ministering angels are the only ones who can be seen physically – all others must be seen prophetically. They are said to have acted as servants to Adam and Eve, cooking their food and serving their wine. Three of them are named as **Aebel**, ANUSH and **Shetel**. Some say that ministering angels are transitory beings, created anew every day.

Mirael, **Miriel** One of the Chiefs and Captains of the Celestial Army in *The Key of Solomon*. However, in the Sloane manuscript *Book of Raziel* he is merely an angel of the eleventh lunar month.

Mithra, **Mihr**, **Mehr** The ancient Iranian god, **Mithras**, at one time worshipped throughout the Roman Empire, and still worshipped in India under the name of **Mitra**, has become in Zoroastrianism a YAZAD (angel) presiding over contracts and the personification of light. He is the lord of ordeal by fire (walking through fire to prove one's innocence, as in the story of Siavash in the *Shahnameh*) and is one of the angels who preside over judgement of the soul at death. Ancient Greeks identified him with Apollo. The sixteenth day of the month is named after him, as is the seventh month, **Mihr**, which runs from 23 September to 22 October. There is a special festival, Mihragan, which is held on the sixteenth day of the seventh month.

Mitzrael, **Mizrael** In the teaching of Kabbalah, Mitzrael is an ARCHANGEL who brings about obedience within hierarchies. He is also one of the seventy-two SHEMHAMPHORAE angels. As a GUARDIAN ANGEL of those born under Capricorn between 16 and 20 January he is said to be an angel of talent, who gives you the skills to succeed in undertakings, particularly in the intellectual sphere.

Modiel An angel of the east of first heaven in the Sloane manuscript *Book of Raziel*. He may be the same as **Moderiel**, an angel of the sun in the *Liber Juratus*.

Monachiel *The Key of Solomon* illustrates the Third Pentacle of Venus and says, 'This, if it be only shown unto any person, serveth to attract love. Its Angel Monachiel should be invoked in the day and hour of Venus, at one o'clock or at eight.'

Monasiel see SAMAEL

Monichion This is one of the angels presiding over Saturday, the day of Saturn or Sabat, according to the *Liber Juratus* and the Sloane manuscript *Book of Raziel*. If invoked appropriately and in a state of purity, they will aid you. It is tempting to identify Monichion with **Monikonet**, angel of the fifteenth hour of Thursday in the *Magical Treatise of Solomon*.

Mons, Angels of The Battle of Mons was one of the earlier mass slaughters of the First World War. The angels who are supposed to have fought on the British side at the Battle of Mons are probably the best known example of the many stories of angels or spirits helping in battle. Such stories go back to earliest records, usually in the form of gods fighting for their believers – the sort of thing found when Homer describes various gods joining in on the side of both the Greeks and the Trojans in the *Iliad*. This is not just a European phenomenon – angels are said to have fought on the side of Mohammed at the

Battle of Badr. However, angels appeared regularly in accounts of battles in Europe in the Middle Ages. The case of the Angels of Mons is particularly interesting as the development of the story – still circulating in popular culture as true when the author was young – has been clearly traced. Arthur Machen published a short story called 'The Bowmen' in the *London Evening News* in September 1914, in which he imagined Agincourt bowmen led by St George fighting on the side of English troops. It was a first-person narrative, and there was nothing other than his well-established reputation as an author, the fact that newspapers regularly published fiction in those days, and common sense, to indicate it was fiction. This was evidently not enough and, six months after British troops had held the German troops who far outnumbered them at the Battle of Mons, stories of divine help began to circulate. Some of these stories featured bowmen as in the original story, some featured angels. This idea of divine intervention on behalf of the British was very useful propaganda, and no doubt helped newspaper circulation. It is possible the troops in their stressed and exhausted condition were also suscepti-ble to suggestion. This is certainly the approach Kipling took when he wrote his ambiguous short story *The Madonna of the Trenches*. The Society for Psychical Research investigated the stories in 1915. Of first-hand testimony they said, 'We have received none at all, and of testimony at second-hand we have none that would justify us in assuming the occurrence of any super-normal phenomenon.' They went on to say the stories relating to battlefield 'visions' which circulated during the spring and summer of 1915, 'prove on investigation to be founded on mere rumour, and cannot be traced to any authoritative source'. Machen always went to great pains to explain that his story was pure fiction, but this made little impact on the growth of an urban myth. Despite the fact that it looks definite that popular imagination had failed to distinguish between fact and fiction, stories of the Angels of Mons have not faded, and many still believe emphatically in their reality.

Montagin According to the Sloane manuscript *Book of Raziel* this is one of the angels with special care of Monday (Luna) who should be invoked to aid works started on that day. In the *Liber Juratus* the form of the name is **Montazyn.**

Monteylyn An angel of the day of Mars (Tuesday) in the Sloane manuscript *Book of Raziel* and also found in the *Liber Juratus.*

Moon Angels In magic the moon is said to have twenty-eight mansions or spheres of influence, one for each day of the lunar month. Each mansion has its GUARDIAN ANGEL and sign of the zodiac. According to Agrippa (with variants from the *Liber Juratus*) the angels are as follows, numbered by mansion: 1. GENIEL; 2. ENEDIEL; 3. ANIXIEL or Amixiel; 4. AZARIEL; 5. GABRIEL or CABRIEL; 6. DIRACHIEL; 7. SCHLIEL or Scheliel; 8. AMNEDIEL; 9. BARBIEL; 10. ARDIFIEL or Ardesiel; 11. NECIEL; 12. ABDISUEL or Abdizuel; 13. JAZERIEL or Iazeriel; 14 ERGEDIEL; 15. ATLIEL or Ataliel; 16. AZERUEL; 17. ADRIEL; 18. EGIBIEL; 19. AMUTIEL; 20 KYRIEL or Kiriel; 21. BETHNAEL;

22. GELIEL; 23. REQUIEL; 24. ABRINAEL; 25. AZAEL or Aziel; 26. TAGRIEL; 27.ATHENIEL; 28 AMNIXIEL. Each angel, their sign and their properties for good and bad are discussed under the individual angel.

Mordad see AMERTAT

Moriel, **Morayeil** An angel of the fourth lunar month according to the *Liber Juratus* and the Sloane manuscript *Book of Raziel*, who if invoked brings benefits. He is also described there as an angel of Friday, the day of Venus. In the *Lemegeton* he is one of the aerial spirits of whom it is said, 'They appear all in A verry Beautifull forme, & verry Courteously, And in yᵉ night as well as in yᵉ day.'

Moroni Moroni is the angel of the Mormons. According to the account in the *Book of Mormon*, Moroni was the son of Mormon and the last of the Nephite prophets as well as their military leader. The Nephites were defeated by the Lamanites, and Moroni and his followers were forced to wander for years until arriving in North America. All this happened in the late fourth and early fifth centuries. After his death Moroni became, like Enoch, an angel. In 1823 Joseph Smith Jr had an encounter with Moroni who showed him where the gold plates on which the *Book of Mormon* was inscribed were buried, although he was not allowed to see the plates until 1827. On this spot, four miles south of Palmyra, New York State, there is now a forty-foot statue of Moroni.

Mubashshir and Bashir In the Shiite branch of Islam, Mubashshir and Bashir are two angels who are sent to comfort the saintly dead. Some say they are aspects of MUNKA AND NAKIR, but others that they are separate angels.

Mucraton A four-winged angel mentioned in the Sloane manuscript *Book of Raziel*.

Mumiah In the Kabbalah, Mumiah is held to be an angel who controls physics and medicine and oversees health and longevity. As the GUARDIAN ANGEL of those born under Pisces between 16 and 20 March he helps one express oneself with conviction and gives the drive to achieve one's goals.

Munka and Nakir These are the angels of mercy of Islamic tradition (they do not feature in the Koran). Their role is to examine the dead in their tomb to judge their faithfulness. Some say that there is only one angel who does this; while others identify Munka and Nakir with the GUARDIAN ANGELS that each man has.

Muracafel An angel of the element water, under the planet Hanina (Sol, the sun), to be invoked when working under this planet, according to the Sloane manuscript *Book of Raziel*.

Murdad see AMERATAT

Muriel Angel with power over the south in the *Key of Solomon*. In Agrippa, Muriel is an angel ruling over the sign of Cancer. Elsewhere, he is variously described as an angel of the month of June, a ruler of the dominions, one who serves under **Veguaniel** as an angel of the third hour of the day, and an angel invoked to obtain a magic carpet. In

other texts the name is a variant of
URIEL.

Murion This is one of the angels
presiding over Saturday, the day of
Saturn, according to the Sloane
manuscript *Book of Raziel*.

Mursiel see VEQUANIEL

Muviel The angel that rules the
nineteenth degree of Leo under OL, in
the *Lemegeton*.

Mycahe According to the Sloane
manuscript *Book of Raziel* this is one of
the angels of Sunday (Solis) who should
be invoked to aid works started on that
day.

Mylba An angel of the south of the
second heaven in the Sloane manuscript
Book of Raziel.

Myriel In the Sloane manuscript *Book
of Raziel* an angel with power over fire
and flame. In the *Liber Juratus* **Myryel** is
an angel of the eleventh lunar month.

Myschiel In the *Liber Juratus* and the
Sloane manuscript *Book of Raziel,* an
angel of the eleventh lunar month. If
invoked in the relevant month, he will
ensure success in your enterprise.

Myssa, **Myssyn** An angel of the sixth
lunar month according to the *Liber
Juratus* and the Sloane manuscript *Book
of Raziel*.

N

Naajah The angel that rules the sixth
degree of Capricorn under CASUJOJAH
and the sixth degree of Aquarius under
AUSIUL, according to the *Lemegeton*.

Naamab, **Naasien** Angels of the third
lunar month according to the Sloane
manuscript *Book of Raziel* and the *Liber
Juratus*. In the latter Naasien appears as
Naasein and **Naaseyn**.

Naamah see AGRAT BAT MAHLAT, AZAEL,
HARUT AND MARUT, SHAMDON

Naaririel YHWH A mighty angel
found in *3 Enoch* and a guard of the
seventh heaven. It is probably a development of the name **Naar**, one of the
names of METATRON.

Nabiafilyn One of the angels of
Wednesday, the day of Mercury, in the
Sloane manuscript *Book of Raziel*.

Naboon An angel of the third lunar
month in the *Liber Juratus* and the
Sloane manuscript *Book of Raziel,*
whose naming brings benefits.

Nabuel An angel of the eighth lunar
month according to the Sloane
manuscript *Book of Raziel*. In the *Liber
Juratus* the name is the much more
elaborate **Nehubaell**.

Nabyalni According to the Sloane
manuscript *Book of Raziel,* this is one of
the angels with special care of Monday
(Luna) who should be invoked to aid
works started on that day. In the *Liber
Juratus* it is **Nabyalyn**.

Naccamarif, Naccameryf and Nacery
Angels of the sixth lunar month
according to the *Liber Juratus* and the
Sloane manuscript *Book of Raziel*, which
says that if they are named 'in each
thing that thou wilt do … thou shalt
profit'.

Nachiel, Nakiel, Nakhiel In Kaballistic
writing, the intelligence of the sun when
it enters the sign of Leo. **Nachal(l)**, who
along with **Nactif** is an angel of the fifth
lunar month according to the *Liber
Juratus* and the Sloane manuscript *Book
of Raziel*, may well be from the same
name.

Nadib An angel of the second lunar
month in the Sloane manuscript *Book of
Raziel*. He is **Nadys** in the *Liber Juratus*.

Nadibael An angel of the eighth lunar
month according to the Sloane
manuscript *Book of Raziel*. He appears
as **Napybael** in the *Liber Juratus* which
suggests a touch of dyslexia somewhere
along the line of transmission.

Naduch An angel of the ninth lunar
month according to the Sloane
manuscript *Book of Raziel*. The name is
Maduch in the *Liber Juratus*.

Nafac An angel of the sixth lunar
month according to the *Liber Juratus*
and the Sloane manuscript *Book of
Raziel*.

Naffrynyn, Naffreynyn An angel of the
day of Mars (Tuesday) in the Sloane
manuscript *Book of Raziel* and in the
Liber Juratus.

Naflia In the Sloane manuscript *Book of
Raziel*, an angel of the tenth lunar

month. If invoked in rites his name will
ensure good results. The name is **Naclya**
in the *Liber Juratus*.

Nagael The angel that rules the second
degree of Gemini under GIEL, according
to the *Lemegeton*.

Nagrasagiel see NASARGIEL

Nagrow An angel of the fourth lunar
month in the Sloane manuscript *Book of
Raziel*. It is **Nagron** in the *Liber Juratus*.

Nahaliel The angel who presides over
streams. The name may mean 'valley of
God'.

Nahymel An angel of the south of the
first heaven in the Sloane manuscript
Book of Raziel.

**Nairyosangha, Neryosang,
Neryosand** Originally a Persian fire god
(and still worshipped in India as
Narayana), now in Zoroastrianism
considered a YAZAD (angel) associated
with prayer.

Nakir see MUNKA AND NAKIR

Namael see SARANDIEL

Nameal see PAMYEL

Namedor see ZAAZENACH

Nameron see ORIEL

Nameroyz see IASSUARIM

Nameton see ABASDARHON

Nanael, Nanel A PRINCIPALITY who is
one of the seventy-two SHEMHAM-

PHORAE angels. In the Kabbalah his domain is that of the philosophers and ecclesiastics and the sciences. As the GUARDIAN ANGEL of those born under Sagittarius between 13 and 16 December he is said to be an angel of perfection who helps the development of the senses, and in the area of law and of order, whether social or personal.

Nangareryn According to the Sloane manuscript *Book of Raziel* this is one of the angels with special care of Monday. He is **Niangaroryn** in the *Liber Juratus*.

Nanylin An angel presiding over Friday, the day of Venus, according to the Sloane manuscript *Book of Raziel*. He is **Namylyn** in the *Liber Juratus*.

Nap An angel of the eighth lunar month in the Sloane manuscript *Book of Raziel*. The name **Aiguap** appears in the same place in the *Liber Juratus*.

Naphael The angel that rules the fifth degree of Scorpio under JOSEL and the fifth degree of Sagittarius under SUIAJASEL, according to the *Lemegeton*.

Narbell, **Narbeyll** An angel of the day of Mars (Tuesday) in the Sloane manuscript *Book of Raziel* and in the *Liber Juratus*.

Narcoriel The angel of the eighth hour in the *Lemegeton*. He has a vast number of attendant angels, among the most important of whom are CAMBIEL, **Cambriel, Nedarym, Astrocon, Marifiel, Dramozyn, Lustifion, Amelson, Lemozar, Xernifiel, Kanorsiel, Bufanotz, Jamedroz, Xanoriz, Jastrion, Themaz, Hobraiym, Zymeloz** and **Gamsiel**.

Narel Angel of the final quarter of the year, according to *1 Enoch* 82.

Nasael The angel that rules the third degree of Virgo under VOIL, according to the *Lemegeton*.

Nasargiel, **Nagrasagiel** This is a lion-headed angel who showed Moses around hell. He shared dominion over the place with **Kipod** and **Sangha**. The origin of this angel may lie with Nergal, a Mesopotamian god who was not only a sun god, but also ruler of the underworld.

Nashriel see MALKIEL

Nasmyel In the Sloane manuscript *Book of Raziel*, an angel of the thirteenth lunar month (March). He appears as **Nosmyel** in the *Liber Juratus*.

Naspaya In the *Liber Juratus* and the Sloane manuscript *Book of Raziel*, an angel of the tenth lunar month.

Naspiel, **Naspyell** An angel of the eighth lunar month according to the *Liber Juratus* and the Sloane manuscript *Book of Raziel*.

Nassa An angel of the sixth lunar month according to the *Liber Juratus* and the Sloane manuscript *Book of Raziel*. **Nassam**, an angel of the eleventh lunar month in both works, may be the same name.

Nastiafori, **Nascyasori** An angel of the first lunar month according to the *Liber Juratus* and the Sloane manuscript *Book of Raziel*.

Nastoriel see DARDARIEL

Nastrus see BARAQIEL

Nastul see SABRATHAN

Nasyel In the *Liber Juratus* and the Sloane manuscript *Book of Raziel* an angel of the eleventh lunar month.

Nathaniel, Natanael In Jewish legend **Nathaniel** was the sixth angel created. He rules over fire, vengeance and hidden things. According to the Sloane manuscript *Book of Raziel* **Natanael** is a 'benign' angel who has 'might in the air' and was a companion and instructor to Solomon.

Natheel The angel that rules the eleventh degree of Aries under AIEL, according to the *Lemegeton*.

Nathmiel see SANIEL

Natriel, Natryel In the *Liber Juratus* and the Sloane manuscript *Book of Raziel*, an angel of the eleventh lunar month.

Naveriel see SARANDIEL

Naveron see ORIEL

Naveroz see DARDARIEL

Naviel The angel that rules the fourth degree of Libra under JAEL, according to the *Lemegeton*.

Naxas An angel of the eighth lunar month according to the Sloane manuscript *Book of Raziel*. In the *Liber Juratus* he is **Nacpas. Nebubael**, who appears in the *Liber Juratus* as **Nehubaell**, belongs with the same month.

Naya'il see LAWIDH

Necamia, Necamya An angel of the first lunar month according to the *Liber Juratus* and the Sloane manuscript *Book of Raziel*.

Necanynael An angel of the element fire, under the planet Zedek (Jupiter), to be invoked when working under this planet, according to the Sloane manuscript *Book of Raziel*.

Nechorym see ABASDARHON

Neciel A MOON ANGEL who rules the eleventh mansion of the moon in Leo. He supports successful journeys, profitable trading and the ransoming of prisoners.

Necyf, Nekyff An angel of the fifth lunar month according to the *Liber Juratus* and the Sloane manuscript *Book of Raziel*.

Necyl According to the Sloane manuscript *Book of Raziel* this is one of the angels of Sunday (Solis) who should be invoked to aid works started on that day.

Nedabor see SANIEL

Nedarym see NARCORIEL

Nediter, Nedyler An angel of the fourth lunar month according to the *Liber Juratus* and the Sloane manuscript *Book of Raziel*.

Nedroz see TARTYS

Nedruan see JEFISCHA

Nefrias see SARANDIEL

Nefta see ASRAEL

Negri In the Sloane manuscript *Book of Raziel*, an angel of the tenth lunar month. He appears as **Neapry** in the *Liber Juratus*.

Nelchael Opinion varies as to the nature of Nelchael. Some see him as a FALLEN ANGEL who teaches demons the knowledge of astronomy, mathematics and geography. Nevertheless he still appears to be one of the seventy-two angels bearing the mystic name of God, SHEMHAMPHORAE. Other say he is still among the THRONES. As GUARDIAN ANGEL of those born under Cancer between 2 and 6 July he is considered an angel of moderation who helps develop a sense of honesty and responsibility and skill in communicating.

Neliel The angel that rules the second degree of Pisces under PASIL, according to the *Lemegeton*. **Nelia**, an angel of the south of the second heaven in the Sloane manuscript *Book of Raziel* may be the same name.

Nemamiah In the Kabbalah Nemamiah is an ARCHANGEL who is guardian of all those who engage in just causes and of admirals and generals. He is also one of the seventy-two angels bearing the mystic name of God, SHEMHAMPHORAE. Others, however, describe him as an angel who defends the rights of children and animals. As a GUARDIAN ANGEL of those born under the sign of Capricorn between 1 and 5 January he is seen as an angel of prosperity who brings tenacity in undertaking tasks, original thinking and success.

Nenael An angel of the north of the second heaven in the Sloane manuscript *Book of Raziel*. **Nenel**, which appears to be the same name, is listed immediately afterwards.

Nepenielin, **Nepenyelyn** According to the *Liber Juratus* and the Sloane manuscript *Book of Raziel,* this is one of the angels with special care of Monday (Luna) who should be invoked to aid works started on that day.

Nephilim, **Nephelim**, **Nephillim** The Nephilim are the offspring of the angels who came to earth, the GRIGORI, and the daughters of men. They were giants; so big, *The Zohar* tells us, that 'the Hebrews were like grasshoppers in comparison', and a violent race with enormous appetites. They first fought each other, then brought conflict and destruction to Mankind. Some say the purpose of Noah's flood was to destroy them. There are many names for them, including **Emim**. As Ginzberg tells us: 'Sometimes they go by the name **Rephaim**, because one glance at them made one's heart grow weak; or by the name **Gibborim**, simply giants, because their size was so enormous that their thigh measured eighteen ells; or by the name **Zamzummim**, because they were great masters in war; or by the name **Anakim** because they touched the sun with their neck; or by the name **Ivvim**, because, like the snake, they could judge the qualities of the soil; or finally, by the name Nephilim, because, bringing the world to its fall, they themselves fell.'

Nephyel An air angel under Sabaday (Saturn), to be invoked when working under this planet, in the Sloane manuscript *Book of Raziel*.

Neqael One of the GRIGORI according to *1 Enoch*.

Nerad An angel of the ninth lunar month in the Sloane manuscript *Book of Raziel*, which says that if they are named 'in each thing that thou wilt do … thou shalt profit'. He appears as **Necad** in the *Liber Juratus*.

Nerastiel see BERATIEL

Neraziel An angel of the element fire, under the planet Noga (Venus), to be invoked when working under this planet, according to the Sloane manuscript *Book of Raziel*. **Nerastiel**, an angel of the twelfth hour serving under BERATIEL in the *Lemegeton*, is probably the same.

Nermas see DARDARIEL

Neryosang, **Neryosand** see NAIRYOSANGHA

Nesquiraf An angel of the fifth lunar month according to the Sloane manuscript *Book of Raziel*, who if invoked brings benefits. He appears as **Nesgnyraf** in the *Liber Juratus*.

Nestoriel see SARANDIEL and SAMAEL

Nestorii see BARAQIEL

Nestoroz see SERQUANICH

Neszomy see ABASDARHON

Netoniel One of the angels whose name is used in the First Pentacle of Jupiter, which is used in hunting for treasure in *The Key of Solomon*.

Netzach In the *Key of Solomon* identified as one of the angels who preside over the ten SEFIROTH.

Neyeyl(l) In the *Liber Juratus* and the Sloane manuscript *Book of Raziel* this is one of the angels of Sunday.

Nike Nike is the Greek embodiment of victory, widely shown in art as a winged figure descending from the heavens offering a wreath to the victors. The best known example is the *Victory of Samothrace* in the Louvre. Such depictions of victory have been enormously influential in the development of the iconography of angels.

Nilaihah see NITH-HAIAH

Nisroc Nisroc or **Nisroch** is in origin an Assyrian god who, like many such deities, takes the form of a winged human with an eagle's head. In the Bible (II Kings 19:37) he is the god in whose temple Sennacherib was worshipping when assassinated by his sons. It is Milton who elevates him to the role 'of Principalities the prime' (other rulers of the PRINCIPALITIES are CERVIAL and HANIEL). In occult lore, however, he is a demon in charge of hell's kitchens.

Nilaihah, **Nithaiah**, **Nith-Haiah** In the Kabbalah this angel is a DOMINION who is invoked by pronouncing any of the divine names together with the first verse of Psalm 9. He is considered a poet angel who prophesies in rhyme. His domain is the occult sciences and wise men who love peace and solitude. As a GUARDIAN ANGEL of those born under the sign of Leo between 23 and 27 July he is said to be an angel of beauty, inspiring a loving nature and a joyous and positive attitude to life.

Nithael Despite the fact that Nithael is said to have joined the rebellion of SATAN and that he now rules in hell over emperors, kings and ecclesiastics of the highest rank, he is still counted among the seventy-two angels who bear the mystic name of God, SHEMHAMPHORAE. As a GUARDIAN ANGEL of those born under Sagittarius between 17 and 21 December, he is described as an angel of profusion who brings long life, good health and worldly success.

Noaphiel One of the angels whose name is used in the Fifth Pentacle of Saturn 'which chaseth away the Spirits which guard treasures' in *The Key of Solomon*. Invocants need to recite from Deuteronomy 10 for effective co-operation.

Nobquin An angel of the west of the fourth heaven in the Sloane manuscript *Book of Raziel*.

Nocpis, **Necpys** An angel of the second lunar month according to the *Liber Juratus* and the Sloane manuscript *Book of Raziel*.

Nonanrin, **Nenanryn** An angel presiding over Friday, the day of Venus, according to the *Liber Juratus* and the Sloane manuscript *Book of Raziel*. **Noraraabilin** or **Narraabylyn** is another Friday angel in these texts.

Noriel, **Noryel** The angel who presides over the fourth lunar month according to the *Liber Juratus* and the Sloane manuscript version of *The Book of Raziel*, through whose power a man may know his future.

Nosmyel see NASMYEL

Nuriel The angel of fire in some traditions. The name comes from *nura*, the Aramaic for 'fire'. Other traditions call MICHAEL or GABRIEL the angel of fire. Nuriel is also described as the angel of hailstorms and in *The Zohar* rules Virgo. He manifests in the form of an eagle.

Nuscifa, **Nastyfa** An angel of the third lunar month serving under AMARIEL, according to the *Liber Juratus* and the Sloane manuscript *Book of Raziel*.

Nyazpatael, **Nyahpatuel** In the *Liber Juratus* and the Sloane manuscript *Book of Raziel*, an angel of the twelfth lunar month, under GABRIEL. If invoked in the relevant month, he will ensure success in your enterprise.

Nybiel A fire angel under Sabaday (Saturn), to be invoked when working under this planet, according to the Sloane manuscript *Book of Raziel*.

Nybirin, **Nybyryn** An angel of the day of Mars (Tuesday) with power over 'red metal' in the Sloane manuscript *Book of Raziel,* who is also a Tuesday angel in the *Liber Juratus*. **Nyrysin** is another Tuesday angel in these texts.

O

Och Och is one of the angels said to be ruler of the sun. He is also said to be able to bestow good health (up to 600 years!) and has influence over alchemy and minerals. He is one of the OLYMPIC SPIRITS who rules 28 of the 196 provinces and ruled the events of the world between 921 and 1410.

Odrael An angel of the east of the first heaven in the Sloane manuscript *Book of Raziel*.

Ofaniel see OPANNIEL

Ofanim see OPHANIM

Ohrmazd, **Ormazd** Another name for the great god of Zoroastrianism Ahura Mazda. See further under DEVAS.

Ol The angel who rules Leo according to the *Lemegeton*.

Oliab, **Olyab** In the *Liber Juratus* and the Sloane manuscript *Book of Raziel*, an angel of the tenth lunar month.

Oliel An angel of the element air, under the planet Hanina (Sol, the sun), to be invoked when working under this planet, according to the Sloane manuscript *Book of Raziel*.

Olympic Spirits According to the sixteenth-century book of magic, the *Arbatel of Magic*, the universe is divided into 196 provinces. These are ruled by spirits (or angels to some) who live in the air and between the planets. The rulers of the Olympic, or Olympian

spirits, also known as Stewards of Heaven are: ARATON or Aratron; BETHOR; PHALEG; OCH; HAGITH; OPHIEL or Prifiel; PHUL.

Omael An angel who is the patron of chemists and also of propagation – both of species and of races. He belongs among the DOMINIONS – although some say he is now a FALLEN ANGEL – and is among the seventy-two angels who bear the mystic name of God, SHEMHAM-PHORAE. As the GUARDIAN ANGEL of those born under Leo between 18 and 22 August he is described as an angel of plenitude who brings wealth and success, as well as fertility and both physical and moral health.

Omary see BARIEL

Omedriel see SABRATHAN

Omeliel One of the angels whose name is used in the Third Pentacle of Saturn; 'good for use at night when thou invokest the Spirits of the nature of Saturn' in *The Key of Solomon*.

Omiel An angel presiding over Thursday, the day of Jove, according to Sloane manuscript *Book of Raziel*. Elsewhere, said to be an angel who mixed with mortals before the Flood, so presumably considered one of the GRIGORI. In the *Lemegeton* Omiel is an aerial spirit of the south-west, who serves in the night under **Asyriel**.

Ononiteon, **Onoxion** These are angels presiding over Saturday, the day of Saturn or Sabat, according to Sloane manuscript *Book of Raziel*. If invoked appropriately and in a state of purity, they will aid you. In the *Liber Juratus* the names are **Monyteon** and **Orleunyon**.

Ophaniel, Opanniel, Ofaniel YHWH
Opanniel combines the job of chief of
the OPHANIM with being the angel in
charge of the phases of the moon. With
the aid of eighty-eight angels he makes
the moon run its course. He has sixteen
faces and one hundred pairs of wings.
His 8,766 eyes match the hours of the
year, but they flash with such power that
not even angels can look at them
without being consumed.

Ophanim, Ofanim In *1 Enoch* the
Ophanim, along with SERAPHIM and
CHERUBIM are 'they who sleep not And
guard the throne of His glory'. They are
many-eyed wheels within wheels in
many texts (derived from the vision in
Ezekiel 10.13), often adorned with
gems, and their task is to carry the
throne of God. Some texts, however,
associate them with THRONES or, as
Milton does, cherubim, while others,
such as *3 Enoch*, have a separate class of
angels called GALGALLIM ('wheels'). In *3
Enoch* they are in the care of the angel
OPHANIEL; 'Every day he stands over
them and tends them and beautifies
them: he praises and arranges their
running; he polishes their platforms; he
adorns their compartments; he makes
their turnings smooth, and cleans their
seats.' They are ranked second by
Maimonides and fifth by *The Zohar* in
the HIERARCHY OF THE ANGELS.

Ophiel An angel whose name is used
for conjuration in the *Key of Solomon*.
Also an OLYMPIC SPIRIT who rules 14 of
the 196 provinces.

Oraios see HORAEUS

Ordibehesht see ASHA VAHISHTA

Oreus see HORAEUS

Orfiel, Oriphiel, Orifel, Orfyll
Considered by some to be an
ARCHANGEL. In the *Lemegeton*, one of
the seven regents of the world and an
angel of the second hour. An angel
presiding over Thursday, the day of
Jove, according to the *Liber Juratus* and
the Sloane manuscript *Book of Raziel*,
but elsewhere said to be an angel of
Saturday. He has also been called the
angel of Saturn.

Oriel The angel of the first Lunar
month according to the *Liber Juratus*
and the Sloane manuscript version of
The Book of Raziel, through whose
power a man may know his future, as
well as having power over water. He also
has power over the element of earth. In
the *Lemegeton*, he is the angel ruling the
tenth hour, attended by thousands of
angels, of whom the most important are
**Armosy, Drabiel, Penaly, Mesriel,
Choreb, Lemur, Ormas, Charny,
Zazyor, Naveron, Xantros, Basilon,
Basilion, Nameron, Kranoti** and
Alfrael.

Orifel see ANACHIEL

Oriphiel see ORFIEL, THRONES

Ormael see JEFISCHA

Ormas see ORIEL

Ormezyn see TARTYS

Ormyel see VATHMIEL

Orphiel see HANIEL

Orychyn In the Sloane manuscript *Book of Raziel* an angel with power over air.

Osflyel An angel presiding over Thursday, the day of Jove, according to Sloane manuscript *Book of Raziel*.

Osmadiel In the *Lemegeton* this is identified as the angel that governs the eighth hour of every day. Among his many attendant angels are **Sarfiel**, **Amalym**, **Chroel**, **Mesial**, **Lantrhots**, **Demarot**, **Janofiel**, **Larfuty**, **Vemael**, **Thribiel**, MARIEL, **Remasyn**, **Theoriel**, **Framion** and **Ermiel**.

Osmyn An angel of the ninth lunar month according to the *Liber Juratus* and the Sloane manuscript *Book of Raziel*.

Ouriel see URIEL

Oyarsa see ELDIL

P

Paafiryn, **Paarfyryn** An angel of the day of Mars (Tuesday) in the Sloane manuscript *Book of Raziel* and in the *Liber Juratus*.

Paajah The angel that rules the ninth degree of Capricorn under CASUJOJAH and the ninth degree of Aquarius under AUSIUL, according to the *Lemegeton*.

Paamiel, **Paamyel** In the *Liber Juratus* and the Sloane manuscript *Book of Raziel*, an angel of the twelfth lunar month. If invoked in the relevant month, he will ensure success in your enterprise.

Pabliel An angel of the west of the fifth heaven in the Sloane manuscript *Book of Raziel*.

Pachayel An angel presiding over Thursday, the day of Jove, according to the Sloane manuscript *Book of Raziel*.

Pacryton, **Pacrifon** This is one of the angels presiding over Saturday, the day of Saturn or Sabat, according to the *Liber Juratus* and the Sloane manuscript *Book of Raziel*.

Pacuel In the Sloane manuscript *Book of Raziel* an angel of the tenth lunar month. He is **Pacrel** in the *Liber Juratus*.

Pacyta An angel of the first lunar month according to the *Liber Juratus* and the Sloane manuscript *Book of Raziel*.

Pagulan One of the angels of the

seventh lunar month according to the Sloane manuscript *Book of Raziel*, which says that if they are named 'in each thing that thou wilt do … thou shalt profit'. The name appears as **Pagnlan** in the *Liber Juratus*.

Pahaliah One of the seventy-two angels who bear the mystic name of God, SHEMHAMPHORAE, he rules theology and morals and is invoked to convert heathens to Christianity. As the GUARDIAN ANGEL of those born under Cancer between 27 June and 1 July he is considered an angel of control, helping towards moderation and fairness and thus successful negotiation.

Paimonaih One of the angels whose name is used in the Second Pentacle of the Sun which 'serveth to repress the pride and arrogance of the Solar Spirits, which are altogether proud and arrogant by their nature,' in *The Key of Solomon*. He may be related to **Paimon**, described variously as King of the North or King of the North West and as a FALLEN ANGEL, who when invoked appears as a young woman with a crown on her head and riding a dromedary camel.

Palatinates An order in the HIERARCHY OF ANGELS, usually identified with POWERS. In the *Greater Key of Solomon* they are invoked to bestow invisibility.

Paliel, **Palyel** An angel of the fifth and eighth lunar months according to the *Liber Juratus* and the Sloane manuscript *Book of Raziel*, who if invoked brings benefits.

Palit see MICHAEL

Palitam, **Palytam** An angel of the eighth lunar month according to the *Liber Juratus* and the Sloane manuscript *Book of Raziel*, which says that if named 'in each thing that thou wilt do … thou shalt profit'.

Palriel An angel of the element earth, under the planet Zedek (Jupiter), to be invoked when working under this planet, according to the Sloane manuscript *Book of Raziel*.

Paltamus An angel of the third lunar month according to the *Liber Juratus* and the Sloane manuscript *Book of Raziel*.

Palthia, **Palatnia**, **Paltnya** An angel of the second lunar month according to the *Liber Juratus* and the Sloane manuscript *Book of Raziel*.

Paltifus, **Paltifur** An angel of the first lunar month according to the *Liber Juratus* and the Sloane manuscript *Book of Raziel*.

Paly An angel of the west of the fifth heaven in the Sloane manuscript *Book of Raziel*. **Palylet** and **Palytam**, angels of the eighth and fifth months in the *Liber Juratus*, may be related.

Pammon see ZAAZENACH

Pamor In *The Key of Solomon*, an angel whose name is invoked when the master is putting on the white linen vestments of power before practising magic.

Pamyel The angel ruling the ninth hour of the night in the *Lemegeton*. His principal followers are **Demaor**, **Nameal, Adrapan, Chermel, Fenadros,**

Vemasiel, Comary, Camary, MATIEL, Zenoroz, Brandiel, Evandiel, Tameriel, Befranzy, Jachoroz, Xanthir, Armapy, Druchas and Sardiel.

Panael The angel that rules the fifth degree of Taurus under TUAL, according to the *Lemegeton*. Elsewhere, he is one of the angelic guards of the north wind.

Pandroz see MENDRION

Pangael The angel that rules the fifth degree of Pisces under PASIL, according to the *Lemegeton*.

Panhiniel, **Pamhiniel** A Thursday angel according to the *Liber Juratus* and the Sloane manuscript *Book of Raziel*.

Pani In *The Key of Solomon*, an angel whose name is invoked when preparing materials for the practice of magic.

Paniel The angel that rules the fifth degree of Gemini under GIEL, according to the *Lemegeton*. Like his near name-sake PANAEL he is also said to be a guardian of the north wind and his name has been found inscribed on a charm to ward off evil.

Panion This is one of the angels presiding over Saturday, the day of Saturn or Sabat, according to the *Liber Juratus* and the Sloane manuscript *Book of Raziel*.

Pansa In the Sloane manuscript *Book of Raziel*, an angel of the tenth lunar month. If invoked in rites his name will ensure good results. In the *Liber Juratus* he appears in the obviously mangled form of **Pmla**.

Pantaceren In the Sloane manuscript *Book of Raziel* an angel with power over air.

Pantan, **Panten** In the *Liber Juratus* and the Sloane manuscript *Book of Raziel*, an angel of the twelfth lunar month. If invoked in the relevant month, he will ensure success in your enterprise.

Panteron, **Pantaron** In the *Liber Juratus* and the Sloane manuscript *Book of Raziel*, both forms are given as an angel of the twelfth lunar month. **Pantaseron**, a four-winged angel mentioned in the Sloane manuscript *Book of Raziel*, may be the same.

Paoiryaenis Star YAZAD (Zoroastrian angel) associated with the Pleiades. In origin he may be the same as the Hindu god Parjanya. He is also known as **Upa-paoiri**.

Papon This is one of the angels presiding over Saturday in the Sloane manuscript *Book of Raziel*. He appears as **Paxon** in the *Liber Juratus*.

Paradiel An angel of the element fire, under the planet Cocab (Mercury), to be invoked when working under this planet, according to the Sloane manuscript *Book of Raziel*.

Parasiel 'Lord and Master of Treasures' and one of the angels whose name is used in the First Pentacle of Jupiter used in hunting for treasure in *The Key of Solomon*. As **Paras** he is an aerial spirit in the *Lemegeton*.

Parciot An angel of the second lunar month according to the Sloane manuscript *Book of Raziel*. He is missing from the *Liber Juratus*, which has only twenty-six angels to cover the twenty-eight days, while *Raziel* has a superabundant thirty.

Parendi A female YAZAD (Zoroastrian angel) of abundance.

Parhaya In the *Liber Juratus* and the Sloane manuscript *Book of Raziel*, an angel of the twelfth lunar month. If invoked in the relevant month, he will ensure success in your enterprise.

Pariel An angel presiding over Thursday, and of the element water under Mars, according to the Sloane manuscript *Book of Raziel*. His name has also been found used on a charm to keep its wearer from harm and as an aerial spirit in the *Lemegeton*.

Parna An angel of the south of the third heaven in the Sloane manuscript *Book of Raziel*.

Parniel see VEQUANIEL

Partriel In the Sloane manuscript *Book of Raziel* an elemental angel with power over the earth.

Parziel The angel that rules the sixth degree of Virgo under VOIL, according to the *Lemegeton*.

Pasaliel An angel of the element water, under the planet Madin (Mars), to be invoked when working under this planet in the Sloane manuscript *Book of Raziel*.

Paschania An angel of the fourth lunar month according to the Sloane manuscript *Book of Raziel*. The name is

Pastama in the *Liber Juratus*.

Pasil, **Pasiel** The angel who rules Pisces according to the *Lemegeton*. In the Kabbalah he has power over hell.

Pasriel see BARAQIEL

Pathiel, **Pata** Known as 'the opener', Pathiel is invoked in magic against forgetfulness and stupidity. He is also invoked at the close of the Sabbath. He is one of the seventy-two angels who bear the mystic name SHEMHAM-PHORAE.

Paticael An angel of the element fire, under the planet Labana (Luna, the moon), to be invoked when working under this planet, according to the Sloane manuscript *Book of Raziel*.

Patiel, **Patyel** In the *Liber Juratus* and the Sloane manuscript *Book of Raziel*, an angel of the twelfth lunar month. The angel that rules the seventh degree of Libra under JAEL, according to the *Lemegeton*.

Patnilin, **Patnelyn** An angel presiding over Friday, the day of Venus, according to the Sloane manuscript *Book of Raziel* and the *Liber Juratus*.

Patrozyn see ABASDARHON

Paxilon, **Paxylon** This is one of the angels presiding over Saturday, the day of Saturn or Sabat, according to the *Liber Juratus* and the Sloane manuscript *Book of Raziel*. The similarly named **Paxonion, or Paxonyon** shares the role.

Pazehemy An angel of the ninth lunar month according to the *Liber Juratus*

and the Sloane manuscript *Book of Raziel.*

Paziael An angel of the element earth, under the planet Noga (Venus), to be invoked when working under this planet, according to the Sloane manuscript *Book of Raziel.*

Pazicaton An angel of the element water, under the planet Labana (Luna, the moon), to be invoked when working under this planet, according to the Sloane manuscript *Book of Raziel.*

Pdgnar An angel of the fifth lunar month according to the Sloane manuscript *Book of Raziel,* who if invoked brings benefits, although the text makes no suggestions as to exactly how one should pronounce such a name. He is a much more manageable **Pegner** in the *Liber Juratus.*

Peciel An angel presiding over Thursday in the Sloane manuscript *Book of Raziel.* There is no corresponding angel in the *Liber Juratus.*

Peacock Angel see MALAK TA'US

Pecyrael An angel of the element air, under the planet Hanina (Sol, the sun), to be invoked when working under this planet, found in the Sloane manuscript *Book of Raziel.*

Pegal One of the angels of Wednesday in the *Liber Juratus* and the Sloane manuscript *Book of Raziel.*

Pegiel The angel that rules the fourteenth degree of Aries under AIEL, according to the *Lemegeton.* This may be the same angel as PECIEL.

Peliel Ruler of the order of VIRTUES and the angel who instructed Jacob. He alternates with **Zekuniel** as the second of the ten angel of the SEFIROTH.

Pemiel see SANIEL

Pemoniel see MENDRION

Penaly see ORIEL

Penargos see SERQUANICH

Penat An angel of the north of the third heaven in the Sloane manuscript *Book of Raziel.* The *Heptameron* adds to this that he rules on Friday.

Penatiel see BERATIEL

Penemue A leader of the GRIGORI, who, according to *1 Enoch,* 'taught the children of men the bitter and the sweet' as well as the art of writing, which was not meant for Mankind.

Peniel Peniel has many different roles in different texts. In the *Heptameron* he is an angel of the third heaven who rules Friday and should be called on from the north; in a French version of the *Key of Solomon* his name is written on a pentacle used on Friday (the day of Venus) in order to get your way with a woman; in the *Lemegeton* he is one of the ten dukes of the night serving under CARABIEL. Some say that it was he who wrestled with Jacob, although this may be due to confusion with the names PELIEL or PENUEL, as this role is also given to CAMAEL, SAMAEL or an anonymous DARK ANGEL. He is also invoked against stupidity. **Penael,** an angel of the north of the third heaven in the Sloane manuscript *Book of Raziel,* may be another example of the name.

Penoles see SABRATHAN

Penuel An ARCHANGEL who is ANGEL OF THE FACE or PRESENCE of God (the meaning of the name), who is also called the Angel of Repentance. In the Bible Penuel is also the place where Jacob wrestled with the angel (or God, depending on your interpretation of the passage – see Exodus 33:14–15 and under DARK ANGEL) and the name of several individuals. Some say this is the same angel as PENIEL.

Pepilon This is one of the angels presiding over Saturday, the day of Saturn or Sabat, according to the Sloane manuscript *Book of Raziel*. If invoked appropriately and in a state of purity, he will aid you. The name is **Polypon** in the *Liber Juratus*.

Perelandra see ELDIL

Periel The angel that rules the eighth degree of Scorpio under JOSEL and the sixth degree of Sagittarius under SUIAJASEL, according to the *Lemegeton*. Elsewhere, it is given as one of the many names of METATRON.

Perman see BARIEL

Permaz see TARTYS

Permiel see VATHMIEL

Permon see DARDARIEL, SANIEL

Persiel see VEQUANIEL

Pesagniyah According to *The Zohar* this is an angel of the south who

controls the keys to the ethereal space. His other role is as the angel in charge of the prayers of those in deep sorrow. When their prayers rise up Pesagniyah takes them, kisses them, and accompanies them to a higher heaven.

Phaleg, Phalec An OLYMPIC SPIRIT who rules 35 of the 196 provinces and ruled the events of the world between AD 431and 920. As ruler of Mars, the planet of the Roman god of war, he is described as the lord of war. He is also the angel of Tuesday, as this is the day of Mars (for although the English get Tuesday from the Germanic god of war Tiu, this is merely a way of equating it with the Latin *martis dies,* 'day of Mars', that gives us French *Mardi* and Spanish *Martes*).

Phanael, Phanuel, Phamael In *3 Baruch* **Phamael** (a Greek corruption of the original **Phanael**) is described as the angel who interprets revelations to those who pass through life rightly, although in *2 Baruch* this task is given to RAMIEL, and in *Daniel* to GABRIEL. Phamael is Baruch's guide to the heavens. In *1 Enoch* **Phanuel** is he 'who is set over the repentance unto hope of those who inherit eternal life'. In the same text, with Gabriel, MICHAEL and RAPHAEL, Phanuel casts AZAZEL and his followers into the fiery abyss. He also stands at the throne of God, alongside the other higher angels. In the *Sibylline Oracles* he is 'one of the five angels who know all the evils that men have wrought'. He is listed among the ANGELS OF THE PRESENCE, and considered by some to be an ARCHANGEL, but in the *Lemegeton* **Phaniel**, another spelling, is a mere servant of the night to CAMUEL. Jean Danielou, in his *Angels and Their*

Missions, says Phanael is the angel of hope. See also FANIEL.

Phoenix In the fourth heaven, among the angelic guardians of the sun, are the Phoenixes and **Chalkydri** or **Kalkydras**. 'And I looked and saw flying spirits, the solar elements, called phoenixes and khalkedras, strange and wonderful. For their form was that of a lion … their head that of a crocodile. Their appearance was multi-coloured, like a rainbow. Their size was 900 measures. Their wings were those of angels, but they have 12 wings each. They accompany and run with the sun, carrying heat and dew and whatever is commanded them from God.' (*2 Enoch* 12) In chapter fifteen they burst into song, flapping their wings and rejoicing in the giver of light. This description is unusual, for it seems to be the only place that the Phoenix appears in the plural, the author ignoring the tradition that there can only be one Phoenix at a time. In *1 Enoch* the Chalkydri are brass serpents, but here they seem to be identical with the Phoenix. The Phoenix is also called 'the guardian of the terrestrial sphere'. Ginzberg tells us that 'he runs with the sun on his circuit, and he spreads out his wings and catches up the fiery rays of the sun. If he were not there to intercept them, neither man nor any other animate being would keep alive. On his right wing the following words are inscribed in huge letters, about four thousand stadia high: "Neither the earth produces me, nor the heavens, but only the wings of fire"'. The Phoenix's food is 'the manna of heaven and the dew of the earth. His excrement is a worm, whose excrement in turn is the cinnamon used by kings and princes.' When Eve gave all the animals some of the fruit of the tree of knowledge, the Phoenix was the only bird that refused to eat any and his reward was eternal life. There is another tradition of Phoenix as the name of a FALLEN ANGEL, once one of the THRONES, who nevertheless hopes to return to heaven after 1,200 years of punishment.

Phorlakh Angel of Earth and one of the angels whose name is used in the Seventh Pentacle of the Sun which, 'If any be by chance imprisoned or detained in fetters of iron, at the presence of this Pentacle, which should be engraved in Gold on the day and hour of the Sun, he will be immediately delivered and set at liberty' in *The Key of Solomon.*

Phorsiel see JEFISCHA

Phul An OLYMPIC SPIRIT who rules 7 of the 196 provinces. He is lord of the moon, and hence of water and Monday.

Phynitiel A fire angel under Sabaday (Saturn), to be invoked when working under this planet, according to the Sloane manuscript *Book of Raziel.*

Pion This is one of the angels presiding over Saturday found in the *Liber Juratus* and the Sloane manuscript *Book of Raziel.*

Pirtophin, **Pyrteplin** A Tuesday angel in the Sloane manuscript *Book of Raziel* and the *Liber Juratus.*

Pistis-Sophia A female AEON, one of the greatest in Gnosticism. She is an embodiment of Wisdom. Some say she sent the serpent to beguile Adam and

Eve in Eden. See further under SOPHIA and SAMAEL.

Plaior In *The Key of Solomon*, an angel whose name is invoked when the master is putting on the white linen vestments of powers before practising magic.

Plamiel see BERATIEL

Platiel see ABASDARHON

Pliset An angel of the second lunar month according to the Sloane manuscript *Book of Raziel,* with the power to grant wishes. The name takes the form **Palilet** in the *Liber Juratus*.

Poiel, **Poyel** Both one of the seventy-two angels of the zodiac and one of the seventy-two who bear the mystic name of God, SHEMHAMPHORAE, Poiel is a PRINCIPALITY who rules over fortune and philosophy. As the GUARDIAN ANGEL of those born under Capricorn between 27 and 31 December he is considered an angel of splendour who gives beauty and health and success in life.

Polypon see PEPILON

Poniel An angel of the north of the third heaven in the Sloane manuscript *Book of Raziel.*

Porackmiel In the Sloane manuscript *Book of Raziel* an angel with power over water.

Powers According to Dionysius the Areopagite, Powers thwart the efforts of demons to overthrow the world. For Pope Gregory the Great, they preside over the demons. In Ephesians 6:12, however, they are regarded as evil and

under the control of the devil: 'the cosmic powers of this present darkness'. They are also listed among those who cannot 'separate us from the love of God in Christ Jesus our Lord' (Romans 8:38–39). In the *Testament of Adam* they are a rank of angels whose job is to keep demons from destroying the world, paying particular attention to humans. In traditional art Powers are sometimes shown in full armour holding on to a chained demon. Otherwise they are identical to DOMINIONS.

Poyel see POIEL

Prasiniel see BARIEL

Pravuil This is the ARCHANGEL who keeps the records in heaven according to *2 Enoch*: 'And the Lord summoned one of his archangels by name Pravuil, whose knowledge was quicker in wisdom than the other archangels, who wrote all the deeds of the Lord; and the Lord said to Pravuil: Bring out the books from my store-houses, and a reed of quick-writing, and give it to Enoch … And Pravuil told me: All the things that I have told you, we have written. Sit and write all the souls of Mankind, however many of them are born, and the places prepared for them to eternity; for all souls are prepared to eternity, before the formation of the world.' (Chapter 22–23)

Praxiel see TARTYS

Prenostix see ZAAZENACH

Prince, **Principalities** Princes or Principalities are a high-ranking choir of angels, found particularly in those texts that describe God in terms of a great ruler surrounded by an angelic court. Their principal function, according to tradition, is the protection of religion. Dionysius the Areopagite says that they watch over the leaders of people and inspire them to make the right decisions. They are also linked with the powers to include evil as well as good spirits (Ephesians 6:12, 2:2). The word 'principalities (Greek *archai*) translates as 'rulers' in English, but can also be rendered ARCHON. They can have various subdivisions such as PRINCE OF TORAH, Prince of the Divine Presence who stands before God himself, Prince of Kingdoms (one for each, although few are named) and Prince of the World – sometimes said to be MICHAEL. Sometimes, however, Prince is merely an honour put before the name of any angel. In *3 Baruch* Principalities bring the virtues of the righteous to Michael in the form of baskets of flowers. Princes are shown in art crowned and armed.

Prince of Torah An angel whose function is to help you understand the deeper meanings of the Torah (the first five books of the Bible) and who prevents you forgetting what you have learned. **Prince of Learning** or **Prince of Wisdom** are alternative titles. Some texts talk of a number of these, but in *3 Enoch* the Prince of Torah is named as Yepipyah or YEPHEPHIYYA, who helped Moses remember the Law he had been given on Sinai.

Princes of the Presence see ANGELS OF THE PRESENCE

Psychopomp(s), **Psychopompoi** (Greek plural) This Greek term simply means one who conducts the soul. The idea of a spiritual guide who helps the soul after death is found in religions throughout the world. In the ancient world HERMES and CHIRON are prominent. In angelic lore SANDALPHON, MICHAEL and AZRAEL are prominent psychopomps.

Puriuel, **Puruel** see DOKIEL

Putti These chubby baby angel figures get their name from the Italian *putto* 'a boy'. They owe more to the iconography of EROS than to traditional angels, and are emphatically male, rather than sexless as the traditional angles are. They are ubiquitous in Renaissance and later art, can still be seen decorating nineteenth-century buildings and turn up in all sorts of unlikely places.

Pyroyinel An angel of the element air, under the planet Madin (Mars), to be invoked when working under this planet, according to the Sloane manuscript *Book of Raziel*.

Q

Qaddisin and Irrin In MERKABAH literature, the Qaddisin and Irrin are two pairs of angels of the highest rank, resident in either the sixth or seventh heaven, who together form God's inner council. They are described in *3 Enoch* as greater than all the other angels 'For each one of them is equal to all the rest together'.

Qafsiel, Qaphsiel see KAFZIEL

Qemuel see CAMAEL

Qeseph and Qispiel Angels whose function is indicated by the meaning of their names, 'Divine Anger'. They are often associated with APH and HEMAH.

Qnatiel An angel of the fifth lunar month according to the Sloane manuscript *Book of Raziel*, who if invoked brings benefits. The name appears as **Guatyell** in the *Liber Juratus*. Similarly, **Qnynzi**, an angel of the same month appears as **Gnynzy**.

Qoriel An angel whose name is inscribed on amulets and magic bowls. He appears in these contexts sometimes as an angel, sometimes as a demon.

Quabriel see SERQUANICH

Quadissa An angel of the third heaven invoked from the east in the Sloane manuscript *Book of Raziel*.

Qualabye An angel of the sixth lunar month according to the Sloane manuscript *Book of Raziel*, which says that if

they are named 'in each thing that thou wilt do … thou shalt profit'. **Gualaly** is the equivalent in the *Liber Juratus*.

Quarshiel An angel associated with the Tabernacle, who is found in a number of medieval texts. His name comes from the biblical word for the boards of acacia wood with which the Tabernacle was constructed.

Queen of the Angels A title most frequently found in the Roman Catholic Church, used of the Virgin Mary. In the Kabbalah the Queen of the Angels is the SHEKINAH, while for Gnostics the title belonged to PISTIS SOPHIA.

Quelamia In the *Book of Raziel* one of the seven THRONES of the first heaven.

Quemon An angel of the second lunar month according to the *Liber Juratus* and the Sloane manuscript *Book of Raziel*, with the power to grant wishes.

Quenol see SABRATHAN

Queriel see VATHMIEL

Quesdor see ABASDARHON

Quesupale An angel of the first lunar month according to the Sloane manuscript *Book of Raziel*. As in other cases a 'q' in this work is a 'g' in the *Liber Juratus*, where the name is **Guespales**.

Quian An angel of the north of the second heaven in the Sloane manuscript *Book of Raziel*.

Quiel An angel of the north in the fifth heaven in the Sloane manuscript *Book of Raziel*.

Quilon This is one of the angels presiding over Saturday in the Sloane manuscript *Book of Raziel*. It is **Quibon** in the *Liber Juratus*.

Quirix see BERATIEL

Quiron, **Quyron** This is one of the angels presiding over Saturday, the day of Saturn or Sabat, according to the *Liber Juratus* and the Sloane manuscript *Book of Raziel*.

Quisiel, **Quisyell** An angel presiding over Thursday, the day of Jove, in the *Liber Juratus* and the Sloane manuscript *Book of Raziel*.

Quor An angel of the first lunar month found in the *Liber Juratus* and the Sloane manuscript *Book of Raziel*.

Quosiel see HANIEL

Quyel An angel of the element earth, under the planet Zedek (Jupiter), to be invoked when working under this planet, according to the Sloane manuscript *Book of Raziel*.

Qwenael An angel of the second lunar month according to the Sloane manuscript *Book of Raziel*. It is a more comfortable **Quenael** in the *Liber Juratus*.

R

Raaciel In the Sloane manuscript *Book of Raziel*, an angel of the tenth lunar month. In the *Liber Juratus the* name is Raacpel.

Raajah The angel that rules the twelfth degree of Aquarius under AUSIUL, according to the *Lemegeton*.

Raamyel An angel of the eighth lunar month according to the Sloane manuscript *Book of Raziel*. He resides in the east of the first heaven.

Rabacyal see DALQUIEL

Rabfilyn An angel of the day of Mars (Tuesday) in the Sloane manuscript *Book of Raziel*. It takes the form **Rabsylyn** in the *Liber Juratus*.

Rabiel An angel of the element earth, under the planet Cocab (Mercury) in the Sloane manuscript *Book of Raziel*. In the *Lemegeton* Rabiel is an aerial spirit of the night who serves the Emperor of the South, **Maseriel**, described as 'of good nature & willingly will doe your will in all things' if invoked.

Rabmia One of the angels of Wednesday in the Sloane manuscript *Book of Raziel*. He does not feature in the *Liber Juratus*.

Racheil An OPHANIM who is the ruler of the planet Venus, hence involved in human sexuality, and as such is the ruler of the day of Venus, Friday, alongside ANAEL and SACHIEL. The connection between these roles is that Venus,

Roman goddess of fertility and love, gives her name to Friday in languages descended from the Latin – hence French *vendredi*, Spanish *viernes*, both from Latin *dies veneris*, 'the day of Venus'. Friday comes from Frigga, the nearest Germanic equivalent goddess to Venus.

Rachmiel An ANGEL OF MERCY and a CHILDBED ANGEL, and sometimes described as a guard of the gates of the east wind.

Raconeal, **Reconcall** This is one of the angels presiding over Saturday in the *Liber Juratus* and the Sloane manuscript *Book of Raziel*.

Racyelyn, **Racyeylyn** An angel of the day of Mars (Tuesday) in the *Liber Juratus* and the Sloane manuscript *Book of Raziel*.

Racynas One of the angels of the seventh lunar month according to the Sloane manuscript *Book of Raziel*, which says that if they are named 'in each thing that thou wilt do … thou shalt profit'. There is some confusion as to the correct form of the name, as the *Liber Juratus* has **Sastyracnas** at this point, which represents two angels in the *Raziel* list – **Safcy** and **Racynas** – run together. However, in both texts there seem to be corruptions and names lost from the list, as *Liber Juratus* only has twenty-three angels to cover the twenty-eight days of the month, while *Raziel* only has twenty-two, despite not having run the names together. The name **Racino**, **Racyno**, given as an angel of the ninth month, is probably the same.

Radiel, **Radyel** An angel of the ninth lunar month according to the *Liber Juratus* and the Sloane manuscript *Book of Raziel*, which says that if named 'in each thing that thou wilt do … thou shalt profit'.

Radweriel, **Radweriel YHWH**, **Radueriel** Radweriel is called the heavenly archivist in *3 Enoch*. His task is to pass the sacred scrolls to the Holy One, who then passes them to the scribes to read out to the Great Law Court of heaven. He is the angel of poetry, and the Talmud says, 'out of every word that goeth forth from his mouth a song-uttering angel is born.' He is said to rank even above METATRON. The name is sometimes seen as an alternative form of VEREVEIL.

Raffeylyn, **Raffylyn** An angel of Tuesday in the Sloane manuscript *Book of Raziel*.

Raftma'il An angel invoked in exorcism in Arabic tradition.

Raguel, **Raguil**, **Ragehyel**, **Ragael** This is the name of one of the two angels who take Enoch up to heaven, and then become the guardians of Enoch according to *2 Enoch*. The other is called SARIEL or **Samuil**. When they first come to Enoch to summon him to heaven, they appear as two men: '… very tall. Their faces shone like the sun, and their eyes were like burning lamps, and fire came forth from their lips; their wings were brighter than gold, their hands whiter than snow.' Raguel is regarded as the angel appointed to watch over the good behaviour of other angels, although the role is expressed rather more fiercely in both *1 Enoch* and one of the Dead Sea Scrolls, which tell us that he 'takes vengeance on the world of the luminaries'. In this role he is guardian of the second heaven (ruled by RAPHAEL), in which FALLEN ANGELS are imprisoned until Judgement. There is one manuscript variant of *Revelation* (not found in the standard text in the Bible) which says that after the sinners have been separated from the virtuous, 'Then shall He send the angel Raguel, saying: Go and sound the trumpet for the angels of cold and snow and ice, and bring together every kind of wrath upon them that stand on the left [sinners].' In the Sloane manuscript *Book of Raziel* he is an angel of the twelfth lunar month and with power over air, found in the east of the fourth heaven.

Rahab Rahab is the Angel of the Sea. One story says that this came about because he rebelled at the creation of the world. For 'God had commanded Rahab to take in the water. But he refused, saying, "I have enough," thus refusing to separate the upper and lower waters. The punishment for his disobedience was death. His body rests in the depths of the sea, the water dispelling the foul odour that emanates from it.' (Ginzberg) He is also said to have been destroyed for trying to stop the Israelites escaping from Pharaoh across the Red Sea. However, although some call him a demon rather than an angel, he is not always bad. When the Book of RAZIEL was stolen and thrown into the sea, it was Rahab who found it and returned it to Adam. There are other stories that after invocation he has restored property lost at sea to its owner.

Rahmiel, **Rhamiel** An ANGEL OF MERCY and of love who is used to protect against the evil eye. Although records of

this angel go back to ancient times, some say Rhamiel is the name of St Francis of Assisi after he went to heaven and became an angel.

Rahtiel, **Rahatiel** The angel of the constellations in *3 Enoch*. Seventy-two angels help him cause the constellations to turn in the heavens every night.

Rahumiel, **Rahumel** An angel of the north of the fourth heaven in the Sloane manuscript *Book of Raziel*. In the *Heptameron* Rahumel is an angel of the fifth heaven among those who rule Tuesday under **Samax**, subject to the east wind and to be invoked from the north.

Rahyeziel In the Sloane manuscript *Book of Raziel*, an angel of the tenth lunar month. If invoked in rites his name will ensure good results. In the *Liber Juratus* he becomes the much grander **Raazyell** (i.e. RAZIEL).

Rakhaniel One of the angels whose name is used in the Fifth Pentacle of Saturn 'which chaseth away the Spirits which guard treasures' in *The Key of Solomon*.

Raliel An angel presiding over Thursday, the day of Jove, according to Sloane manuscript *Book of Raziel*.

Raloyl An angel of the element fire, under the planet Madin (Mars), to be invoked when working under this planet, according to the Sloane manuscript *Book of Raziel*.

Ram, **Ramasdon** An angel of the first lunar month according to the *Liber Juratus* and the Sloane manuscript *Book of Raziel*. See also RAMAN, below.

Raman, **Ram** YAZAD (Zoroastrian angel) presiding over Joy or Felicity, who works with VOHU MANO. He gives his name to the twenty-first day of the month.

Ramatiel An angel of the element air, under the planet Cocab (Mercury), to be invoked when working under this planet, according to the Sloane manuscript *Book of Raziel*.

Ramaziel see TARTYS

Rameel One of the GRIGORI, 'a chief of ten', according to *1 Enoch* 6.

Ramesiel see SABRATHAN

Ramiel, **Raamiel**, **Ramael** The angel of the thunder in *3 Enoch*, but in *2 Baruch* the interpreter of visions for the righteous and governor of true visions, who interprets Baruch's vision for him. In Milton's *Paradise Lost* Ramiel is a FALLEN ANGEL routed by ABDIEL, a role taken from the *Apocalypse of Baruch*. In the *Sibylline Oracles* Ramiel leads souls to judgement.

Ramlel One of the GRIGORI, 'a chief of ten', according to *1 Enoch* 6.

Ramnel A Thursday angel in the Sloane manuscript *Book of Raziel*. He is **Ramuel** in the *Liber Juratus*.

Rancyl According to the Sloane manuscript *Book of Raziel* this is one of the angels of Sunday. The name is **Raneyl** in the *Liber Juratus*.

Ranfiel, **Ransyel** In the *Liber Juratus* and the Sloane manuscript *Book of Raziel*, an angel of the eleventh lunar month.

Ranks of Angels see HIERARCHY OF ANGELS

Raphael, **Rafael** Raphael, whose name means 'God healed' in Hebrew, has been classed variously among the CHERUBIM or OPHANIM, and as a PRINCE of the VIRTUES, DOMINIONS and POWERS and a WATCHER, but is most widely known as an ARCHANGEL, alongside MICHAEL and GABRIEL. In the Roman Catholic Church, 29 September is celebrated as the feast day of these three archangels, the only ones mentioned by name in the Bible. Even Raphael's status as a biblical angel is disputed, as he appears only in *The Book of Tobit*, recognised as biblical by the Roman Catholic Church, but relegated to the Apocrypha by others.

In *The Book of Enoch* and the Dead Sea scrolls, Raphael is said to rule the spirits of men, but as his name suggests, elsewhere he is most closely associated with healing. In *The Book of Tobit* he befriends Tobias, and helps him catch a giant fish and to use parts of it for healing, using the gall to cure the blindness of his father Tobit, and burning the entrails to defeat the devil Asmodeus. It is not until his adventures are over that the kind companion and guide reveals his true nature to Tobias. In doing so he reveals another of his important functions, to note the prayers of the righteous, and present them to God, for he tells Tobit, 'I am Raphael, one of the seven holy angels, which present the prayers of the saints, and go in before the glory of the Holy One.' (Tobit 12:15) In the *Testament of Solomon* we are again told that Raphael thwarts Asmodeus, and that the fish that needs to be used for healing is the 'sheatfish', a large kind of catfish, found only in the rivers of Assyria, an area that

Asmodeus also haunts. In the Kabbalah, Raphael is believed to have healed the pain felt by Abraham as a result of his adult circumcision and elsewhere he has been credited with healing Jacob's thigh after his night-long struggle with the angel (see Genesis 32; DARK ANGEL) and to be the angel who troubles the healing pool at Bethesda (John 5). There is a tradition that he gave Noah a book on medicine to take on the Ark, although another story says Raphael founded the knowledge of medicine when he taught Noah about all the medicinal plants after the flood. Noah wrote his advice down, and this work underlies all subsequent medicine. Another aspect of his healing role is as healer of the earth, for he is said in the *Book of Enoch* to have healed the earth when it was defiled by the sins of the FALLEN ANGELS. This makes him popular with those concerned with the present state of the earth. He is also the patron of the blind, of nurses, and of doctors, and is called the Angel of Compassion.

His role as companion, instructor and guide found in the *Book of Tobit* makes him patron of happy meetings and of travellers. He has a darker aspect, also found in *Enoch*, as a guide to Sheol, the underworld. In this aspect he becomes the ANGEL OF DEATH, and can be identified with IZRAIL, the Angel of Death in the Holy Koran.

A more romantic story makes him the angel whom God sent to Solomon in reply to his prayers, with a magic ring which allowed him to command the devils or DJINN (depending on which version you follow). With the power of this ring Solomon was able to finish building the Temple at Jerusalem.

Raphael has a multitude of other aspects, among which he has been described as Regent of the Sun; Governor of the South; Guardian of the West; Overseer of the Evening Wind; as the angel of prayer, love, joy, light, science and knowledge. He is one of the six Angels of Repentance and has also been credited with being the guardian of the Tree of Life.

Another Jewish legend says the archangel Raphael was originally called **Labbiel.** When God was creating Man, the bands of angels under Michael and Gabriel were destroyed with fire when they objected. Having seen this happen, Labbiel advised his followers to support God's actions in order to save themselves from a similar fate. 'Thereupon God changed Labbiel's name to Raphael, the Rescuer, because his host of angels had been rescued by his sage advice. He was appointed the Angel of Healing, who has in his safe-keeping all the celestial remedies, the types of the medical remedies used on earth.' (Ginzberg)

He is again the angel of the sun in the Sloane manuscript of *The Book of Raziel* (see also ANGELS OF THE SUN). The same text describes him as an angel of fire and flame and of the air, alongside Gabriel, Michael, **Cherubyn** (?Cherubim) **Ceraphin** (?Seraphim), ORYCHYN, PANTACEREN, MICRATON, MANDALFON, PARACHIEL, Ragehyel (see under RAGUEL) and TOBIEL. See also under AZAZEL. In the *Testament of Solomon* Raphael can tame the female demon Obyzouth, who strangles babies at birth. Some identify him as the archangel of Mercury, and thus Wednesday. The *Lemegeton* says that Raphael is the sovereign prince of the east with **Miel** and SERAPHIEL as Princes under him, who is to be invoked when dealing with those zodiac signs of the air (Gemini, Libra and Capricorn). He also has dominion over science, knowledge in general and love. In art, Raphael is usually shown in his role of companion to Tobias, so is dressed as a traveller. He may be carrying a medicine box.

Raphiel The angel that rules the eighth degree of Taurus under TUAL and the eighth degree of Gemini under GIEL, according to the *Lemegeton*. Were it not for the very minor role he has, one would assume this is simply a form of RAPHAEL.

Rapinis, **Rapynis** In the *Liber Juratus* and the Sloane manuscript *Book of Raziel*, an angel of the tenth lunar month.

Rapion, **Rapyon** An angel of the sixth lunar month according to the *Liber Juratus* and the Sloane manuscript *Book of Raziel*.

Rapithwin YAZAD (Zoroastrian angel) presiding over the period of the day from noon to 3pm. As 'Lord of the Noonday Heat', it is his warmth that enables plants to grow. During the five months of winter Rapithwin retreats to the underworld and keeps the subterranean waters warm so the roots of the plants will not freeze. At that time his role above ground is taken by a YAZAD known as the second HAWAN. He also rules the North Star (Polaris) and the planet Kevan (Saturn) and leads the Chieftains of the Sky (see further under TISHTRYA).

Rartudel A Thursday angel in the Sloane manuscript *Book of Raziel*. He is not in the *Liber Juratus* list.

Rasanstat Female YAZAD (Zoroastrian angel) whose name means 'truth, justice'. She gives her name to the eighteenth day of the month in the Zoroastrian religious calendar.

Raseroph An angel of the sixth lunar month according to the Sloane manuscript *Book of Raziel*, which says that if they are named 'in each thing that thou wilt do … thou shalt profit'. **Raserch** appears in the same position in the *Liber Juratus*.

Rasfia One of the angels of Wednesday, the day of Mercury, according to the Sloane manuscript *Book of Raziel*. The name appears as **Nafya** in the *Liber Juratus*.

Rashn, **Rashne**, **Rashnu** YAZAD (Zoroastrian angel) of Justice. He judges souls of the deceased before the bridge (known as the Chinvat Bridge) which leads to heaven and the abyss. Like so many figures who judge the souls of the dead, such as the ARCHANGEL MICHAEL, he carries golden scales with which he weighs the souls of the dead. He works with the AMESHA SPENTA AMERETAT. He gives his name to the eighteenth day of the month in the Zoroastrian religious calendar.

Rasiel, **Rashiel**, **Raasiel** The angel of earthquakes (with ZIIEL overseeing earth tremors) in some traditions, although others name him Angel of the Whirlwind. The name comes from the Hebrew for 'quaking'.

Rasliel One of the angels of the eighth lunar month according to the Sloane manuscript *Book of Raziel*, which says that if they are named 'in each thing that thou wilt do … thou shalt profit'.

Rasoiel In the Sloane manuscript *Book of Raziel* an angel with power over fire and flame.

Rassy An angel of the sixth lunar month according to the *Liber Juratus* and the Sloane manuscript *Book of Raziel*.

Rata Female YAZAD (Zoroastrian angel) personifying charity. She is known as **Rati** in India.

Rathanael An angel in the *Testament of Solomon* who has the power to thwart the two-headed female demon Enepsigos.

Rathiel The angel that rules the ninth degree of Virgo under VOIL, according to the *Lemegeton*.

Ratziel The angel that rules the eighth degree of Pisces under PASIL, according to the *Lemegeton*.

Rayziel see JEFISCHA, MENDRION

Raziel Shortly after Adam was expelled from paradise, the angel Raziel came to him and gave him a book. 'In the moment when Adam took the book, a flame of fire shot up from near the river, and the angel rose heavenward with it. Then Adam knew that he who had spoken to him was an angel of God, and it was from the Holy King Himself that the book had come, and he used it in holiness and purity.' (Ginzberg) The book contains all celestial and earthly wisdom, 'and it teaches also how to call upon the angels and make them appear before men, and answer all their questions.' The angels were so jealous of the wisdom that Adam learnt from the

book that they stole it and threw it in the sea. But God sent RAHAB, the Angel of the Sea, to fetch it back to Adam. The Hebrew text we know today as *Sefer Raziel* or *The Book of Raziel* was already in circulation by the thirteen century. It is often attributed to Eleazar of Worms (*c* 1160–1237), and he may indeed have been one of several people who had a hand in writing it. Such was the fame of this work as the ultimate source for invoking angels, that its name was widely used. The sixteenth-century English-language *Book of Raziel* (British Library Sloane Manuscript 3826, referred to throughout this book as the Sloane manuscript *Book of Raziel*, and discussed further in the Introduction), which bears only a loose connection with the difficult work generally known today as *Sefer Raziel,* is one such work. An invaluable source of information on sixteenth-century angelology, it includes such forms of Raziel's name as **Razelius**, **Rasziel**. Elsewhere, Raziel is reported to be the angel of hidden regions and the guardian of the secrets of the universe. He plays an important role in magic, as is to be expected from the angel who introduced such mysteries to man. In the Kabbalah he is the guardian of the second SEFIRA. Maimonides says Raziel is the chief of the ERELIM, and the herald of God, as well as the teacher of Adam. Others call him a CHERUB or one of the OPHANIM and describe him as having blue wings, a glowing yellow aura around his head and wearing a grey robe which appears to have liquid-like properties. Others say that he stands close by God's throne, and therefore hears and writes down everything that is said and discussed. In popular culture the name Raziel is found as the protagonist of the successful series of computer games called *The Legacy of Kain*, but this has nothing to do with the angelic Raziel.

Razishta Chista see CHISTA

Rebiel The angel that rules the eleventh degree of Scorpio under JOSEL, according to the *Lemegeton*.

Refacbilion This is one of the angels presiding over Saturday in the Sloane manuscript *Book of Raziel*. If invoked appropriately and in a state of purity, they will aid you.

Regael The angel that rules the eleventh degree of Sagittarius under SUIAJASEL, according to the *Lemegeton*.

Regnia, Regnya An angel of the second lunar month according to the *Liber Juratus* and the Sloane manuscript *Book of Raziel*, with the power to grant wishes.

Rehael One of the POWERS who bear the mystic name of God, SHEMHAMPHORAE, he has as his domain health and longevity, and he inspires respect for parents. As a GUARDIAN ANGEL of those born under Libra between 4 and 8 October he is seen as an angel of strength who gives the energy and the strength to handle one's problems alone.

Reiiel, Reiyel A DOMINION who is one of the seventy-two SHEMHAMPHORAE angels. GUARDIAN ANGEL of those born under the sign of Leo between 13 and 17 August, he is considered an angel of knowledge, giving the wisdom to anticipate the course of events and attain one's goal.

Reivtip see ALIMON

Rekhodiah One of the angels whose names are used in the Second Pentacle of the Sun which 'serveth to repress the pride and arrogance of the Solar Spirits, which are altogether proud and arrogant by their nature' in *The Key of Solomon*.

Relion, Relyon This is one of the angels presiding over Saturday in the *Liber Juratus* and the Sloane manuscript *Book of Raziel*.

Remafidda, Remafydda An angel of the fourth lunar month according to the *Liber Juratus* and the Sloane manuscript *Book of Raziel*.

Remasyn see OSMADIEL

Remcatheyel According to the Sloane manuscript *Book of Raziel*, this is one of the angels of Sunday (Solis). He appears as **Reniayeyll** in the *Liber Juratus*.

Remiel, Eremiel, Jeremiel An angel whose duty it is to watch over the souls in Hades. The name appears as Remiel in texts such as *2 Baruch*; as Eremiel in the *Apocalypse of Zepaniah*, while in *4 Ezra* he is Jeremiel. *1 Enoch* 20 presents problems, for while many reference works will tell you that Remiel is described there as 'one of the holy angels, whom God set over those who rise', this entry is only found in one manuscript, although it was included in Charles's translation. Other manuscripts make no mention of Remiel. Elsewhere, Remiel shares rule over thunder with RAMIEL and URIEL and is said to be the one who leads souls to judgement and rules over those awaiting resurrection.

Rengliel The angel that rules the tenth degree of Scorpio under JOSEL, according to the *Lemegeton*.

Rephaim see NEPHILIM

Reprobated Angels At a Church council
in 745 led by Pope Zachary, seven angels
were reprobated – that is to say, rejected
as worthless for failing to pass the test of
authenticity. It was declared that the only
angels who could be venerated were
those found in the Bible – that is to say
MICHAEL, GABRIEL and RAPHAEL, a view
that is still the rule in the Roman
Catholic Church. Seven angels in
particular were rejected: URIEL, RAGUEL,
Inias, ADIMUS, SIMIEL or **Semibel**,
Tubuael or **Tubaeus** and **Sabaothe** or
Saboac (presumably the same as
SABAOTH). The reprobation was a
response to a growing interest in angels
and a multiplication of those who were
revered, which, it was feared, was the
path away from monotheism to idol
worship. At the same council two
prominent bishops who advocated angel
worship were excommunicated.

Requiel A MOON ANGEL who rules the
twenty-third mansion of the moon in
Capricorn. He helps the sick find health
and the freeing of prisoners, but also
promotes divorce.

Resegar, **Rasegar** An angel of the
second lunar month according to the
Liber Juratus and the Sloane manuscript
Book of Raziel, who has the power to
grant your wishes.

Resfilin An angel presiding over Friday,
the day of Venus, according to the Sloane
manuscript *Book of Raziel*. He is
Reffylyn in the *Liber Juratus*.

Reycat An angel of the fifth lunar month

according to the *Liber Juratus* and the
Sloane manuscript *Book of Raziel*.

Reyn A Tuesday angel in the Sloane
manuscript *Book of Raziel*. The name is
Veyn in the *Liber Juratus*.

Rhamiel see RAHMIEL

Riajah The angel that rules the twelfth
degree of Capricorn under CASUJOJAH,
according to the *Lemegeton*.

Rikbi'el YHWH In *3 Enoch*, an angel of
the mystic Jewish tradition of the
MERKABAH (Chariot) which gives adepts
access to heaven. His name means
'chariot of God' and he is in charge of
the wheels of the chariot. He is described
as chief of the GALGALLIM.

Rimezyn see JEFISCHA

Rinafonel An angel of the element
water, under the planet Cocab
(Mercury), to be invoked when working
under this planet, according to the
Sloane manuscript *Book of Raziel*.

Rizoel An angel invoked in the
Testament of Solomon to get rid of
Soubelti, a demon who causes shivering
and numbness.

Robica, **Robyca** An angel of the first
lunar month according to the *Liber
Juratus* and the Sloane manuscript *Book
of Raziel*.

Rochel This angel helps to find lost
objects as well as being one of the
seventy-two angels bearing the mystic
name of God, SHEMHAMPHORAE. As the
GUARDIAN ANGEL of those born under
Pisces between 1 and 5 March he is said

to be an angel of equilibrium who creates a balance between the masculine and feminine sides of a person and resolves conflict.

Roelhaiphar One of the angels whose name is used in the Fifth Pentacle of Saturn 'which chaseth away the Spirits which guard treasures' in *The Key of Solomon*.

Rofiniel, **Rofynyel** An angel presiding over Thursday, the day of Jove, according to the *Liber Juratus* and the Sloane manuscript *Book of Raziel*.

Romiel, **Romyel** In the *Liber Juratus* and the Sloane manuscript *Book of Raziel* the angel with power over the twelfth lunar month. If invoked in the relevant month, he will ensure success in your enterprise. In the *Lemegeton* Romiel is an attendant angel of BERATIEL, the angel of the twelfth hour of the day. See also BERATIEL.

Roncayl According to the Sloane manuscript *Book of Raziel* this is one of the angels of Sunday (Solis) who should be invoked to aid works started on that day. He is **Romayl** in the *Liber Juratus*. **Ronmeyeyl** is another Sunday angel who appears as **Ronayeyll** in the *Liber Juratus*.

Roqniel In the Sloane manuscript *Book of Raziel* an angel with power over fire and flame. The correct form of the name may be **Roquiel**, which is found elsewhere in magic.

Rorafeyl A Tuesday angel in the Sloane manuscript *Book of Raziel*. The name is **Rarafeyll** in the *Liber Juratus*.

Rubi In 'The Second Angel's Story' in

Thomas Moore's 1823 poem *The Loves of the Angels* inspired by the story of the GRIGORI, Rubi is a WATCHER who falls through love of the mortal woman Lilis.

Rubycyel, **Rubyeyel** An angel presiding over Thursday, the day of Jove, according to the *Liber Juratus* and the Sloane manuscript *Book of Raziel*.

Rudefor see ZAAZENACH

Ruffaraneylyn An angel of the day of Mars (Tuesday) in the Sloane manuscript *Book of Raziel*. In the *Liber Juratus* the name becomes two angels **Ruffar** and **Aneylyn**.

Ruhiel the angel of the wind in *3 Enoch*. The name comes from a Hebrew word meaning 'wind'.

Rulbelyn, **Rubbelyn** A Tuesday angel in the *Liber Juratus* and the Sloane manuscript *Book of Raziel*.

Rumael, **Rumjal** Two of the GRIGORI according to *1 Enoch*.

Ruman In Islamic tradition, an angel who greets sinners when they arrive in hell. He then sits them down and makes them write out in full detail every sin they committed on earth. Since he has knowledge of every single sin, this can take some time. The sinner is then handed over to MUNKIR AND NAKIR for punishment.

Ruva'il An angel invoked in exorcism in Arabic tradition.

Rymaliel see SABRATHAN

S

Saamyel see SAMYEL

Sababiel, Sabybyall One of the angels of the seventh lunar month according to the *Liber Juratus* and the Sloane manuscript *Book of Raziel*.

Sabael An angel in the *Testament of Solomon* who can imprison the demon Sphendonael, who causes tumours and tetanus. Most reference books give the name as SABRAEL, which is how the name appears in the 1898 translation by F C Conybeare, but modern editions of the text are clear that the name is Sabael.

Sabaoth In the Gnostic *The Hypostasis of the Archons*, Sabaoth is the offspring of the Satan-figure Samael-Ialdaboath and Matter. When SAMAEL is cast into the underworld for setting himself up as God, Sabaoth repents and as a reward is made ruler of the seventh heaven, with a four-faced chariot of CHERUBIM, and an infinity of angels to attend him. The name is frequent in Gnostic texts and used in incantations and amulets. For example, according to the *Testament of Solomon,* to expel the demon Katanikotael, who causes domestic strife, from your home you should write on seven laurel leaves 'Angel, Eae, Ieo, Sabaoth, imprison Katanikotael', then soak the leaves in water and sprinkle the house with the water. And to expel Saphthorael, who causes dissensions in the minds of men, a person should wear an amulet bearing the words 'Iae, Ieo, sons of Sabaoth' round his neck. Sabaoth is listed among the ANGELS OF THE PRESENCE and is also one of the names of God, but he was also among the REPROBATED ANGELS.

Sabathiel The angel of the planet Saturn, who is said in the Kabbalah to receive divine light from the holy spirit and reflect it on to those who come under him. He stands continually in the presence of God.

Sabbath As well as being the day of rest and worship, Sabbath is also embodied as the Angel of the Sabbath, who was enthroned before God on the first ever Sabbath (the seventh day of creation), when the other angels paraded before him, singing the praises of God. This angel also helped save Adam from hell when he was expelled from paradise, by interceding with God on his behalf.

Sabiel The first of the personalised angels of the ten holy SEFIROTH. In magic he is the angel that rules the twenty-fifth degree of Gemini under GIEL, according to the *Lemegeton*, while as **Sabeél** he is an angel of Mars and hence Tuesday in the *Magical Treatise of Solomon.*

Sablo In Gnostic writings an AEON who is often associated with ABRAXIS and GAMALIEL. He offers protection.

Sabrael An angel who shares leadership of the TARSHISHIM with **Tarsheil**. He is often confused with SABAEL.

Sabrathan The angel who rules the first hour of the night, according to the *Lemegeton*. He has a horde of attendant angels, the most important being **Domaras, Domoras, Amerany, Penoles, Mardiel, Nastul, Ramesiel,**

Omedriel, **Franedac**, **Chrasiel**, **Dormason**, **Hayzoym**, **Emalon**, TURTIEL, **Quenol** and **Rymaliel**.

Sacadiel, **Sacadyel** In the *Liber Juratus* and the Sloane manuscript *Book of Raziel*, an angel of the thirteenth lunar month (March). If invoked in the relevant month, he will ensure success in your enterprise.

Sacciniel, **Saccynyel** An angel presiding over Thursday in the *Liber Juratus* and the Sloane manuscript *Book of Raziel*.

Sacdon One of the angels of the seventh lunar month according to the *Liber Juratus* and the Sloane manuscript *Book of Raziel*, which says that if they are named 'in each thing that thou wilt do … thou shalt profit'.

Sachiel, **Zadkiel** The ARCHANGEL of Jupiter, invoked for the upholding of justice, law and order, wisdom, humour, abundance, success and generosity. An angel of the ninth lunar month according to the Sloane manuscript *Book of Raziel*. In the same source, he appears as **Saciel**, the angel of the seventh lunar month (although the name is given as **Suryel** in the *Liber Juratus*), through whose power a man may know his future, and in the form **Sachquiel** as an angel presiding over Thursday, the day of Jove. SATQUIEL appears to be the same angel in this text as he is also given Mercury, but in other texts may be distinct. The *Heptameron*, however, disagrees, as it says Sachiel is one of three angels of Friday/Venus. He is given yet more roles as the angel that rules the third degree of Taurus under TUAL and the first and fourth degrees of Cancer under CAEL, according to the

Lemegeton. As **Sachael**, he is the angel that rules the third degree of Gemini under GIEL, according to the same work, which seems to regard them as distinct angels. As ZADKIEL he is an ANGEL OF MERCY, who is also listed by some among the archangels, while others say Sachiel is one of the CHERUBIM.

Sacstoyeyn According to the *Liber Juratus* and the Sloane manuscript *Book of Raziel* this is one of the angels with special care of Monday.

Saddaniel An angel of the element fire, under the planet Hanina (Sol, the sun), to be invoked when working under this planet, according to the Sloane manuscript *Book of Raziel*.

Sadiel An angel of the south of the third heaven in the Sloane manuscript *Book of Raziel*. The angel that rules the seventeenth degree of Leo under OL, according to the *Lemegeton* as well as a duke of the night under the Emperor of the South, GEDIEL.

Sadiniel see VEQUANIEL

Sadriel Sadriel is the angel of order, and one of the rulers of the seven heavens, although it is difficult to find more information about him. He has been widely used by gamers and fantasy fans in their fictions.

Saeliah see SEELIAH

Saeprel An angel of the north of the fifth heaven in the Sloane manuscript *Book of Raziel*.

Safcy see RACYNAS

Safe An angel of the fifth lunar month found in the Sloane manuscript *Book of Raziel*. The name is **Sase** in the *Liber Juratus*.

Saffeyeyl, **Saffyell**, **Safyel** According to the *Liber Juratus* and the Sloane manuscript *Book of Raziel*, this is one of the angels of Sunday (Solis) who should be invoked to aid works started on that day. The name is also found inscribed on charms.

Safida, **Safyda** An angel of the fourth lunar month according to the *Liber Juratus* and the Sloane manuscript *Book of Raziel*, who if invoked bring benefits.

Sagansagel see SASNIGIEL

Sagel The angel that rules the sixteenth degree of Cancer under CAEL, according to the *Lemegeton*.

Sagiel The angel that rules the fourteenth degree of Leo under OL, in the *Lemegeton*. See also under BARAQIEL.

Sagnel The angel that rules the twelfth degree of Aries under AIEL, according to the *Lemegeton*.

Sagnessagiel see SASNIGIEL

Sahael The angel that rules the third degree of Libra under JAEL, according to the *Lemegeton*.

Sahaman An angel of the ninth lunar month found in the Sloane manuscript *Book of Raziel*.

Sahel The angel that rules the fifth degree of Leo under OL, in the *Lemegeton*.

Sahgragynyn According to the *Liber Juratus* and the Sloane manuscript *Book of Raziel*, this is one of the angels with special care of Monday.

Sahuhaf In the *Liber Juratus* and the Sloane manuscript *Book of Raziel*, an angel of the eleventh lunar month. If invoked in the relevant month, he will ensure success in your enterprise. **Sahumiel** in *Raziel*, **Sahinyel** in *Juratus*, is a companion.

Salainel An angel of the element earth, under the planet Noga (Venus), to be invoked when working under this planet, according to the Sloane manuscript *Book of Raziel*.

Salamiel see SEMYAZA

Salathiel, **Salatheel** One of the great ministering ARCHANGELS who aid the repentant. He one also one of the angels said to rule the spheres. In the *Book of Adam and Eve* he and SURIEL rescue Adam and Eve from a high mountain where SATAN had lured them.

Salgiel see SHALGIEL

Salion, **Salyon** This is one of the angels presiding over Saturday according to the *Liber Juratus* and the Sloane manuscript *Book of Raziel*. If invoked appropriately and in a state of purity, they will aid you.

Saloniel An angel of the element water, under the planet Noga (Venus), to be invoked when working under this planet, in the Sloane manuscript *Book of Raziel*.

Salor An angel of the third lunar month

in the Sloane manuscript *Book of Raziel*, whose naming brings benefits. Once again there has been confusion in the word breaks between *Raziel* and the *Liber Juratus*, for the former has Salor followed by another angel called **Hac**, while the latter has one angel called **Saforac**. Counting angels does not help, for even with the loss of one name, the *Liber Juratus* still has thirty angels to cover the twenty-eight days of the lunar month.

Salttri An angel of the sixth lunar month according to the Sloane manuscript *Book of Raziel*, which says that if they are named 'in each thing that thou wilt do … thou shalt profit'. The name is **Salhy** in the *Liber Juratus*.

Samael, Sammael, Samyel, Camael
Samael has possibly the richest and most contradictory set of stories about him of any angel. Some identify him with SATAN, saying that Samael was his angelic name, but others are definite that Satan's angelic name was SATERNAIL. He certainly has many roles that overlap with those ascribed to Satan and with SEMYAZA, but has positive roles as well. The name probably means either 'poison of God' or 'the blind one'. Since the ANGEL OF DEATH is sometimes said to administer poison, Samael is sometimes identified as that angel. In the Gnostic text *The Hypostasis of the Archons*, Samael is the name of the first ARCHON, and the name is said to mean 'god of the blind'. In this work, Samael, also known as IALDABOATH, proclaimed himself the true god to his seven offspring. In response Zoe (Greek for 'Life') the daughter of PISTIS-SOPHIA ('Faith-Wisdom) breathed into his face; her

breath became a fiery angel 'and cast him down into Tartaros below the Abyss'. He appears as **Samma'el**, Prince of the Accusers in *3 Enoch* 14 (compare the role of Satan in Job). He is also the Prince of Rome, regarded as the great enemy at the time of writing. Daily, he sits alongside DUBBIEL and Satan to write down the sins of Israel. They pass the writing tablets to the SERAPHIM to pass on to God, but the Seraphim burn them instead. Some say he is the angel who wrestled with Jacob, although others say this is PENIEL. He has been described as having twelve wings.

On an astronomical level he is called the ruler of Mars, which, as this is the planet of war, accounts for his being called an angel of evil. However, the influence of Mars can be turned instead to energising and bringing vitality, determination and, as Clare Nahmad says, 'a fighting spirit harmonized by love, quickening lethargic resignation into transfiguring action'. In kabbalistic vision he is seen in his original glory, ablaze with jewels and precious crystals, before humanity degraded his energies. He can be the leopard-bodied Count Palatine of hell or a bejewelled archangel of the divine presence. Nahmad also describes him as one 'on whom we should call for courage, empowerment, protection of the innocent, willpower, stimulative energy,' and says that we should call on him for help in manual jobs as Mars is the planet of energy, enthusiasm and drive.

Samael figures widely in magic books. In a slip of the pen *The Lemegeton* calls him **Samuel** at one point, although there is no doubt that it is Samael that is meant. In this work he is the angel who rules the first hour of the day. His chief dukes (who each have

171

another 444 servants following them) are **Ameniel, Charpon, Darosiel, Monasiel, Brumiel, Nestoriel, Chremas** and **Meresyn.** The text invokes him as 'Thou mighty and blessed angel Samael' and calls him a servant of mercy and of the most high God when conjuring him to 'descend and shew your self visible and perfectly in a pleasant and comely form before me in this Cristall stone: to the sight of my Eyes speaking with a voyce Intelligible and to my apprehension: shewing, declaring & accomplishing all my desires that I shall aske or Request of you both herein and in whatsoever Truths or things else that is Just and lawfull before the presence of Almighty god.' In the Sloane manuscript *Book of Raziel* Samael is an elemental angel with power over the earth. He shares power over the west with ADTRIEL and JOEL. Samyel, an angel of the south of the third heaven in the same work, is probably identical. See also AGRAT BAT MAHLAT

Samael is one of the most frequently found names in modern literary treatments of angels. The Black Huntsman in Weber's opera *Der Freischütz* is called SAMIEL. Samael is Lucifer's original name in Neil Gaiman's *Sandman* graphic novels; features as a name in Jordan's *Wheel of Time* series and as the name of a character in the computer game *Discworld Noir*, based on Terry Pratchett's *Discworld* novels; features in a number of role-playing games and is the name of a rock group, to list but a few examples.

Samahazai see SEMYAZA, AZAZEL

Samangaluf, Semangelof see SANSANUI

Samax see RAHUMIEL

Samayelyn An angel of the day of Mars (Tuesday) in the *Liber Juratus* and the Sloane manuscript *Book of Raziel*.

Samelon see ABASDARHON

Sameon see SANIEL

Sameriel see MENDRION

Sameron see BERATIEL

Samerym see ABASDARHON

Samhiel, Samhyell In the *Liber Juratus* and the Sloane manuscript *Book of Raziel*, an angel of the eleventh lunar month. If invoked in the relevant month, he will ensure success in your enterprise.

Samiel The angel that rules the sixth degree of Aquarius under AUSIUL, according to the *Lemegeton*. In the *Sibylline Oracles* he is one of the angels who lead souls to judgement. It is also a form of the name SAMAEL.

Samil see ARAEBEL

Samkiel An angel of destruction in *3 Enoch*. He is in charge of the souls of the intermediate – that is, those whose good and bad parts are just about in balance, so that they count as neither righteous nor wicked. Samkiel, whose name comes from a word for 'support', takes them down to hell, where their souls are purified by fire.

Samlazaz One of the GRIGORI, 'a chief of ten', according to *1 Enoch 6*.

Sammael see SAMAEL

Samsaweel or **Samsapeel** One of the GRIGORI who taught Mankind the signs of the sun (*1 Enoch* 6).

Samtiel An angel of the sixth lunar month according to the Sloane manuscript *Book of Raziel*. He is **Sanytyell** in the *Liber Juratus*. This suggests that at some point there was a manuscript where Samtiel was read as Sanitiel (or vice versa) before the 'i's were changed to 'y's, as in handwriting 'm' and 'ni' or 'in' are often indistinguishable.

Samuel see SAMAEL

Samuil see SARIEL

Samyel, Saamyel An angel of the fourth lunar month according to the *Liber Juratus* and the Sloane manuscript *Book of Raziel*. However, the name can also be a form of both SAMAEL and SAMIEL, and the divisions between these similar-sounding angels are very blurred.

Samysarach An angel of the third lunar month according to the *Liber Juratus* and the Sloane manuscript *Book of Raziel*.

Sanael see SANIEL

Sandalon A four-winged angel mentioned in the Sloane manuscript *Book of Raziel*. The name should probably be identified with SANDALPHON.

Sandalphon, Sandalfon Some describe Sandalphon as the chief of the GUARDIAN ANGELS, as well as giving him the titles **Master of Song, Angel of Glory** and **Angel of Prayer**. His support of the repentant has led to him being called **The Angel of Tears**. He is one of the most significant angels in Kabbalah. He is counted by some among the ANGELS OF THE PRESENCE. Others say he is the great prophet Elijah, who after being carried alive up to heaven in a fiery chariot was transformed into Sandalphon, just as Enoch was transformed into METATRON. Because of this he is called Metatron's twin (one possible interpretation of the name is 'co-brother'). In this role he stands at the crossways of paradise to guide the pious to their appointed places. Accounts stress his great size. One of his tasks is to weave the prayers of the faithful into garlands for God. In magic Sandalfon also has power over air. He figures prominently in modern literary treatments of angels: Longfellow wrote a poem called *Sandalphon*, where he is called 'Angel of Glory' and 'Angel of Prayer'; he figures in *Neon Genesis Evangelon* and a number of other fantasy works.

Sanfael An angel presiding over Thursday, the day of Jove, according to the *Liber Juratus* and the Sloane manuscript *Book of Raziel*.

Sanficiel An angel of the east of the fifth heaven in the Sloane manuscript *Book of Raziel*.

Sangariel An angel who guards the portals of heaven, whose name is used for conjuration in the *Key of Solomon*.

Sangha see NASARGIEL

Sangiel The angel that rules the fourth degree of Virgo under VOIL, according to the *Lemegeton*.

Saniel The angel who rules the sixth hour of the day according to the *Lemegeton*. He has many angels under him, the chief of whom are **Arnebiel**, **Charuch, Medusiel, Nathmiel, Pemiel**, GAMIEL, **Jenotriel, Sameon, Trasiel, Xamyon, Nedabor, Permon, Brasiel, Camosiel** and **Evadar. Sanael**, an angel of the south of the third heaven in the Sloane manuscript *Book of Raziel*, is likely to be an alternative spelling. Sanael is also the angel that rules the third degree of Pisces under PASIL, according to the *Lemegeton*.

Sansanui, Sansenoy One of the three angels (the others being **Sennoi, Sanuy** or **Senoy** and **Samangaluf** or **Semangelof**) said in Jewish tradition to have brought Adam's first wife Lilith back to him when she first left him. Lilith was later rejected by Adam and became a demon who preys on infants (see CHILDBED ANGELS). In another version of the story she is said to have fled to the Red Sea and then mated with Asmodeus and other demons and given birth to innumerable children. The three angels are said to have threatened to kill one hundred of Lilith's children for each day she stayed away from Adam. But Lilith refused to return and said that from then on she would prey on the descendants of Adam and Eve. Because of his earlier role, Sansanui's name and those of the other two angels was used on charms as a protection against her. **Sansani** or **Sansany**, an angel of the eighth lunar month in the *Liber Juratus* and the Sloane manuscript *Book of Raziel*, appears to be the same name.

Saoriel An angel of the south of the fourth heaven in the Sloane manuscript *Book of Raziel*.

Sapiel In the Sloane manuscript *Book of Raziel* an angel with power over water. In the *Heptameron* he is described as an angel of the fourth heaven. He is ruler of the Lord's Day as well as a GUARDIAN ANGEL to be invoked from the north.

Sapsi An angel of the sixth lunar month according to the Sloane manuscript *Book of Raziel*. The name is **Saspy** in the *Liber Juratus*.

Saracus An angel of the fourth lunar month according to the *Liber Juratus* and the Sloane manuscript *Book of Raziel*.

Sarafil, Sarafin see ISRAFIL

Sarakika'il An angel invoked in exorcism in Arabic tradition.

Saranana The *Lemegeton* says that this is an angel that can be invoked to control the loss or gain of wealth. When conjured it appears as a child or small woman, dressed in green and silver, wearing a wreath of bay leaves decorated with white and green flowers, and leaves a sweet smell behind.

Sarandiel Angel of the twelfth hour of the night according to the *Lemegeton*. His main attendant angels are ADONIEL, **Damasiel**, AMBRIEL, **Meriel, Denaryz, Emarion, Kabriel, Marachy, Chabrion, Nestoriel, Zachriel, Naveriel, Damery, Namael, Hardiel, Nefrias, Irmanotzod, Gerthiel, Dromiel, Ladrotzod** and **Melanas.**

Saraqael, **Saraquel**, **Sanakiel** An ARCHANGEL who in *1 Enoch* and one of the Dead Sea Scrolls is set over the spirits that sin. Elsewhere Saraqael is listed amongst the ANGELS OF THE PRESENCE, or described as the ruler of the MINISTERING ANGELS who presides over their councils and who shares the rule of Aries with **Sataaran**.

Sarasael An angel who appears only in *3 Baruch*, where he reveals to Noah that the vine that SATAN had planted in paradise and used to deceived Adam and Eve was washed out of paradise by the Flood. He instructs Noah to plant the vine and cultivate it, for the wine it makes will eventually be transubstantiated into the blood of God, just as Jesus Christ's sacrifice will eventually enable Man to return to the paradise that the vine helped them be expelled from.

Sardiel see PAMYEL

Sarfiel see OSMADIEL

Sargnamuf, **Sarananuf** In the *Liber Juratus* and the Sloane manuscript *Book of Raziel*, an angel of the tenth lunar month.

Sargolais An angel identified by Alma Daniel, Timothy Wyllie and Andrew Ramer in their influential book *Ask Your Angels* as their companion angel during the writing of the book. Sargolais, they say, is pronounced sar-go-lie-iss. This angel has been cited in a number of other modern works on angels.

Sarican, **Sarycam** One of the angels of the seventh lunar month according to the *Liber Juratus* and the Sloane manuscript *Book of Raziel*.

Sariel, **Seriel**, **Samuil** Sariel is the name of one of the two angels who take Enoch up to heaven, and then become the guardians of Enoch according to *2 Enoch*. The other is called RAGUEL or Raguil. Confusingly, as Seriel, which appears to be the same name, he is described as one of the GRIGORI who taught Mankind the signs of the moon. In a fragment known as *The War of the Sons of Light against the Sons of Darkness*, one of the Dead Sea Scrolls, Sariel is a WARRIOR ANGEL, one of the four angelic leaders of the forces of good. In occultism he is one of the nine angels of the summer equinox, governor of the sign of Aries, shares power over the south with **Corabiel** and MICHAEL, or is an angel of the ninth lunar month. **Sereriel**, an angel of the first lunar month, may be the same name.

Sarman In the *Liber Juratus* and the Sloane manuscript *Book of Raziel*, an angel of the tenth lunar month. If invoked in rites his name will ensure good results.

Sarmas An angel of the eighth lunar month according to the Sloane manuscript *Book of Raziel*. The name is **Saneinas** in the *Liber Juratus*.

Sarmon see ZAAZENACH

Sarmozyn see SERQUANICH

Saron This is one of the angels presiding over Saturday, the day of Saturn or Sabat, according to the *Liber Juratus* and the Sloane manuscript *Book of Raziel*. If invoked appropriately and in a state of purity, he will aid you.

Sarosh see SRAOSHA

Sarsac An angel of the fourth lunar month according to the *Liber Juratus* and the Sloane manuscript *Book of Raziel*.

Sarsaf An angel of the second lunar month in the Sloane manuscript *Book of Raziel*. The name is **Sarsall** in the *Liber Juratus*.

Sasael The angel that rules the seventh degree of Cancer under CAEL, according to the *Lemegeton*.

Sasajah The angel that rules the seventh degree of Capricorn under CASUJOJAH, according to the *Lemegeton*.

Sasci, **Sascy** An angel of the eighth lunar month in the *Liber Juratus* and the Sloane manuscript *Book of Raziel*.

Sasnigiel YHWH A mighty angel in *3 Enoch*. It appears to be a form of the name **Seganzagel** one of the names of METATRON. Some books give this name as **Sagnessagiel**, and it is also found as **Sagansagel**. He is a prince of wisdom and chief of the angelic guard of the seventh heaven.

Sasquiel The angel of the fifth hour of the day in the *Lemegeton*.

Sasuagos, **Susuagos** In the *Liber Juratus* and the Sloane manuscript *Book of Raziel*, an angel of the thirteenth lunar month (March). If invoked in the relevant month, he will ensure success in your enterprise.

Sasuyel The angel with power over the second lunar month according to the *Liber Juratus* and the Sloane manuscript version of *The Book of Raziel*, through whose power a man may know his future.

Sataaran see SARAQAEL

Satael An angel of Tuesday in the *Heptameron*.

Satan, **Shaitan**, **Shaytan** The name Satan means 'the adversary' or 'the accuser'. In early Jewish writing he is not a FALLEN ANGEL, but the prosecutor in the court of heaven, and the word is not a name but a job description, the prime original role of Satan(s) being to accuse Mankind or the individual soul, before the Mercy Seat. He is found in a similar role when he is sent to test Job in the Book of Job. In *3 Enoch* Satan sits alongside DUBBIEL and Samael every day to write down the sins of Israel. They pass the writing tablets to the SERAPHIM to pass on to God, but the Seraphim burn them instead. In the New Testament this has changed and he becomes Satan with a capital S and the enemy of God, with titles such as 'Prince of the world' (John 16:11), 'Prince of the power of the air' (Ephesians 2:2) and 'the father of lies and murder' (John 5:19; see the story of Cain, below).

In angelic form he was the greatest of the angels in heaven, with twelve wings, instead of the normal six. According to some, the reason he and his followers were cast out of heaven was because Satan refused to bow down to the newly created Adam, a story which is also told of IBLIS. Another story, which identifies Satan with Samael, makes Satan a seducer of the fallen Eve, and Cain, her first child and the man who introduces murder to the world, the fruit of their union. 'Cain's descent from Satan,' says Ginzberg, 'was revealed in his seraphic appearance.'

Because the name was originally descriptive, it gets attached to a number of other FALLEN ANGELS or similar figures who lead man astray, such as AZAZAEL, SATANAIL, Samael and Iblis. So confused is the identification of 'Satan' with these figures that the proper name can vary in different translations of the same work, so that, for example in *3 Baruch* the name of Satan is given as SATANAEL in the Slavonic translation but as Samael in the Greek one. This is less surprising when one realises that both Jewish and Muslim texts often speak of 'the Satans' in the plural. Satan, according to some traditions, was originally called Satanael, but lost the –el element so common in angel names and meaning 'God', when he fell. In *Jubilees* and other texts he is called MASTEMA. The identifi-cation with LUCIFER is due to a misreading of the text where the name occurs. Some texts say that Satan's pride stems from the fact that he was the first angel created, although others say he was created on the sixth day. Shaytan or Shaitan is the Arabic spelling of the name and, while particularly associated with Iblis, is again used as a description, rather than a name (see also under IFRIT and KARIN). Some identify the MALAK TA'US with Satan.

Satanael, **Satanail** Satanael is leader of the GRIGORI according to *2 Enoch* 18. Others say it is SEMYAZA. Satanael is said to have been the original name of SATAN, but he was deprived of the divine ending –el when he fell.

Satarel One of the GRIGORI, 'a chief of ten', according to *1 Enoch* 6.

Satavaesa, **Sataves** A star YAZAD (Zoroastrian angel). He is the chieftain of the west and associated with the planet Anahid (Venus). (See further under TISHTRYA).

Satiel The angel that rules the second degree of Leo under OL, according to the *Lemegeton*.

Saton, **Santon** An angel of the second lunar month according to the *Liber Juratus* and the Sloane manuscript *Book of Raziel* with the power to grant wishes.

Satpach An angel of the sixth lunar month according to the *Liber Juratus* and the Sloane manuscript *Book of Raziel*, which says that if they are named 'in each thing that thou wilt do … thou shalt profit'.

Satquiel, **Satquel** *3 Enoch* says Satquiel is an angelic PRINCE, who is in charge of the fifth heaven, Maon. In the Sloane manuscript of *The Book of Raziel* he is the angel of the planet Jupiter (or Zedek) so he should probably be identified with SACHIEL in this instance. Confusingly, the same paragraph describes him as angel of Mercury (Cocab), although elsewhere the manuscript gives this role to MICHAEL. He is also described there as an angel of the east of the third heaven. The *Liber Juratus* includes Satquiel in elaborate instructions which involve inscribing angel names on magic symbols, and also calls him the angel of Jupiter and thus of Thursday and gives his seal or sigil.

Satuel An angel of the ninth lunar

month according to the *Liber Juratus* and the Sloane manuscript *Book of Raziel*.

Satyn In the Sloane manuscript *Book of Raziel*, an angel of the eleventh lunar month. If invoked in the relevant month, he will ensure success in your enterprise. The name is **Satymn** in the *Liber Juratus*.

Satziel The angel that rules the sixth degree of Scorpio under JOSEL and the sixth degree of Sagittarius under SUIAJASEL, according to the *Lemegeton*.

Savael The angel that rules the nineteenth degree of Cancer under CAEL, according to the *Lemegeton*.

Savanghi see VISYA

Savaniah In *The Key of Solomon* an angel whose name appears on the Third Pentacle of Mercury.

Saviel The angel that rules the twentieth degree of Leo under OL, according to the *Lemegeton*.

Saziel The angel that rules the fifth degree of Libra under JAEL, according to the *Lemegeton*.

Schemhamphorae see SHEMHAM-PHORAE

Schioel In *The Key of Solomon* an angel whose name appears on the First Pentacle of the Moon, which 'serveth to open doors, in whatever way they may be fastened'. Some say he helps win lawsuits and legal protection

Schliel, Scheliel A MOON ANGEL who rules the seventh mansion of the moon in Gemini. While he has a malign influence on rulers, he supports profit, friendship and lovers.

Sealtiel Considered by some to be an ARCHANGEL with special care of contemplation and worship. He is one of several angels credited with having stopped Abraham from sacrificing Isaac (Genesis 22:12). He is also said to be angel of the Spheres, Spring and Thursday.

Sedim see AZAEL

Seeliah, Saeliah, Sehaliah, Sealiah This angel is said to be able to give long life and happiness and to improve the health of those that invoke him. He governs vegetation. He is also one of the seventy-two angels who bear the mystic name of God, SHEMHAMPHORAE. As the GUARDIAN ANGEL of those born under the sign of Scorpio between 3 and 7 November he is described as an angel of awakening who brings to fruition dormant qualities.

Sefira, Sephira (plural Sefirot(h), Sephiroth) In the Kabbalah the Sefiroth are the ten emanations by which the infinite interacts with the finite. They are ways of making the intangible and incomprehensible nature of the divine graspable by the human mind. There are said to be ten holy and ten unholy Sefira. The ten holy ones come from God's right side and the unholy ones from his left. Each has its own ARCHANGEL. Although there are variations, this is the most common list of the Holy Sefiroth: 1) KETHER, The Crown, archangel METATRON; 2) **Chockmah**, Wisdom, archangel

RAZIEL; 3) BINAH, Intelligence, Understanding, archangel TZAPHQIEL; 4) **Chesed**, Love, Mercy, archangel TZADKIEL; 5) GEBURAH, Strength, archangel CAMAEL; 6) TIPHARETH, Beauty, Compassion, archangel RAPHAEL; 7) NETZACH, Victory, archangel HANIEL; 8) **Hod**, Splendour, archangel MICHAEL; 9) YESOD, Foundation, Archangel GABRIEL; 10) MALKUTH, Kingdom, Archangels METATRON and SANDALPHON. There is more doubt about the names of the Unholy Sefiroth, which are averse to the Holy ones, but some say they are: 1) Thaumiel; 2) Chaigdiel; 3) Sathariel or Sheireil; 4) Gamchicoth or Gog Sheklah; 5) Golab; 6) Togarini; 7) Harab Serap; 8) SAMMAEL; 9) GAMALIEL; 10) **Lilith**.

Seganzagel see SASNIGIEL

Seheiah An angel who can bring protection against fire and sickness and bestows longevity. As the GUARDIAN ANGEL of those born under Leo between 7 and 12 August he is said to be an angel of protection who watches over travellers and guards against natural disasters.

Sekiel The angel that rules the eleventh degree of Leo under OL, according to the *Lemegeton*.

Sekinah, **Shekinah** In mystic texts the Sekinah is the visible manifestation of God's presence (but most emphatically not God Himself). There is a tradition that angels feed on the radiance that comes from it. In *3 Enoch* we are told that from the day that God banished Adam and Eve from the Garden of Eden, the Sekinah resided on a cherub

beneath the Tree of Life. Some interpret the Sekinah as a feminine principle, and describe her as 'the bride of God'.

Semeol One of the angels of Wednesday, the day of Mercury, according to the *Liber Juratus* and the Sloane manuscript *Book of Raziel*.

Semhahylyn, **Shemhazylyn** According to the *Liber Juratus* and the Sloane manuscript *Book of Raziel* this is one of the GUARDIAN ANGELS with special care of Monday.

Semjaza see SEMYAZA

Semquiel An angel of the first lunar month according to the Sloane manuscript *Book of Raziel*. The name takes the form **Seniquiel** in the *Liber Juratus*.

Semyaza, **Semyaz**, **Shemhazai**, **Semiaza**, **Semjaza**, **Shamazya** In *1 Enoch 6* Semyaza is the leader of the GRIGORI, the fallen WATCHERS: 'In those days, when the children of man had multiplied, it happened that there were born unto them handsome and beautiful daughters. And the angels, the children of heaven, saw them and desired them; and they said to one another, "Come, let us choose wives for ourselves from among the daughters of man and beget us children." And Semyaz, being their leader, said unto them, "I fear that perhaps you will not consent that this deed should be done, and I alone will become responsible for this great sin." But they all responded to him, "Let us all swear an oath and bind everyone among us by a curse not to abandon this suggestion but to do the deed".' As a result 200 angels came down to earth to consort with the women, and Prometheus-like, taught Mankind all sorts of skills that were beforehand secrets of heaven. Indeed, in some accounts it is this betrayal of secret knowledge which is the great sin of the FALLEN ANGELS rather than their sexual activity. The subject of just how angels and humans have sex has been, however, the source of much discussion among theologians. Each of the Grigori taught Mankind particular skills. Semyaza, called by some **Satanael** or **Salamiel**, and by Ginzberg Shemhazai, taught Mankind enchantment and 'the cutting of roots', which perhaps means making magic potions, according to tradition, although *1 Enoch* ascribes this to other Grigori. The offspring of the angels and women were the giant NEPHILIM, who brought violence and destruction to earth until eliminated by the Flood. At this point in the story as told in *1 Enoch,* AZAZEL rather takes over as the villain from Semyaza. All that *1 Enoch* has to add is that Semyaza will see his children destroyed and that God orders MICHAEL to take Semyaza and his followers and 'bind them for seventy generations underneath the rocks of the ground until the day of their judgment and of their consummation, until the eternal judgement is concluded. In those days they will lead them into the bottom of the fire – and in torment – in the prison where they will be locked up forever.'

Others tell a different version of the story. Ginzberg says, 'When the angels came to earth, and beheld the daughters of men in all their grace and beauty, they could not restrain their passion. Shemhazai saw a maiden named Istehar, and he lost his heart to her. She promised to surrender herself to him, if first he taught her the Ineffable Name, by means of which he raised himself to heaven. He assented to her condition.' But once she knew it, she pronounced the Name, and herself ascended to heaven, without fulfilling her promise to the angel. God said, 'Because she kept herself aloof from sin, we will place her among the seven stars, that men may never forget her,' and she was put in the constellation of the Pleiades. (A similar story is told of HARUT AND MARUT.)

According to another story Ginzberg tells, based on *The Zohar*, Shemhazai has two sons by a daughter of Eve. 'These two sons of Shemhazai, **Hiwwa** and **Hiyya** by name, dreamed dreams. The one saw a great stone which covered the earth, and the earth was marked all over with lines upon lines of writing. An angel came, and with a knife obliterated all the lines, leaving but four letters upon the stone. The other son saw a large pleasure grove planted with all sorts of trees. But angels approached bearing axes, and they felled the trees, sparing a single one with three of its branches. When Hiwwa and Hiyya awoke, they repaired to their father, who interpreted the dreams for them, saying, "God will bring a deluge, and none will escape with his life, excepting only Noah and his sons." When they heard this, the two began to cry and scream, but their father consoled them: "Soft, soft! Do not grieve. As often as men cut or haul stones, or launch vessels, they shall invoke your names, Hiwwa! Hiyya!" This prophecy soothed them.'

Even Semyaza's ultimate fate is debated, for one version says that he repented, although Azazel did not, and hung himself upside-down from the constellation of Orion, suspended between heaven and earth. For the role of **Samahazai** in Robertson Davies' novel *The Rebel Angels* see under AZAZEL.

Senael The angel that rules the second degree of Virgo under VOIL, according to the *Lemegeton*.

Sengael The angel that rules the eighth degree of Leo under OL, according to the *Lemegeton*.

Sennoi, **Senoy**, **Sanuy** see SANSANUI

Sephatia, **Sephatya** An angel of the first lunar month according to the *Liber Juratus* and the Sloane manuscript *Book of Raziel*.

Sephiroth see SEFIRA

Serael An angel of the north of the fourth heaven in the Sloane manuscript *Book of Raziel*.

Seraphim According to Isaiah 6:2–7, each in this highest category of angels has six wings: 'with two they covered their faces, and with two they covered their feet, and with two they flew'. They resemble here the six-winged god El/Kronos mentioned by Eusebius of Caesarea (*Praeparatio Evangelica* 1.10.36–38) as worshipped in the Middle East. As the Seraphim surround the throne of the Lord, they call to one another: 'Holy, holy, holy is the Lord of hosts; the whole earth is full of his glory,' lines that are incorporated into the liturgy at the beginning of the Eucharistic Prayer. In the visions of Enoch and other MERKABAH literature, the Seraphim are regularly mentioned as surrounding the throne of God,

singing his praises. They are often described as frightening: 'the fiery seraphim fixed their gaze on me, I shrank back trembling and fell down stunned by the radiant appearance of their eyes and the bright vision of their faces' (*3 Enoch* 1). This can have its advantages, for there is a Jewish tradition, according to Ginzberg, that once a year the Seraphim approach the world of spirits, and intimidate them so that they fear to do harm to men. *3 Enoch* 26 says there are four Seraphim, one for each of the winds of the world. They have six wings for the six days of Creation, sixteen faces, and shine so brightly that even the CHERUBIM cannot look at them. The name Seraph is based on the word for 'to burn', and *3 Enoch* says they are so called because they burn the tablets on which SATAN, SAMMAEL and DUBBIEL write down the sins of Israel. These are passed to the Seraphim to pass on to God, but they make sure that they never reach Him. In the *Testament of Adam* they serve the inner chamber of the Lord. In some magic texts they are described as having power over the air. They are ranked fifth by Maimonides and third by *The Zohar* in the HIERARCHY OF THE ANGELS, but the standard Christian hierarchy, based on Dionysius, makes them the highest rank of all. In art, Seraphim are traditionally shown with bright red wings of which they have one, two or three pairs. They often are simply a face surrounded by wings, but if shown with bodies they may have bare feet and may carry a sword or a candle.

Serapiel, **Seraphiel** *3 Enoch* describes Serapiel as the prince of the SERAPHIM; 'His face is like the face of angels, and his body is like the body of eagles.' He teaches the other Seraphim how to sing the praise of God. In the Sloane manuscript *Book of Raziel* he is an angel of the north of the fourth heaven. JAHOEL has also been called chief of the Seraphim.

Seriel see SARIEL

Serquanich The angel in charge of the third hour of the night 'who hath 101,550 servant Dukes and servants to attend him,' according to the *Lemegeton*. The chief of these are **Menarym, Chrusiel, Penargos, Amriel, Demanoz, Nestoroz, Evanuel, Sarmozyn, Haylon, Quabriel, Thurmytz, Fronyzon, Vanosyr, Lemaron, Almonoyz, Janothyel, Melrotz** and **Xanthyozod**.

Sersael The angel that rules the tenth degree of Cancer under CAEL, according to the *Lemegeton*.

Serviel see VEQUANIEL

Sethiel The angel that rules the thirteenth degree of Cancer under CAEL, according to the *Lemegeton*. **Setiel**, the angel that rules the twenty-second degree of Gemini under GIEL is probably the same angel.

Shahrewar see KHSHATHRA VAIRYA

Shalgiel, Salgiel The angel of the snow according to texts such as *3 Enoch*.

Shamdon One of the GRIGORI, who was led astray by the wanton behaviour of the beautiful **Naamah**, the lovely sister of Tubal-cain and, by her, became the father of the devil Asmodeus.

Shamiel According to Ginzberg, 'the

august Divine herald, the angel Sham'iel, steps to the windows of the lowest heaven to hearken to the songs, prayers, and praises that ascend from the synagogues and the houses of learning, and when they are finished, he announces the end to the angels in all the heavens.' Only then can the angels in heaven start their songs of praise to God. There is a Syriac charm in which he is one of the angels invoked alongside MARIEL to 'bind, ban, stop the mouth and tongues of evil men, jealous and wicked judges, emirs, satraps, governors, men in authority, rulers and chiefs, executioners, prefects, the foreigner, the gentile, the infidel. I bind the mouths of all wicked judges, and all the sons of Adam and Eve, evil ones, men, women, and children; I bind their tongues and lips, their minds and thoughts, those of wicked ones, rebels, judges, court-officials, and prefects; and the lips of the emir, prefects, executioners, satraps, and rulers.'

Shamsiel, Shamshiel, Simsiel The angel of the day whose name comes from the Hebrew for 'sun'. However, some traditions give **Yomiel**, based on the Hebrew *yom* 'day', as the angel of the day. One of the ANGELS OF PARADISE who guards Eden, Shamshiel was Moses' guide when he was taken up to heaven. In *The Zohar* he is chief of 365 legions of angels and is one of two aids to URIEL in battle. However, according to *1 Enoch*, he fell with the GRIGORI and later taught Mankind to understand the signs of the sun. The name is also quite widely known as the fourth angel in the anime series *Neon Genesis Evangelion*, the second one that Shinji has to fight.

Sharka'il An angel invoked in exorcism

in Arabic tradition.

Shaytan see SATAN

Shekinah see SEKINAH

Shemeshiel One of the angels whose name is used in the Second Pentacle of the Sun which 'serveth to repress the pride and arrogance of the Solar Spirits, which are altogether proud and arrogant by their nature' in *The Key of Solomon*.

Shemhamphorae Exodus 23:21 tells us that God's name dwells in His angels. *Shem* is Hebrew for 'name' and in angel names indicates the name of God. The *phorae* part comes from Greek, indicating 'bearing'. These seventy-two angels bear the many names of God found in the Hebrew scriptures. Each angel has a verse from the Bible which illustrates one aspect of God's name and nature and both name and verse are much used in magic, and knowledge of the names of God, both secret and revealed, is considered to confer great power. As English lacks the richness of synonyms found in Hebrew, these names are simply translated as 'Lord'. The exact names and actual number of these angels vary, but a standard list, although it has some contradictory repetitions, is as follows. Each angel is given with its name and the biblical verse in English. **Vehujah**, whose verse is 'Thou, O Lord, art my guardian, and exaltest my head.' **Ieliel**, whose verse is 'Do not remove Thy help from me, O Lord, and look to my defence.' **Sirael**, whose verse is 'I shall say so to the Lord, Thou art my guardian, my God is my refuge, and I shall hope in Him.' **Elemijel**, whose verse is, 'Turn, O Lord, and deliver my soul, and save me for Thy mercy's sake.' **Lelahal**, whose verse is 'Let him who lives in Zion sing unto the Lord, and proclaim His goodwill among the peoples.' **Achajah**, whose verse is 'The Lord is merciful and compassionate, long-suffering and of great goodness.' MAHASIAH, whose verse is 'I called upon the Lord and he heard me and delivered me from all my tribulations.' CAHATEL, whose verse is 'O come let us adore and fall down before God who bore us.' HAZIEL, whose verse is 'Remember Thy mercies, O Lord, and Thy mercies which have been forever.' ALADIAH, whose verse is 'Perform Thy mercies upon us, for we have hoped in Thee.' **Laviah**, whose verse is 'The Lord liveth, blessed is my God, and let the God of my salvation be exalted.' HAHAIAH, whose verse is 'Why has Thou departed, O Lord, so long from us perishing in the times of tribulation.' **Jezalel**, whose verse is 'Rejoice in the Lord, all ye lands, sing, exult, and play upon a stringed instrument.' MEBAHEL, whose verse is 'The Lord is a refuge, and my God the help of my hope.' HARIEL, whose verse is 'The Lord is a refuge for me and my God the help of my hope.' HAKAMIAH, whose verse is 'O Lord, God of my salvation, by day have I called to Thee, and sought Thy presence by night.' LEUVIAH, whose verse is 'O Lord our Lord, How wonderful is Thy name in all the world.' CALIEL, whose verse is 'Judge me, O Lord according to Thy loving kindness, and let not them be joyful over me, O Lord.' **Luviah**, whose verse is 'I waited in hope for the Lord, and He turned to me.' PAHALIAH, whose verse is 'I shall call upon the name of the Lord, O Lord free my soul.' **Nelakhel**, whose verse is 'In Thee also have I hoped, O Lord, and said, Thou art my God.'

Jajajel, whose verse is 'The Lord keep thee, the Lord be thy protection on thy right hand.' MELAHEL, whose verse is 'The Lord keep thine incoming and thine outgoing from this time forth for evermore.' **Hahajah**, whose verse is 'The Lord is well pleased with those that fear Him and hope upon His mercy.' **Haajah**, whose verse is 'I have called unto Thee with all my heart and shall tell forth all Thy wonders.' **Nithhaja**, whose verse is 'I shall acknowledge Thee, O Lord, with all my heart, hear me, O Lord, and I shall seek my justification.' **Jerathel**, whose verse is 'Save me, O Lord, from the evil man and deliver me from the wicked doer.' **Sehijah**, whose verse is 'Let not God depart from me, look to my help, O God.' **Rejajel**, whose verse is 'Behold, God is my helper, and the Lord is the guardian of my soul.' OMAEL, whose verse is 'For thou art my strength, O Lord, O Lord, Thou art my hope from my youth.' LECABEL, whose verse is 'I shall enter into the power of the Lord, my God, I shall be mindful of Thy justice only.' VASARIAH, whose verse is 'For the word of the Lord is upright, and all his words faithful.' **Jehuvajah**, whose verse is 'The Lord knows the thoughts of men, for they are in vain.' LEHAHIAH, whose verse is 'Let Israel hope in the Lord from this time forth and for evermore.' CHAVAKIAH, whose verse is 'I am joyful, for the Lord hears the voice of my prayer.' **Manadel**, whose verse is 'I have delighted in the beauty of Thy house, O Lord, and in the place of the habitation of Thy glory.' **Aniel** (HANIEL), whose verse is 'O Lord God, turn Thy power towards us, and show us Thy face and we shall be saved.' HAAMIAH, whose verse is 'For Thou art my hope, O Lord, and Thou hast been

my deepest refuge.' REHAEL, whose verse is 'The Lord has heard me and pitied me and the Lord is my helper'. **Jejazel**, whose verse is 'Why drivest Thou away my soul, O Lord, and turnest Thy face from me?' HAHA(H)EL, whose verse is 'O Lord, deliver my soul from wicked lips and a deceitful tongue'. MICHAEL, whose verse is 'The Lord protects thee from all evil and will protect thy soul.' **Vevaliah**, whose verse is 'I have cried unto Thee, O Lord, and let my prayer come unto Thee.' **Jelabiah**, whose verse is 'Make my wishes pleasing unto Thee, O Lord, and teach me Thy judgements.' **Sealiah** (see SEELIAH), whose verse is 'If I say that my foot is moved, Thou wilt help me of Thy mercy.' ARIEL, whose verse is 'The Lord is pleasant to all the world and His mercies are over all His works.' ASALIAH, whose verse is 'How wonderful are Thy works, O Lord, and how deep Thy thoughts.' MICHAEL(again), whose verse is 'The Lord hath made thy salvation known in the sight of the people and will reveal His justice.' **Vehael** (VEHUEL), whose verse is 'Great is the Lord and worthy to be praised, and there is no end to His greatness'. DANIEL, whose verse is 'The Lord is pitiful and merciful, long-suffering and of great goodness.' HAHASIAH, whose verse is 'Let the Lord be in glory for ever and the Lord will rejoice in His works.' IMAMIAH, whose verse is 'I shall make known the Lord, according to His justice, and sing hymns to the name of the Lord, the greatest.' NANAEL, whose verse is 'I have known Thee, O Lord, for Thy judgments are just, and in Thy trust have I abased myself.' NITHAEL, whose verse is 'The Lord hath prepared His seat in heaven and His rule shall be over all.' MEBAHIAH, whose verse is 'Thou remainest for ever, O Lord, and Thy memorial is from generation to generation.' **Polial**, whose verse is 'The Lord raiseth up all who fall and setteth up the broken.' **Namamiah**, whose verse is 'They who fear the Lord have hope in the Lord, He is their helper and their protector.' **Jejalel**, whose verse is 'My soul is greatly troubled, but Thou, O Lord are here also.' HARAEL or Harahel, whose verse is 'From the rising of the Sun to the going down of the same, the word of the Lord is worthy to be praised.' MITZRAEL, whose verse is 'The Lord is just in all His ways and blessed in all His works.' UMABEL, whose verse is 'Let the name of the Lord be blessed from this time for evermore.' **Iahael**, whose verse is 'See, O Lord, how I have delighted in Thy commandments according to Thy life-giving mercy.' **Anaviel**, whose verse is 'Serve ye the Lord with gladness and enter into His sight with exultation.' **Mehikiel**, whose verse is 'Behold the eyes of the Lord are upon those that fear Him and hope in His loving kindness.' DAMABIAH, whose verse is 'Turn, O Lord, even here also, and be pleased with Thy servants'. **Meniel**, whose verse is 'Neither leave me, Lord, nor depart from me.' **Ejael**, whose verse is 'Delight in the Lord and He will give thee petitions of thy heart.' **Habujah**, whose verse is 'Confess to the Lord, for He is God, and his mercy is for ever.' **Roehel**, whose verse is 'The Lord is my inheritance and my cup and it is Thou who restorest mine inheritance.' JABAMIAH, whose verse is 'In the beginning God created the heaven and the earth.' **Hajael**, whose verse is 'I shall confess to the Lord with my mouth and praise Him in the midst of the multitude.' **Mumijah**, whose verse is 'Return to thy rest, my soul, for the Lord doeth thee good.'

Shemhazai see SEMYAZA

Shetel see ANUSH, MINISTERING ANGELS

Shoperial see SOPERIEL

Sidriel The angel prince in charge of the first heaven, Wilon, a name that comes from the Latin *velum* 'curtain, veil'. There are two interpretations of this veil: either that this forms the division between the heavens and earth, hiding the Divine from Man; or else that its opening and shutting gives us night and day.

Silat see DJINN

Simapesiel One of the GRIGORI according to *1 Enoch*.

Simiel, Simyllyel An angel of the element earth, under the planet Labana (Luna, the moon), to be invoked when working under this planet, according to the Sloane manuscript *Book of Raziel*. He is also a REPROBATED ANGEL.

Simkiel Chief of the ANGELS OF DESTRUCTION in *3 Enoch*. As well as destroying Man he can purify him.

Simsiel see SHAMSIEL

Sirens In Greek myth sirens are birds with beautiful women's heads, although in later traditions they became women with fishes' tails or in other words mermaids. In their earlier form they are well known in legend as temptresses with beautiful voices who tried to lure sailors, such as Odysseus, to their doom. However, in religion they were associated with the souls of the dead, and were invoked at the moment of death. As such, they have obvious links to ANGELS OF DEATH. The ALKASNOSTS appear to be a transitional form between siren and angels.

Sitael Sitael is invoked to overcome adversity. He is a SERAPH and one of the seventy-two angels of the zodiac and the seventy-two SHEMHAMPHORAE. As the guardian angel of those born under Aries between 1 and 4 April he is said to be an angel of bloom who bestows idealism combined with the practical skills to put it into effect.

Skellig In David Almond's prize-winning novel *Skellig* (1998), this is the name, as nearly as Michael the boy who finds him can tell, of the person he finds in a dilapidated garage. Skellig is a dirty, sick, degraded and depressed figure, who could pass for a tramp, were it not for something strange about him. At the same time as Michael and a friend are caring for Skellig, Michael's little sister is desperately ill. At the point at which she starts to recover, Skellig too turns from despondency to joy as angel wings burst from his back and he recovers his true nature. In this book, written for older children, but much admired by adults, Almond spells nothing out. Skellig is not metaphor or GUARDIAN ANGEL, but just is. It is left to the reader to interpret as he wants.

Snynyel An angel presiding over Thursday in the Sloane manuscript *Book of Raziel*.

Sodiel, **Sodyel** An angel of the eighth lunar month according to the *Liber Juratus* and the Sloane manuscript *Book of Raziel*, which says that if they are named 'in each thing that thou wilt

do ... thou shalt profit.'

Solomon's Seal According to legend, found for example in the *Testament of Solomon* (written some time between the first and third century AD), when King Solomon was building the Temple in Jerusalem, God sent MICHAEL to give him a magic ring with which he could control demons by the use of magic words, by knowing the correct angel to control the demon and by 'sealing' it with the ring. These demons were then set to use their super-human strength to help build the Temple, or were even built into the structure itself. While traditionally the ring was said to bear the name of God, in Europe the sign on the seal has usually been thought to be the pentagram – the five-pointed star. In the East, it is usually thought of as the six-pointed star formed by two interlocking triangles – what is nowadays usually called the Star of David. (The Star of David has only been thought of as a symbol of Jewry in Europe since the nineteenth century.) This six-pointed star has been widely used as a symbol of good fortune, divine providence, abundance and above all protection since at least Roman times, and was not associated with any race or religion. It is found throughout the Middle East on everything from mosques and synagogues to daily tableware. As a symbol of protection it was particularly used at points that could provide an entry point for evil. These again could vary enormously in scale, to include anything from a city's gates to garments to door locks. The symbols are much used in magic.

Somahi In the Sloane manuscript *Book of Raziel*, an angel of the tenth lunar month. **Sanihay** is the form in the *Liber Juratus*.

Sonatas An angel of the west of the fourth heaven in the Sloane manuscript *Book of Raziel*.

Soperiel and **Shoperial YHWH** In *3 Enoch* 'He who puts to death' and 'He who makes alive' are the two scribe angels in the celestial law courts. The one keeps a record of all those who die; the other a record of those who are subsequently granted eternal life. They stand upon wheels of storm, and write with a quill of fire.

Sophia This is the Greek word for wisdom, familiar from the churches dedicated to Santa Sophia, the Holy Wisdom. The word is feminine in Greek, and she is always interpreted as female. In the Kabbalah she appears as **Binah** (see under SEFIRA). Some see her as the goddess principle in the divine and show her as a crimson-robed angel sitting in glory upon a throne. New Age angelologists see her as the angel of the earth, a female ARCHANGEL of all wisdom, compassion and grace. She is associated variously with MICHAEL, RAPHAEL and in her guise of PISTIS-SOPHIA with SAMAEL.

Sophiel Angel of the Fourth Pentacle of the Moon in *The Key of Solomon*, which says it 'giveth the knowledge of the virtue of all herbs and stones; and unto whomsoever shall name him, he will procure the knowledge of all.' In the Kabbalah he is the intelligence of Jupiter. He is also said to be GUARDIAN ANGEL of fruit and fruit trees.

Soqedhozi YHWY In *3 Enoch*, the

angel in the celestial law courts whose job it is to exercise impartiality as he weighs men's merits in the scales, resisting the urging of SOTERASIEL and ZEHANPURYU.

Soquiel An angel of the south of the first heaven in the Sloane manuscript *Book of Raziel*, who is also listed among those in the west of the first heaven.

Sornadaf An angel of the first lunar month according to the *Liber Juratus* and the Sloane manuscript *Book of Raziel*.

Sosel see JOSEL

Soterasiel A 'great, terrible, and honoured Prince' in *3 Enoch*. He is the accuser in the celestial law courts, who stands for strict justice, and the punishing of men in the four rivers of burning fire. He is opposed by ZEHANPURYU.

Spenta Armaiti Like all Zoroastrian AMESHA SPENTAS (ARCHANGELS) Spenta Armaiti has numerous names. In the Middle Persian Pahlavi she is **Spandarmad** or **Espandarmaz**, in modern Persian she is **Esphand** and in Armenia she is known as **Spendaramet**. Her name means 'Holy Devotion' or 'Holy Serenity'. She is in charge of the earth and is also the guardian of herdsmen and farmers. She has been equated with the Greek goddess Demeter, for she can be interpreted as an earth and fertility goddess, and is described as a daughter of **Ahura Mazda**. She was the fourth Amesha Spenta created and she works with ABAN, an angel of water.

Sraosha, **Sarosh**, **Srosh** Meaning 'Hearkening', this is the name of a spirit being who guards the soul for three days after death in Zoroastrianism. He is usually considered a YAZAD, but some rank him as an AMESHA SPENTA. His name is given to the seventeenth day of the month.

Stelmel, **Steluyel** In the *Liber Juratus* and the Sloane manuscript *Book of Raziel*, an angel of the thirteenth lunar month (March). If invoked in the relevant month, he will ensure success in your enterprise.

Stemehilyn According to the Sloane manuscript *Book of Raziel* this is one of the angels of Monday who should be invoked to aid works started on that day. The name appears as **Semyhylym** in the *Liber Juratus*.

Strubiel see VATHMIEL

Suciel, **Sucyel** An angel of the eighth lunar month according to the *Liber Juratus* and the Sloane manuscript *Book of Raziel*, which says that if they are named 'in each thing that thou wilt do … thou shalt profit'.

Sugni An angel of the first lunar month in the *Liber Juratus* and the Sloane manuscript *Book of Raziel*.

Suiajasel The angel who rules Sagittarius according to the *Lemegeton*.

Suiel see ZIIEL

Suncacer An angel of the west of the fifth heaven in the Sloane manuscript *Book of Raziel*.

Supernaphim In the *Urantia Book* these have been identified as a rank of angels above even the SERAPHIM, which are 'greater in the vastness of their being than the physical universe', and are the essence of perfection.

Suriel A Prince of ANGELS OF THE PRESENCE and an ANGEL OF THE FACE as well as an angel of healing. Also an ANGEL OF DEATH who was sent to fetch the soul of Moses. His relationship with Moses went back in time, for some say that Suriel was the angel who instructed Moses (although some say this was ZAGZAGAEL). He also helps the penitent. In magic he is one of the angels of the seventh lunar month and his name is used in protective charms. When invoked he can take the form of an ox. There is some confusion between Suriel and SACHIEL.

Suruel An alternative name for URIEL.

Suryah A Prince of the Divine Presence, who has the privilege of serving in the immediate presence of God.

Syymelyel, **Syumelyel** An angel presiding over Thursday, the day of Jove, according to the *Liber Juratus* and the Sloane manuscript *Book of Raziel*.

Szarhyr, **Szarzyr** An angel of the third lunar month in the *Liber Juratus* and the Sloane manuscript *Book of Raziel*.

Szeyyeil, **Szeyeyll** An angel presiding over Friday, the day of Venus, according to the *Liber Juratus* and the Sloane manuscript *Book of Raziel*.

Szif In the Sloane manuscript *Book of*

Raziel, an angel of the tenth lunar month. In the *Liber Juratus* what appear as two separate angels in *Raziel*, **Gasta** and Szif, have become one angel called **Gastaset**.

Szucariel One of the angels of the seventh lunar month according to the Sloane manuscript *Book of Raziel*. In the *Liber Juratus* this has become an unconvincing **Szcaryell**.

T

Tabiel In the Sloane manuscript *Book of Raziel*, an angel of the eleventh lunar month. The name is **Talyel** in the *Liber Juratus*.

Tablic An angel of the fifth lunar month in the *Liber Juratus* and the Sloane manuscript *Book of Raziel*, who if invoked brings benefits.

Tachael The angel that rules the eighteenth degree of Pisces under PASIL, according to the *Lemegeton*.

Tadqiel One of the ten ARCHANGELS in the Kabbalah.

Tafti see ALIMON

Tagas In *3 Enoch* Tagas is described as so great an angel that even the four great ARCHANGELS, MICHAEL, GABRIEL, RAPHAEL and URIEL, bow down to him.

Tagiel The angel that rules the twelfth degree of Scorpio under JOSEL, according to the *Lemegeton*.

Tagriel A MOON ANGEL who rules the twenty-sixth mansion of the moon in the transition between Aquarius and Pisces. He destroys buildings and prisons, but causes harmony, and health in prisoners. He is also the chief angelic guard of either the second or seventh heaven. Although Agrippa gives the name as Tagriel, the *Liber Juratus* calls him **Sagriel**.

Tahiel The angel that rules the seventeenth degree of Taurus under TUAL and the seventeenth degree of Gemini under GIEL, according to the *Lemegeton*.

Talgnaf, Talguaf In the *Liber Juratus* and the Sloane manuscript *Book of Raziel*, an angel of the eleventh lunar month. If invoked in the relevant month, he will ensure success in your enterprise.

Talgylnenyl, Talgylueyl According to the *Liber Juratus* and the Sloane manuscript *Book of Raziel* this is one of the angels of Sunday (Solis) who should be invoked to aid works started on that day.

Taliahad Angel of water and one of the angels whose names are used in the Seventh Pentacle of the Sun, which 'If any be by chance imprisoned or detained in fetters of iron, at the presence of this Pentacle, which should be engraved in Gold on the day and hour of the Sun, he will be immediately delivered and set at liberty' in *The Key of Solomon*.

Taliel The angel that rules the first degree of Sagittarius under SUIAJASEL, according to the *Lemegeton*.

Talrailanrain, Talraylanrayn An angel presiding over Friday, the day of Venus, according to the *Liber Juratus* and the Sloane manuscript *Book of Raziel*.

Tamael The angel that rules the eleventh degree of Libra under JAEL in the *Lemegeton*. Elsewhere, he is described as a Friday angel of the third heaven, who is invoked from the east.

Tamaini, Tamaano see MILKIEL

Tameriel see PAMYEL, TARTYS

Tamiel, Tamel, Temel One of the GRIGORI, simply 'a chief of ten', according to some translations of *1 Enoch* 6, but the one who taught Mankind astronomy in the most recent scholarly edition. In the *Lemegeton*, he is the angel that rules the thirteenth degree of Aquarius under AUSIUL. Elsewhere, he is an angel of the deep. **Tamtiel**, in the Sloane manuscript *Book of Raziel*, an angel of the thirteenth lunar month (March), may be a misreading of the same name, as may **Temael**, the angel that rules the second degree of Capricorn under CASUJOJAH, in the *Lemegeton*.

Tangiel The angel that rules the tenth degree of Virgo under VOIL, according to the *Lemegeton*.

Tankafil An angel invoked in exorcism in Arabic tradition.

Tapsarim, Tipsarim A Hebrew word meaning 'scribe' or 'officer' used of angels. In some texts it is used to mean angels in general; in others, such as *3 Enoch*, it is used for a class of angel 'greater than all the ministering angels that serve before the throne of glory'.

Tarael An angel presiding over Thursday in the Sloane manuscript *Book of Raziel*. He is not in the *Liber Juratus*.

Tarajah The angel that rules the ninth degree of Pisces under PASIL, according to the *Lemegeton*.

Taramel An angel of the east of the third heaven in the Sloane manuscript

Book of Raziel.

Tarfanyelyn, **Tralyeylyn** An angel of the day of Mars (Tuesday) in the *Liber Juratus* and the Sloane manuscript *Book of Raziel.*

Tarmanydyn According to the *Liber Juratus* and the Sloane manuscript *Book of Raziel*, this is one of the angels with special care of Monday.

Tarmytz see MENDRION

Tarshishim Derived from a Hebrew word meaning 'Those of Chrysolite', these are one of many classes of angels derived from the description of the Chariot of the Lord (see MERKABAH) in Ezekiel. They have two leaders, **Tarshiel** and SABRAEL.

Tartalyn An angel of the day of Mars (Tuesday) in the *Liber Juratus* and the Sloane manuscript *Book of Raziel.*

Tartys The angel who governs the second hour of the night according to the *Lemegeton*. He has 101,550 attendant angels, of whom the most important are **Almodar, Famoriel, Nedroz, Ormezyn, Chabriz, Praxiel, Permaz, Vameroz, Emaryel** or **Ematyel, Fromezyn, Ramaziel, Granozyn, Gabrinoz, Mercoph, Tameriel, Venomiel, Jenaziel** and **Xemyzin.**

Taryestorat An angel of the east of the third heaven in the Sloane manuscript *Book of Raziel.*

Tashiel The angel that rules the thirteenth degree of Capricorn under CASUJOJAH, according to the *Lemegeton*.

Tata'il An angel invoked in exorcism in Arabic tradition.

Tatgiel An angel of the third lunar month according to the Sloane manuscript *Book of Raziel* whose naming brings benefits.

Tatrasiel or **Tutrasiel YHWH** This is the name of a mighty angel found in *3 Enoch* and other works. It is also found as one of the names of God. It has been suggested that the ultimate source of the name is the Greek *tetras*, 'four', a reference to the four root letters of the root for God, YHWH, which are shared with the most senior angels.

Tediel The angel that rules the twelfth degree of Sagittarius under SUIAJASEL, according to the *Lemegeton*.

Teiaiel This angel shares with IEIAIEL dominion over the future. He also a throne and oversees travelling by sea and commercial transactions.

Teliel The angel that rules the first degree of Scorpio under JOSEL, according to the *Lemegeton*.

Temael, **Temel** see TAMIEL

Temas see BARIEL

Temelion This is one of the angels presiding over Saturday in the Sloane manuscript *Book of Raziel*. **Tonelyn**, which has drifted rather far from Temelion, is the form in the *Liber Juratus*.

Temeluch, Temeluchus, Temleyakos A caretaking angel who cares for the newborn and the baby. In sharp contrast to this, also found as the name of a merciless angel of hell who torments with fire. All souls are delivered to him on the death of the body.

Tenebiel, **Tenebyel** In the *Liber Juratus* and the Sloane manuscript *Book of Raziel*, an angel of the twelfth lunar month. If invoked in the relevant month, he will ensure success in your enterprise.

Terathel, **Ierathel**, **Yeratel**, **Yerathel** In older manuscripts the capital letters T and Y are easily confused, which explains the variations in this name. He is counted among the DOMINIONS and supports light, civilisation and liberty. As a GUARDIAN ANGEL of those born under Leo between 2 and 6 August he is accounted an angel of hope who brings about optimism, joy and peace.

Tesael The angel that rules the third degree of Aquarius under AUSIUL, according to the *Lemegeton*.

Tetragram see YHWH

Tezael The angel that rules the ninth degree of Taurus under TUAL, according to the *Lemegeton*.

Thanatos Thanatos (Death) and **Hypnos** (Sleep) were the Greek equivalents of the ANGELS OF DEATH. They were not generally seen as fearsome, but as kindly spirits, working together. Hypnos could use either his wand or his wings to put someone to sleep and then he and Thanatos could carry off the soul of the dead to the underworld. Although Euripides did put Death on stage as the black-robed figure carrying

a sword, familiar in popular epictions of death, usually Thanatos and Hypnos were shown in art as long-haired youths with magnificent wings sprouting from their shoulders. In other words, except for the fact that they are often unclothed, they are identical to standard Western depictions of angels. This iconography, along with that of other winged spirits of Greece and Rome has had much more influence on our modern Western idea of what an angel looks like than the typical Middle Eastern idea of an angel.

Tharsis see ELEMENTALS

Theliel The angel invoked in magic to win the love of a desired woman.

Themaz see NARCORIEL

Themiton This is one of the angels presiding over Saturday, the day of Saturn or Sabat, according to the Sloane manuscript *Book of Raziel*. If invoked appropriately and in a state of purity, they will aid you.

Theoriel see OSMADIEL

Thesfealin, **Thefelyn** An angel presiding over Friday, the day of Venus, according to the *Liber Juratus* and the Sloane manuscript *Book of Raziel*.

Thribiel see OSMADIEL

Thrones Thrones are not found as a class of angels in the very earliest Jewish texts, but are in the New Testament and become popular in the Middle Ages. They seem to derive from the description of the empty thrones around the Ancient of Days in the Book of Daniel

7:9. They are mentioned in Colossians 1:16 as part of God's creation in Christ. According to Jewish legend there are seventy such beings. Dionysius the Aeropagite ranks them third in the HIERARCHY OF ANGELS. They guard the gate of the holy of holies and stand before the throne of the Lord in the *Testament of Adam*. Some are numbered among the FALLEN ANGELS. The dominant characteristic of those still in heaven is steadfastness. Their leader is variously cited **Oriphiel**, **Zabkiel** or **Zaphkiel**. In art, Thrones are sometimes depicted as fiery wheels, with four wings full of eyes. They can also be shown as angels carrying thrones or scales, which represent their role in divine justice.

Thulcandra see ELDIL

Thurmytz see SERQUANICH

Thuros see VATHMIEL

Tibiel The angel that rules the twentieth degree of Libra under JAEL, according to the *Lemegeton*.

Tiiel The angel that rules the nineteenth degree of Virgo under VOIL, according to the *Lemegeton*.

Tinsiel An angel of the element fire, under the planet Zedek (Jupiter), to be invoked when working under this planet, according to the Sloane manuscript *Book of Raziel*.

Tiogra, **Tyagra** One of the angels of Wednesday, the day of Mercury, according to Sloane manuscript *Book of Raziel*.

Tipareth, **Tiphereth** Representing beauty and compassion, this is one of the angels who preside over the ten SEFIROTH.

Tipsarim see TAPSARIM

Tishtrya, **Tisrya**, **Tishtar**, **Tir**, **Tiri** This is the YAZAD (Zoroastrian angel) presiding over the star Sirius (Canis Major) and directing rain (and thus fertility), who is addressed as 'resplendent and glorious'. In Zoroastrian cosmology RAPITHWIN is leader of the Chieftains of the Sky, while Tishtrya is the Chieftain of the East and associated with the planet Tir (Mercury). SATAVAESA is the Chieftain of the West and the planet Anahid (Venus), VANANT the Chieftain of the South and the planet Ohrmazd (Jupiter), and HAPTORING the Chieftain of the North and the planet Warharan (Mars). Tishtrya is associated with the AMESHA SPENTA HAURVETAT. He leads the divine armies against the forces of evil and is an antagonist of the DAEVA Apaosa. The fourth month, Tir, which runs from 22 June to 22 July is dedicated to him, as is the thirteenth day of the month. In origin, he seems to be a development of the Babylonian god Nabu, who ruled over Mercury and presided over scribes. In Persian-Islamic mythology Tir (**Attarod** in Arabic) is still the lord of the scribes. There is a similar Star Yazad, **Tishtryaeinis**, associated with Canis Minor.

Tiszodiel, **Tylzdyell** An angel of the eighth lunar month according to the *Liber Juratus* and the Sloane manuscript *Book of Raziel*.

Titomon This is one of the angels presiding over Saturday according to the

Sloane manuscript *Book of Raziel*. It appears as **Tyfonyon** in the *Liber Juratus*.

Tobiel, **Tobyell** In the Sloane manuscript *Book of Raziel* and the *Liber Juratus* an angel with power over air. This may be a form of TUBIEL.

Toniel An angel of the element earth, under the planet Labana (Luna, the moon), to be invoked when working under this planet, according to the Sloane manuscript *Book of Raziel*.

Torayeil In the Sloane manuscript *Book of Raziel*, this is one of the angels of Sunday.

Toripiel, **Toupyel** An angel presiding over Thursday in the Sloane manuscript *Book of Raziel* and the *Liber Juratus*. **Traacyel** is a fellow Thursday angel.

Trajael The angel that rules the ninth degree of Libra under JAEL, according to the *Lemegeton*.

Tralyelyn, **Tralyeylyn** An angel of the day of Mars (Tuesday) in the *Liber Juratus* and the Sloane manuscript *Book of Raziel*.

Trasiel see SANIEL

Tsadkiel see TZADKIEL

Tual The angel who rules Taurus according to the *Lemegeton*.

Tuberiel see ZAAZENACH

Tubeylyn An angel of the day of Mars (Tuesday) in the *Liber Juratus* and the Sloane manuscript *Book of Raziel*.

Tubiel In the *Heptameron* Tubiel is 'head of the sign of the Summer' while in the *Liber Juratus* he is one of a number of angels who 'do rewle and governe in the somer tyme'. He is also said to be invoked for the return of small birds to their owners.

Tufiel An angel of the element earth, under the planet Zedek (Jupiter), to be invoked when working under this planet, according to the Sloane manuscript *Book of Raziel*.

Tulmas see BARAQIEL

Tumael One of the GRIGORI according to *1 Enoch*.

Turael, **Turel** One of the GRIGORI, 'a chief of ten', according to *1 Enoch* 6. **Turiel**, cited as a messenger of the spirits of the planet Jupiter and of the angel SACHIEL, is presumably a different angel.

Turmiel see BARIEL

Turtiel, **Tutiel** Tutiel is an angel presiding over Thursday in the Sloane manuscript *Book of Raziel*. Turtiel, in the *Lemegeton* an attendant angel under SABRATHAN, may be the same.

Tutrasiel see TATRASIEL

Tyel An angel of the north of the second heaven in the Sloane manuscript *Book of Raziel*.

Tymel An angel presiding over Thursday, the day of Jove, according to Sloane manuscript *Book of Raziel*.

Tzadkiel, **Tsadkiel** The ruler of the

planet Jupiter who was one of the instuctors of Abraham. He is also called a guardian of the east wind.

Tzakiel The angel that rules the seventh degree of Virgo under VOIL, and the ninth degree of Scorpio under JOSEL, according to the *Lemegeton*.

Tzangiel The angel that rules the sixth degree of Sagittarius under SUIAJASEL, according to the *Lemegeton*.

Tzapheal The angel that rules the sixth degree of Pisces under PASIL, according to the *Lemegeton*.

Tzaphkiel One of the ten ARCHANGELS in the Kabbalah, ruler of the ERELIM.

Tzaphniel An angel whose name is used in conjuration in the *Key of Solomon*, particularly when trying to make a magic carpet.

Tzaphqiel One of the ten ARCHANGELS in the Kabbalah, ruler of the ERELIM.

Tzedeqiah One of the angels whose name is used in the First Pentacle of Jupiter, used in hunting for treasure in *The Key of Solomon*.

Tzisiel The angel that rules the sixth degree of Gemini under GIEL, according to the Lemegeton.

U

Uachayel, **Uardayheil** Friday angels in the Sloane manuscript *Book of Raziel*. The names that appear in their place in the *Liber Juratus* are good illustrations of how easily names can be scrambled. If we take the *Raziel* names as correct for the sake of argument (there is no real way of verifying which is the more accurate), Uachayel appears in *Juratus* as **Bacapel**. At first this looks totally unconnected, but it is possible to see how one could have changed into the other. The first thing one needs to remember is that in medieval handwriting a 'v' and a 'u' were not distinguished. A 'v' was simply the form of the letter used at the start of a word, the other being used in the middle of the word, regardless of the sound involved (this fact needs to be remembered when dealing with any angel whose name begins with either of these letters). The *sound* of a 'b' and a 'v' are very close, so if the name were written down from dictation or had been learnt orally – not unusual at a time when everything had to be handwritten – then the confusion between a v/u and b quite easily explains the change of the first letter. The change of 'ch' to 'c' is easier. In Latin a 'ch' is pronounced with the sound of a 'k' – think of *choir* and *chorus* – so it is quite simple for the sound of ch = k to be written down as a simple 'c'. The change of 'y' to 'p', however, depends on the copying of a written text, for this is quite a common confusion in the names in the two manuscripts, and the forms or the letters could be similar in Medieval handwriting. Since these changes involve both spoken and written texts, this proves that there are at least two stages of transmission between the manuscripts, one spoken and one written. In fact the evidence of other major differences in the lists of names for angels of the months and days suggests that the common manuscript may well have been much further back than that. Uardayheil becomes two angels, **Verday** and **Heyll**, in *Juratus*, which is much easier to understand, for we have seen a number of cases where the break between names makes one of two angels or vice versa. With the potential confusion between 'u' and 'v' and the normal variations allowed in spelling at this time, the transformation is easily understood.

Uetamuel An angel of the north of the second heaven in the Sloane manuscript *Book of Raziel*.

Uiotan In the Sloane manuscript *Book of Raziel* an angel with power over water.

Umabel Umabel rules over physics and astronomy as well as being one of the seventy-two SHEMHAMPHORAE angels. As the GUARDIAN ANGEL of those born under Aquarius between 21 and 25 January he is considered an angel of sensitivity. He favours both abstract intellectual activity and the practical application of natural sensitivity.

Umariel see ABASDARHON

Unaraxxydin According to the Sloane manuscript *Book of Raziel*, this is one of the angels of Sunday (Solis) who should be invoked to aid works started on that day.

Unascaiel An angel of the north of the first heaven in the Sloane manuscript *Book of Raziel*.

Unleylyn An angel of the day of Mars (Tuesday) in the Sloane manuscript *Book of Raziel*. It is spelt **Vnlylyn** in the *Liber Juratus*.

Upa-paoiri see PAOIRYAENIS

Urallim An angel of the north of the first heaven in the Sloane manuscript *Book of Raziel*.

Uranacha An angel of the east of the fifth heaven in the Sloane manuscript *Book of Raziel*.

Uraniel see IASSUARIM

Uriel, **Ouriel** Uriel is one of the most important of the angels, often listed as one of the four ARCHANGELS, alongside MICHAEL, GABRIEL and RAPHAEL. Although listed among the REPROBATED ANGELS in 745, he was reinstated and now counts as a saint of the Roman Catholic Church. He has been variously classified among the CHERUBIM and the SERAPHIM, but is most usually called an archangel. He is said by some sources to be one of four who stand in the presence of the Lord (an ANGEL OF THE PRESENCE) and to be an ANGEL OF THE FACE. He is also listed among the ANGELS OF DESTRUCTION. He has an important role as an instructing angel, being an interpreter of prophesies, having both explained Ezra's vision to him and brought Abraham out of Ur. He is associated with poetry in this role. He is also one of several angels who are identified as the one who wrestled with Jacob (see under DARK ANGEL).

He is one of the seven archangels listed in *1 Enoch*, where Uriel watches over this world and over the underworld and is the ruler of the stars and planets, guiding their courses. In the *Sibylline Oracles* he is one of the angels who lead souls to judgement. He instructs Enoch in this knowledge, and also explains the punishment of the GRIGORI. We also learn there that Uriel was sent to Noah to announce to him that the earth would be destroyed by a flood, and to teach him how to save his own life, and that he governs the east with Gabriel and Raphael.

In the form Ouriel he appears in the *Testament of Solomon* where he thwarts the demon Ornais, who has been tormenting Solomon's favourite, the master-workman's little boy. Ornais claims to be descended from an archangel himself, and to have the power to 'strangle those who reside in Aquarius because of their passion for women whose zodiacal sign is Virgo. Moreover, while in a trance I undergo three transformations. Sometimes I am a man who craves the bodies of effeminate boys and when I touch them, they suffer great pain. Sometimes I become a creature with wings flying up to the heavenly regions. Finally, I assume the appearance of a lion.' Once he has used his magic ring to control Ornais, Solomon sets him to cut stones for the Temple. Once Ouriel has subdued Ornais, he fetches Beelzeboul the Prince of Demons to Solomon, who is also set to work on the temple. This text adds that he can thwart the evil star called Error, who leads man's minds away from religion, as well as a demon called Artosael. A Dead Sea Scroll describes him as 'one of the holy angels who is over the world and over

Tartarus'. *The Lemegeton* says that Uriel is of the west, and governs the earthly signs of the zodiac (Taurus, Virgo and Capricorn) with CASSIEL, SACHIEL and ASSIEL as Princes under him.

Urpeniel In the Sloane manuscript *Book of Raziel* an angel with power over water.

Usaryeyel, **Usararyeyll** An angel of the day of Mars (Tuesday) in the *Liber Juratus* and the Sloane manuscript *Book of Raziel*.

Ushahin and Ushah Ushahin is the YAZAD (Zoroastrian angel) who presides over the first watch (Gah) of the day from midnight to daybreak, while Ushah is the female Yazad of the dawn.

Usiel see UZZIEL

Uslael An angel of the west of the fifth heaven in the Sloane manuscript *Book of Raziel*.

Utisaryaya One of the angels of the seventh lunar month according to the Sloane manuscript *Book of Raziel*. It is **Ulysacyaia** in the *Liber Juratus*, somebody at some point having forgotten to cross a 't' and confused an 'r' and a 'c'.

Uzerin YAZAD (Zoroastrian angel) presiding over the fourth watch of each day, which runs from 3pm to sunset.

Uzzah, **Uzza** In *3 Enoch*, a trio of angels Uzzah, AZZAH and AZAEL oppose Enoch's elevation to METATRON, although when God stands firm, they prostrate themselves to him. They are described as laying charges against

Enoch, which associates them with the SATAN-figure SAMMAEL who is described as 'Prince of the Accusers'. These three are also credited with corrupting Mankind by teaching them sorcery.

Uzziel, Usiel Uzziel and Usiel sometimes seem to be the same angel, and sometimes two separate ones. He is listed among the ANGELS OF MERCY under METATRON, and is called both a CHERUB and chief of the VIRTUES. In the *Book of Raziel* he is one of seven angels who stand before the throne of God as well as being one of nine set over the four winds. However, in the Kabbalah he is listed among the GRIGORI.

V

Vaanyel see VANIEL

Vabiel The angel that rules the fourteenth and the twenty-fourth degrees of Taurus under TUAL and the fourteenth degree of Gemini under GIEL, according to the *Lemegeton*.

Vagael, Vagel The angel that rules the eighteenth degrees of Scorpio under JOSEL and of Sagittarius under SUIAJASEL, and the twenty-fourth degree of Aries under AIEL, according to the *Lemegeton*.

Vahajah The angel that rules the fifteenth degree of Pisces under PASIL, according to the *Lemegeton*.

Vahuel, Vehuel GUARDIAN ANGEL of those born under Sagittarius between 23 and 27 November, he is one of the PRINCIPALITIES as well as a SHEMHAM-PHORAE angel.

Valar see GANDALF

Vameroz see TARTYS

Vanant, Vanand A YAZAD (Zoroastrian angel) identified with the star Vega and ruler of the planet Ohrmazd (Jupiter). He is the Chieftain of the South (see further at TISHTRYA).

Vanescor see ABASDARHON

Vanesiel see VATHMIEL

Vaniel The angel that rules the fourth degree of Aries under AIEL, according to the *Lemegeton*. **Vaanyel**, an angel of the south of the fourth heaven in the Sloane manuscript *Book of Raziel*, looks like a corruption of the same name.

Vanosyr see SERQUANICH

Vaol In *The Key of Solomon* an angel whose name appears on the First Pentacle of the Moon, which 'serveth to open doors, in whatever way they may be fastened'.

Varcan see ANDAS

Variel The angel that rules the seventeenth degree of Libra under JAEL, according to the *Lemegeton*.

Varkan see ANDAS

Varmay see BARAQIEL

Vasariah, **Variariah** In the Kabbalah an angel that rules over nobles, justice, magistrates and lawyers. He is also among the seventy-two bearers of the mystic name of God SHEMHAMPHORAE. As the GUARDIAN ANGEL of those born under the sign of Virgo between 29 August and 2 September he is said to be an angel of favours who help find advantages in everything in life and brings happiness.

Vastamel An angel of the south of the third heaven in the Sloane manuscript *Book of Raziel*.

Vathmiel The angel of the fourth hour of the day according to the *Lemegeton*. Chief of his many followers and servant are **Armmyel, Larmich, Marfiel, Ormyel, Zardiel, Emarfiel, Permiel, Queriel, Strubiel, Diviel, Jermiel, Thuros, Vanesiel, Zasviel** and **Hermiel**.

Vayu Also known as **Wad**, **Gowad** and **Govad**, this is a YAZAD (Zoroastrian angel) personifying the wind or atmosphere. He was a co-worker of the AMESHA SPENTA HAURVETAT.

Vaziel The angel that rules the sixteenth degree of Virgo under VOIL, according to the *Lemegeton*.

Veal An angel of the north of the fifth heaven in the Sloane manuscript *Book of Raziel*.

Veallum An angel of the north of the first heaven in the Sloane manuscript *Book of Raziel*.

Veguaniel see MURIEL

Vehiel In *The Key of Solomon* an angel whose name appears on the First Pentacle of the Moon, which 'serveth to open doors, in whatever way they may be fastened'.

Vehuel A PRINCIPALITY who is both one of the seventy-two angels of the zodiac and one of the seventy-two SHEMHAMPHORAE angels. As a GUARDIAN ANGEL of those born under Sagittarius between 23 and 27 November he is described as an angel of splendour who encourages creativity and self-confidence and a capacity for enjoyment.

Vehuiah In the Kabbalah this is one of the eight SERAPHIM who govern the first rays of the sun. He is invoked to fulfil prayers. As a GUARDIAN ANGEL of those born under Aries between 21 and 25 March he is described as an angel of success who helps a person be loved and esteemed.

Vemael see OSMADIEL

Vemasiel see PAMYEL

Venesiel see BARAQIEL

Venomiel see TARTYS

Ventariel see MENDRION

Vequaniel In the *Lemegeton*, the angel of the third hour of the day, the chief of whose many servants are called **Asmiel**, **Persiel**, **Mursiel**, **Zoesiel**, **Drelmech**, **Sadiniel**, **Parniel**, **Comadiel**, **Gemary**, **Xantiel**, **Serviel** and **Furiel**.

Verascyer An angel of the south of the fourth heaven in the Sloane manuscript *Book of Raziel*.

Veremedyn According to the *Liber Juratus* and the Sloane manuscript *Book of Raziel*, this is one of the GUARDIAN ANGELS of Sunday (Solis) who should be invoked to aid works started on that day.

Verethraghna The YAZAD of victory. He is the best-armed of all the Zoroastrian heavenly beings, the swiftest and the strongest, and represents the healing power of strength and fitness. He destroys malice. In the *Khorda Avesta* prayer of sacrifice to him he is described as manifesting in a succession of forms – as wind, a bear, a bird, a bull, a boar, a youth, a warrior with a golden sword and more, each one an embodiment of physical perfection and vigour. He is the divinity of the sacred Vrahran Fire. He is also associated with the resurrection of the soul and with metal-working. The twentieth day of the month in the Zoroastrian religious calendar is named

for him. He was also recognised as a co-worker of the AMESHA SPENTA ASHI VANGHUHI.

Vereveil In accounts of the experiences of Enoch based on the old translation of *2 Enoch,* this is the name of the ARCHANGEL who instructs Enoch about the nature of heaven. The modern translation gives the name as **Vrevoil**, but notes that there are many different versions of the name in different manuscripts, adding 'The other numerous variants in the spelling are not material. The name is otherwise unknown.' Other forms are **Vretel** or **Vretiel**. This angel is described in the texts as 'swifter in wisdom that the other archangels, who records all the Lord's deeds'. See also under RADWERIEL.

Veualiah, **Veuliah** One of the nine VIRTUES, this angel oversees high affairs of state such as the power of empires and of kings. As a GUARDIAN ANGEL of those born under Scorpio between 24 and 28 October he is considered an angel of victory who helps in struggles and towards a happy and fulfilled life.

Victory see NIKE

Virtues These angels rank fifth in the traditional HIERARCHY OF THE ANGELS. According to Hebrew tradition, their principal duty is to work miracles on earth. They are also associated with the performance of magic. The two angels ('two men in white robes') standing by the apostles at the moment of Jesus' ascension into heaven are traditionally regarded as Virtues (Acts 1:10). In traditional art Virtues may be dressed as bishops and carry a lily or a red rose as a symbol of Christ's passion; otherwise they are shown as DOMINIONS.

Visya and Savanghi These two YAZATAS (Zoroastrian angels) are invoked together. The first governs settlements and the second the trade that people conduct there.

Vixalimon, Vyxasmyon This is one of the angels presiding over Saturday according to the *Liber Juratus* and the Sloane manuscript *Book of Raziel*. If invoked appropriately and in a state of purity, they will aid you.

Vohu Mano, Vohu Manah, Vohuman A Zoroastrian AMESHA SPENTA – the equivalent of an ARCHANGEL– whose name means 'Good Mind', or 'Good Purpose'. In later Middle Persian or Pahlavi documents the name appears as Vohuman, and its modern Persian form is **Bahman** (also found as **Barman** and **Bahrman**). Bahman gives his name to the eleventh month that runs for thirty days from 21 January, and he is sometimes equated in Islam with JIBRIL. He is a protector of animals, particularly cattle, and is held to symbolise creative goodness and the concept of Asha, a term which can be translated in a variety of ways: cosmic order, righteous-ness, the sacred, purity, law. **Aka Manah** ('Evil Mind') was created by **Angra Mainya** (the Zoroastrian devil) to oppose Vohu Mano. He is second in command, next to his father, Angra Mainya, in the host of demons. In the final conflict of this present cycle, Aka Manah will be overcome by Vohu Mano, and Angra Mainya will become powerless and flee.

Voices see APPARITIONS

Voil The angel who rules Virgo according to the *Lemegeton*.

Vretel, Vretiel, Vrevoil see VEREVEIL

Vulcaniel see ABASDARHON

W

Wad see VAYU

Warrior Angels According to Claire Nahmad, at times of great need your GUARDIAN ANGEL can summon Warrior Angels to fight on your behalf. They are said to wear headdresses and armour and to be of enormous strength and size.

Watchers While in most texts 'Watchers' is the translation of GRIGORI, the FALLEN ANGELS who taught technical skills to mankind as well as corrupting them, in a few texts they are either a class of angels or a separate order, who have an important function in the divine law courts. There are two Watchers and two Holy Ones who stand by the Glory Throne, giving council to God. In the court they themselves can issue verdicts and pronounce judgements. Each of them has seventy names, one for each of the languages on earth.

Wheels see OPHANIM, GALGALLIM

X

Xamyon see SANIEL

Xanoriz see NARCORIEL

Xanthir see PAMYEL

Xanthyozod see SERQUANICH

Xantiel see VEQUANIEL

Xantropy see ABASDARHON

Xantros see ORIEL

Xaphan see ZEPHON

Xaphania In Philip Pullman's *The Amber Spyglass* (volume three of the *His Dark Materials* trilogy) Xaphania is a WARRIOR ANGEL fighting on the part of those opposing the corrupted forces of heaven. She also helps Will and Lyra, Pullman's Adam and Eve, who this time save the world by falling, to come to terms with the need to separate. When she arrives she is described as having 'the light of another world shining on her. She was unclothed, but that meant nothing: what clothes could an angel wear anyway, Lyra thought? It was impossible to tell if she was old or young, but her expression was austere and compassionate, and both Will and Lyra felt as if she knew them to their hearts.' At the heart of the work is the question of Dust (inspired by the dark matter of modern physics), and the disastrous effects of its loss through windows between parallel worlds. It is Xaphania who explains the nature of Dust to the children in a passage that seems to express Pullman's strong views on morality and human responsibility. 'Understand this,' said Xaphania: 'Dust is not a constant. There's not a fixed quantity that has always been the same. Conscious beings make Dust – they renew it all the time, by thinking and feeling and reflecting, by gaining wisdom and passing it on.

'And if you help everyone else in your worlds to do that, by helping them to learn and understand about themselves and each other and the way everything works, and by showing them how to be kind instead of cruel, and patient instead of hasty, and cheerful instead of surly, and above all how to keep their minds open and free and curious … Then they will renew enough to replace what is lost through one window. So there could be one left open.' At first the children think this means that they can continue to see each other, but then realise they must sacrifice their love to allow the dead to escape from their dismal underworld to be reunited with the universe.

Xatinas In the Sloane manuscript *Book of Raziel*, an angel of the tenth lunar month. If invoked in rites his name will ensure good results.

Xemyzin see TARTYS

Xernifiel see NARCORIEL

Xerphiel see ZAAZENACH

Xysuylion This is one of the angels presiding over Saturday, the day of Saturn or Sabat, according to Sloane manuscript *Book of Raziel*.

Y

Yabtasyper In the *Liber Juratus* and the Sloane manuscript *Book of Raziel,* an angel of the thirteenth lunar month (March).

Yael An angel of the west of the fourth heaven in the Sloane manuscript *Book of Raziel.*

Yafrael In the Sloane manuscript *Book of Raziel* an angel with power over fire and flame.

Yahel An angel whose name is inscribed in the Fourth Pentacle of the Moon in *The Key of Solomon* to give protection against sorcery.

Yahoel Both the name of an ARCHANGEL, and also given in *3 Enoch* as a name of METATRON. In the *Apocalypse of Abraham* **Jaoel** (see JAHOEL), another form of the name, is Abraham's heavenly guide. He is identified as the Angel of the Lord of whom it is said in Exodus 23:20–21 that God's name is 'in him'.

Yalsenac An angel of the eighth lunar month according to the *Liber Juratus* and the Sloane manuscript *Book of Raziel.*

Yamiel An angel with power over the north, according to the Sloane manuscript *Book of Raziel.*

Yamla An angel of the sixth lunar month according to the *Liber Juratus* and the Sloane manuscript *Book of Raziel*, which says that if they are named 'in each thing that thou wilt do ... thou shalt profit'.

Yanael An angel of the north of the second heaven in the Sloane manuscript *Book of Raziel*.

Yariel, **Yaryel** An angel of the first lunar month according to the *Liber Juratus* and the Sloane manuscript *Book of Raziel*.

Yas An angel of the west of the fourth heaven in the Sloane manuscript *Book of Raziel*.

Yashiel In *The Key of Solomon,* an angel whose name appears on the First Pentacle of the Moon, which 'serveth to open doors, in whatever way they may be fastened'.

Yasmyel In the *Liber Juratus* and the Sloane manuscript *Book of Raziel*, an angel of the thirteenth lunar month (March). If invoked in the relevant month, he will ensure success in your enterprise.

Yassar An angel of the sixth lunar month in the *Liber Juratus* and the Sloane manuscript *Book of Raziel*.

Yatayel In the Sloane manuscript *Book of Raziel* an elemental angel with power over the earth.

Yayac An angel of the third lunar month according to the Sloane manuscript *Book of Raziel*.

Yayel(l) In the *Liber Juratus* and the Sloane manuscript *Book of Raziel* an angel of the thirteenth lunar month (March).

Yazads Yazads are the Zoroastrian equivalent of ANGELS. Meaning 'adorable ones', it is thought that Yazads have their origin in pre-Zoroastrian gods, and would therefore originally have been classed with the DAEVAS. They were, however, reincarnated as angels – created spiritual beings, worthy of being honored or praised. Like the AMESHA SPENTAS they personify abstract ideas and virtues, or concrete objects of nature. The Yazatas try to help people and to protect them from evil. They are also known as **Eyzads**. In Manicheism some of the Yazads were elevated to the rank of gods, while at the same time clergy and the elect could be honoured by the title of Yazad.

Yaziel An angel of the first lunar month according to the Sloane manuscript *Book of Raziel*. In the *Liber Juratus* he is **Zaziel**.

Yebel An angel presiding over Thursday, the day of Jove, according to the *Liber Juratus* and the Sloane manuscript *Book of Raziel*.

Yefefiah see YEPIPYAH

Yehoc An angel of the second lunar month according to the Sloane manuscript *Book of Raziel* with the power to grant wishes.

Yehudiah GUARDIAN ANGEL of those born between 3 and 7 September, under Virgo. He is also charged with bearing the souls of the dead to heaven.

Yeiayel see IEIAIEL

Yeialel see IEILAEL

Yelahiah, Yelaiah see IELAHIAH

Yelbrayeyl, Yelbrayeyell According to the *Liber Juratus* and the Sloane manuscript *Book of Raziel* this is one of the angels of Sunday (Solis) who should be invoked to aid works started on that day. **Yeocyn** is another Sunday angel.

Yepipyah, Yephephiyya, Yefefiah A PRINCE OF TORAH, and one of the ANGELS OF THE FACE and ANGELS OF THE PRESENCE. He is said to have taught the Kabbalah to Moses.

Yeratel, Yerathel see TERATHEL

Yesararye An angel of the west of the second heaven in the Sloane manuscript *Book of Raziel*.

Yesmactria, Yesmachia An angel of the first lunar month according to the Sloane manuscript *Book of Raziel*.

Yesod In the *Key of Solomon* identified as one of the angels who preside over the ten SEPHIROTH.

YHWH The four consonants that form the Hebrew root of the true name of God. In addition, in some traditions the highest ARCHANGELS all carry these four letters (known as the **Tetragram**) added to their personal name. In the Great Law Court of heaven only these angels – seventy-three of them by some traditions – are allowed to speak.

Ykiel An angel of the element water, under the planet Zedek (Jupiter), to be invoked when working under this planet, in the Sloane manuscript *Book of Raziel*.

Ymel, Ynel An angel presiding over Thursday, the day of Jove, according to the *Liber Juratus* and the Sloane manuscript *Book of Raziel*.

Yoas An angel of the sixth lunar month according to the *Liber Juratus* and the Sloane manuscript *Book of Raziel*, which says that if they are named 'in each thing that thou wilt do … thou shalt profit'.

Yoel, Yel In the Sloane manuscript *Book of Raziel*, an angel of the thirteenth lunar month (March). If invoked in the relevant month, he will ensure success in your enterprise.

Yomiel, Yomyael see JOMJAEL, SHAMSIEL

Yryniel An angel of the element water, under the planet Zedek (Jupiter), to be invoked when working under this planet, according to the Sloane manuscript *Book of Raziel*.

Ysar An angel of the third lunar month according to the *Liber Juratus* and the Sloane manuscript *Book of Raziel*, whose naming brings benefits.

Z

Zaapiel, **Zafiel** The angel of the hurricane in texts such as *3 Enoch*. The form Zaapiel comes from the Hebrew word *za'ap* which can mean either 'rage, anger' or 'storm, hurricane'. Zaapiel is also an ANGEL OF DESTRUCTION, who takes the souls of those condemned in the heavenly courts down to Sheol and beats them with rods of burning coals.

Zaazenach In the *Lemegeton*, the angel of the sixth hour of the night. Among his multitude of following angels are **Amonazy**, **Menoriel**, **Prenostix**, **Namedor**, **Cherasiel**, **Dramaz**, **Tuberiel**, **Humaziel**, **Lanoziel**, **Lamerotzod**, **Xerphiel**, **Zeziel**, **Pammon**, **Dracon**, **Gematzod**, **Enariel**, **Rudefor** and **Sarmon**.

Zabaniyah In Islamic folklore, the nineteen angels who guard hell under their chief, MALIK.

Zabdiel With ADRIEL and YAMIEL, an angel with power over the north, according to the Sloane manuscript *Book of Raziel*.

Zabkiel see THRONES

Zacdon An angel of the sixth lunar month according to the *Liber Juratus* and the Sloane manuscript *Book of Raziel*.

Zachariel Zachariel has been classed variously as one of the ARCHANGELS, DOMINIONS, and POWERS, and is called by some Ruler of the Second Heaven. He is also known as the angel of Jupiter and Thursday (in the *Liber Juratus* and elsewhere) and a governor of the world, a follower of MENDRION, and angel of the seventh hour of the night in the *Lemegeton*.

Zachiel The angel that rules the seventeenth degree of Virgo under VOIL, as well as the nineteenth degrees of Scorpio under JOSEL and of Sagittarius under SUIAJASEL, according to the *Lemegeton*. Elsewhere, he is ruler of the sixth heaven.

Zachriel see SARANDIEL

Zaciel The angel that rules the fifth degree of Aries under AIEL, according to the *Lemegeton*.

Zacrias A prophetic angel in Carlos Ruiz Zafón's 2001 novel, *The Shadow of the Wind*.

Zadiel The angel that rules the twenty-fifth degree of Aries under AIEL, according to the *Lemegeton*.

Zadkiel Zadkiel is, according to the Kabbalah, the leader of the nine angels who make up the choir of DOMINIONS. Zadkiel has also been called the leader of the HASHMALIM, although this is more often said to be **Hashmal**. He is guardian of memory and of mercy. The **Lesser Zadkiel** is an angel who features in Robertson Davies' 1985 novel *What's Bred in the Bone*, alongside another fictional angel, the **Daimon Maimas**. For other instances of the name Zadkiel see under SACHIEL.

Zafiel, **Zefael** The angel of the showers in the *Book of Enoch*. In the Sloane manuscript *Book of Raziel*, an angel of the eleventh lunar month.

Zagiel The angel that rules the fifteenth degree of Gemini under GIEL and the twenty-first degree of Taurus under TUAL, according to the *Lemegeton.*

Zagzagael An ANGEL OF THE FACE and OF THE PRESENCE, PRINCE OF THE TORAH and of Wisdom. Zagzagel speaks seventy languages, as does METATRON. When not in the Presence of God, he guards the fourth heaven. He was a teacher of Moses, and one of the angels who brought his soul to heaven.

Zahra see HARUT AND MARUT

Zakkiel see ZAQUIEL

Zakun see LAHASH

Zakzaki'el YHWH A mighty angel in *3 Enoch*, whose job it is 'to record the merits of Israel upon the throne of glory'.

Zalibron, **Zelybron** This is one of the angels presiding over Saturday, the day of Saturn or Sabat, according to Sloane manuscript *Book of Raziel* and the *Liber Juratus.*

Zam see ZAMYAT

Zamiel, **Zamayl**, **Zamel**, **Zaamiel** The angel of the hurricane in some traditions, in others, of the whirlwind, although some attribute this role to RASIEL. The name comes from the Hebrew *za'am*, 'indignation' and implies 'Divine Indignation', which is what these phenomena must have seemed like. In the Sloane manuscript *Book of Raziel*, he is an angel of the eleventh lunar month

and of Sunday. If invoked at the relevant time, he will ensure success in your enterprise. He resides in the south of the first heaven. Compare ZAPPIEL.

Zamirel One of the angels of Wednesday, the day of Mercury, according to the Sloane manuscript *Book of Raziel.* He does not feature in the *Liber Juratus* list.

Zamyat, **Zam** Female YAZAD (Zoroastrian angel) presiding over the earth. The tewnty-eighth day of the month in the Zoroastrian religious calendar is named after her. She works with the AMESHA SPENTA AMERETAT.

Zamzummim see NEPHILIM

Zaphiel An angel found in *3 Enoch*. His name comes from the Hebrew for 'rage' and he represents divine wrath. Some call him ruler of the CHERUBIM (Milton describes him as 'of cherubim the swiftest wind') and prince of the planet Saturn. In another tradition, he was the teacher of Noah, and in yet another one of the three leaders of the months. There is also a fallen Zaphiel – see under BARAQIEL.

Zaphkiel see CASSIEL, THRONES

Zaqlel One of the GRIGORI, 'a chief of ten', according to *1 Enoch* 6.

Zaquiel, **Zakkiel** Zaquiel is described as an angel of the east of the fifth heaven in the Sloane manuscript *Book of Raziel.* Elsewhere, in the form Zakkiel, he is described as the angel of the storm.

Zarael, **Zarafil** Two Sunday angels in the Sloane manuscript *Book of Raziel.*

Only Zarafil is in the *Liber Juratus*.

Zarall A cherub who, with his twin JAEL, guards the Ark of the Covenant.

Zaraph In 'The Third Angel's Story' in Thomas Moore's 1823 poem *The Loves of the Angels* inspired by the story of the GRIGORI, Zaraph is a SERAPH who falls through love of the mortal woman Nama.

Zardiel see VATHMIEL

Zarfaieil According to the Sloane manuscript *Book of Raziel*, this is one of the GUARDIAN ANGELS of Sunday (Solis). He is **Zarsayeyll** in the *Liber Juratus*.

Zarialin, **Zaryalyn** An angel presiding over Friday, the day of Venus, according to the *Liber Juratus* and the Sloane manuscript *Book of Raziel*.

Zasviel see VATHMIEL

Zavael The angel that rules the sixteenth degree of Pisces under PASIL, according to the *Lemegeton*. Davidson describes him, rather than ZAMIEL, as the angel of whirlwinds.

Zazriel YHWH A mighty PRINCE of the angels found in *3 Enoch*.

Zazyor see ORIEL

Zebaliel An angel of the element water, under the planet Madin (Mars), to be invoked when working under this planet, according to the Sloane manuscript *Book of Raziel*.

Zebuleon One of the nine 'angels who are over the consummation' (the end of the world) in the Greek *Apocalypse of Ezra*, about whom nothing more is known.

Zechiel An angel whose name is used for conjuration in the *Key of Solomon*.

Zegiel The angel that rules the twelfth degree of Taurus under TUAL, according to the *Lemegeton*.

Zehanpuryu YHWH In the celestial law courts when SOTERASIEL, the accuser, exercising strict justice, tries to have souls cast into the rivers of fire, Zehanpuryu acts as the defender, urges mercy and quenches the rivers. As such he is classed as an ANGEL OF MERCY.

Zekuniel see PELIEL

Zemoel see BARIEL

Zenam An angel of the third lunar month according to the Sloane manuscript *Book of Raziel* and the *Liber Juratus*.

Zenoroz see PAMYEL

Zephania(h) see ISHIM

Zephon, **Xaphan** One of the ANGELS OF PARADISE, in some accounts. But in others, particularly in the spelling Xaphan, he is known as an angel who joined SATAN in his rebellion and suggested that they pursue their cause by setting fire to heaven. However, before they could do this they were cast into the abyss, and he now fans the fires in hell.

Zetha see HARBONAH

Zethiel The angel that rules the eighteenth degree of Libra under JAEL, according to the *Lemegeton*.

Zewaiel In *3 Enoch*, the angel in charge of terrors and commotions. The name comes from the Hebrew for 'terror'.

Zeziel see ZAAZENACH

Ziiel, **Suiel** Angel in charge of earth tremors according to *3 Enoch* 14. The name may be a corruption of *Zewa'i'el*, from the Hebrew for 'earthquake'.

Ziqiel Angel in charge of comets in *3 Enoch* 14.

Zoaziel An angel of the east of the fifth heaven in the Sloane manuscript *Book of Raziel*. He is probably the same angel as **Zoesiel** (see VEQUANIEL).

Zodiel see JEFISCHA

Zotiel An angel mentioned in *1 Enoch* as dwelling in the east of heaven, near the Garden of Righteousness. He is only mentioned in early texts, and Enoch is said to 'pass over' him. Ufologists who wish to identify angels with extraterrestrial events have, for some reason, identified Zotiel as a possible spaceship. He is classed as one of the ANGELS OF PARADISE.

Zsmayel In the Sloane manuscript *Book of Raziel,* an angel with power over water.

Ztaziel An angel of the element air, under the planet Labana (Luna, the moon), to be invoked when working under this planet, according to the Sloane manuscript *Book of Raziel.*

Zumech In *The Key of Solomon*, an angel whose name is invoked when preparing materials for the practice of magic.

Zupa An angel of the west of the fifth heaven in the Sloane manuscript *Book of Raziel.*

Zuriel A leader of the PRINCIPALITIES and ruler of the sign of Libra. He is invoked against stupidity, and his name appears on amulets for protection in childbirth.

Zymeloz see NARCORIEL

Descriptive Bibliography and Further Reading

The works in this list are grouped by type of text and by the short form used to refer to them in the dictionary.

Pseudepigrapha

Charlesworth *The Old Testament Pseudepigrapha,* edited by James H Charlesworth. Two volumes. Doubleday 1983. This is now the standard edition of these texts, replacing R H Charles *Apocrypha and Pseudepigrapha of the Old Testament.* Two volumes. Oxford 1913. Much of the latter can now be found online. By far the best place to look for on-line editions of these works is the Early Jewish Writings site http://www.earlyjewishwritings.com. This excellent site will link you to texts and study material both on- and off-line. It should however be noted that on-line versions are, because of copyright, older and much less trustworthy versions than those in Charlesworth.

Individual Texts

Apocalypse of Abraham. This dates from the first to second century AD and survives in both Slavonic and Greek versions, although the original language was probably Hebrew. It can be found in Charlesworth, and a partial text on-line at http://www.oxleigh.freeserve.co.uk/pt01c.htm.

Apocalypse of Baruch. Also known as *3 Baruch* and the *Greek Apocalypse of Baruch.* This dates from the first to third century AD and survives both in Slavonic and in Greek, the probable original language. In Charlesworth and in Charles's translation at http://carm.org/ lost/3barauch.htm.

Apocalypse of Ezra. Also called the *Greek Apocalypse of Ezra* and the *Revelation of Esdras.* It was written in Greek some time between the second and ninth century AD. It can be found in Charlesworth and an older translation under the title *Word and Revelation of Esdras* at http://ccel.org./fathers2/ANF-08/anf08-106.htm.

Apocalypse of Zephaniah. Preserved in a fragmentary form made up of a passage quoted in Greek (probably the original language) by Clement of Alexandria and two fragments of manuscript written in different dialects of Coptic in Charlesworth. The same text is on-line

at http://userpages.burgoyne.com/
bdespain/progress/progzeph.htm.

Book of Adam and Eve, also called *Life of
Adam and Eve.* Written in the first century AD. Survives in Greek and Latin
texts, as well as translations in
Armenian and Slavic and other languages. The original was probably in
Hebrew. In Charlesworth and widely
available on-line.

1 Enoch, also known as the *Ethiopic
Apocalypse of Enoch.* Written some time
between the second century BC and the
first century AD. The only complete versions are in the Ge'ez language of
Ethopia, although there are fragments
in Aramaic, Greek and Latin. The original language is not surely known, but it
may have been written in a mixture of
Hebrew and Aramaic. In Charlesworth,
and Charles' translation at
http://reluctant-messenger.com/
bookofenoch.htm.

2 Enoch, also known as *The Book of the
Secrets of Enoch* or the *Slavonic
Apocalypse of Enoch.* Written in the first
century AD and surviving in two versions in Slavonic. The original language
in not known. In Charlesworth and on-
line in Charles's translation at http://
members.iinet.net.au/%7Equentinj/
Christianity/2Enoch.html.

3 Enoch, also known as the *Hebrew
Apocalypse of Enoch.* Written in the fifth
to sixth century AD and surviving in the
original Hebrew. In Charlesworth.
There is no on-line version at the time
of writing.

Jubilees or the *Book of Jubilees.* Written
in the second century BC. It survives in

many languages, including the original
Hebrew. In Charlesworth and also on-
line at http://www.ccel.org/c/charles/
otpesudepig/jubilee in R H Charles's
translation.

Philo wrote in Greek in the third to
second century BC. There are other
works attributed to him, also known as
Pseudo-Philo, from the first century AD.
These writings are available in
Charlesworth and via the Early Jewish
Writings web-site.

Sibylline Oracles. Written from the
second to the seventh centuries AD.
They are in Greek and have been
worked on by a number of people, both
Jewish and Christian. In Charlesworth,
and there is a nineteenth-century translation at http://www.sacred-texts.com/
cla/sib/.

Testament of Abraham. Written in the
first or second century AD. It survives in
numerous languages, and was probably
originally in Greek. In Charlesworth,
and a translation of unknown prove-
nance at http://www.newadvent.org/
fathers/1007.htm.

Testament of Adam. Written in the
second to fifth century AD. Surviving in
numerous languages including Greek
and Arabic. The best manuscripts are in
Syriac which was probably the original
language. In Charlesworth, but there is
no full text on-line.

Testament of Solomon. Written between
the first to third centuries AD in Greek.
In Charlesworth. The old translation by
F C Conybeare, from the *Jewish
Quarterly Review,* October 1898, is on-
line at http://www.esotericarchives.com/

solomon/testamen.htm with modern footnotes.

Works of Incantation and Magic

The most important source for these works is at the Esoteric Archives at http://www.esotericarchives.com/esoteric.htm, which has an extensive library of these works, plus useful information and links.

Agrippa, Henry Cornelius, (1486–1535) *De Occulta Philosophia* and other writings available via the Esoteric Archives or in several printed editions including *Three Books of Occult Philosophy* James Freake and Donald Tyson, Llewellyn Books 2000.

Arbatel of Magic (1573). Available via Esoteric Archives.

Grimoir Verum. Available (in Italian) via Esoteric Archives.

Abano, Peter de, *Heptameron or Magical Elements.* Available in the English translation of 1655 via the Esoteric Archives.

The Key of Solomon the King or Clavicula Salomenis translated by S Liddell Macgregor Mathers 1888. Available at http://www.sacred-texts.com/grim/kos/.

Lemegeton Clavicula Solomonis or the Lesser Key of Solomon http://www.esotericarchives.com/solomon/lemegeton.htm. A considerably enlarged edition of the *Lesser Key of Solomon* is now available edited by Joseph Peterson from Weiser Publishers.

Liber Juratus or the Sworne Booke of Honorius. This was translated into English in the fourteenth century. Available via Esoteric Archives.

Names of Angels and Demons from the Magical Treatise of Solomon (Harleian MS 5596). An internet text based on Richard Greenfield's *Traditions of Belief in Late Byzantine Demonology,* (Amsterdam: Hakkert, 1988) is at http://www.esotericarchives.com/solomon/mts.htm.

Sepher Rezial Hemelach: The Book of the Angel Rezial. Translated by Steve Savedow (Red Wheel/Weiser 2001). A very literal translation of the 1701 Hebrew text of the Book of Raziel.

Book of Raziel British Library Sloane MS 3826. Transcribed, annotated, and introduced by D Karr 2003. Part One: http://www.esoteric.msu.edu/VolumeV/Raziel1.html. Part Two: http://www.esoteric.msu.edu/VolumeV/Raziel2.html.

Syriac charms: The Book of Protection, Being a Collection of Charms Now edited for the First Time from Syriac Manuscripts. Hermann Gollancz, London (1912), available via Esoteric Archives.

Other Books Mentioned in the Text

Davidson, Gustav, *A Dictionary of Angels including the Fallen Angels.* Free Press, 1971 (1967). The founding dictionary of angels, which still has much to recommend it, but depending on out-of-date sources.

Dionysius the Areopagite, *Celestial Hierarchy.* English translation on-line at http://www.esoteric.msu.edu/VolumeII/ CelestialHierarchy.html.

Fludd, Robert, *Utriusque cosmi majoris et minoris historia* (1619). There are no modern versions of this work.

Ginzberg, Louis, *Legends of the Jews* (1909). The text of this wonderful book is widely available on-line, including at http://www.sacred-texts.com/jud/loj/.

Heywood, Thomas, *Hierarchy of the Blessed Angels* (1635). There is no modern edition of this work. It is available on-line by subscription only.

Hypostasis of the Archons. An early Gnostic text available at http://www. gnosis.org/naghamm/hypostas.html.

Nahmad, Claire, *Summoning Angels: How to Call on Angels in Every Life Situation.* Watkins Publishing (2004).

Origen, *Contra Celsum.* Translated by H Chadwick, Cambridge University Press 1953. On-line at http://www. newadvent.org/fathers/0416.htm.

Paradise Lost, John Milton. First published in 1667, this epic poem is widely available both in print and on-line.

Tertullian, *Adversus Marcionem.* Edited and translated by Ernest Evans, Oxford University Press 1972, on-line at http://www.tertullian.org/articles/evans _marc/evans_marc_00index.htm.

General Reference Works and Websites

The Encyclopaedia of Islam 1959. Edited by B Lewis, C Pellat and J Schacht. Published by Brill, latest updated version available on CD or on-line by subscription at http://www.encislam. demo.brill.nl/ inhoudDemo.htm. (Hughes, T P *Dictionary of Islam* London (1895) is a poor substitute, but part of it is on-line at http://answering-islam.org.uk/ Books/Hughes/).

The Encyclopedia Iranica, an ongoing work at http://www.iranica.com/index. html, is excellent for Zoroastrianism and related subjects. Otherwise there are many good sites for Zoroastrianism. www.avest.org makes a good starting point.

Guiley, Rosemary Ellen, *The Encyclopedia of Angels.* Checkmark Books, second edition 2004.

Esoterica, an on-line peer-review journal at http://www.esoteric.msu.edu/ is an excellent starting point for those wishing to study the subject in depth.

The Jewish Encyclopedia. Originally published 1901–6, this is now available on-line at http://www.jewishencyclopedia. com/index.jsp.

Karr, D, *The Study of Solomonic Magic in English*. www.digital-brilliance.com/kab/karr/tssmie.pdf.

http://khidr.org/index.htm is the starting point for those wishing to learn more about Al-Khidr, the Green Man.

Wikipedia. http://en.wikipedia.org/wiki/Main_Page is an excellent source for treatment of named angels in popular culture.

Other Books

Book of Tobit in the *Apocrypha*, 1611 translation, revised 1894, OUP.

Hotam Khatam Suleiman: King Solomon's Seal. Edited by Rachel Mulstein, Tower of David Museum of the History of Jerusalem, 1997.

Loves of the Angels. Poems by Thomas Moore 1823 online at http://www.cimmay.com/moore.htm.

Olyan, Saul M, *A Thousand Thousands Serve Him: Exegesis and the Naming of Angels in Ancient Judeaism*. Tubingen, 1993.

Thorndike, Lynn, *The History of Magic and Experimental Science*. Three volumes. Columbia University Press, 1922–34.

Angel Attributes

This list does not include the multiple angels of the hours, months, seasons, moon or minor angels of the plants and zodiac, or the minor angels, all of which would have made the list unmanageable.

Abyss see Abaddon, Phanuel, Zephon
Adversity see Caliel, Sitael
Agriculture see Cahatel, Habuhiah, Lecabel, Michael
Air see Aiel, Andas, Arfig, Atel, Baraqiel, Bengariel, Beriel, Camirael, Carbiel, Chasen, Elementals, Flatoniel, Gabriel, Gael, Karason, Loriqniel, Machatan, Michael, Micraton, Nephyel, Oliel, Orychyn, Pantaceren, Pecyrael, Pyroyinel, Raguel, Ramatiel, Raphael, Sandalphon, Seraphim, Tobiel, Ztaziel
Alchemists see Anixiel, Och
Anger see Affafniel, Aph, Hemah, Qeseph and Qispiel, Zaapiel
Animal rights see Nemamiah, Vohu Mano
Animals see Hariel
Annunciation see Gabriel
Aquarius see Ausiul, Cabriel, Cambiel, Uriel
Aries see Aiel, Machidiel, Michael, Saraqael, Sariel
Arts see Haamiah, Hariel

Babies see Caretaking Angels, Childbed Angels, Temeluch
Banking see Anauel
Birds see Anpiel
Blind see Raphael, Samael
Buildings see Adriel

Business see Anauel, Ieiaiel

Cancer see Cael, Gabriel, Muriel
Capricorn see Anapel, Casujojah, Haniel, Uriel
Chemists see Omael
Childbirth see Armisael, Childbed Angels, Zuriel
Children's rights see Nemamiah
Choirs see Jahoel
Civilisation see Haaiah, Terathel
Comets seee Ziqiel
Commerce see Anauel
Compassion see Hanael, Raphael, Tiphareth, Sophia
Conception see Armisael, Lailah
Constellations see Kokabel, Rahtiel
Contemplation see Cassiel, Sealtiel
Contemplatives see Iahhel

Day see Shamsiel, Yomiel
December see Haniel
Death see Angel of Death
Divine Wrath see Zaphiel
Doctors see Raphael
Dreams see Duma

Earthquake see Rashiel, Ziiel
East see Uriel
Ecology see Raphael
Escape see Michael
Evening Wind see Raphael
Evil eye see Rahmiel

Family see Jeliel
February see Baraqiel
Fertility see Abdisuel, Alimiel,

Borachiel, Hellison, Lebes
Fire see Adonai, Arel, Dalquiel, Dokiel, Gabriel, Michael, Nuriel
Fish see Dagiel
Fishermen see Arariel
Forgetfulness see Ansiel, Pathiel
Fortune see Poiel
France see Hakamiah
Friendship see Amnediel
Fruit see Sophiel
Future see Teiaiel

Gemini see Giel
Glory see Sandalphon

Hail see Baradiel, Nuriel
Happiness see Eiael
Harmony see Cassiel, Mahasiah
Harvests see Amnixiel
Healing and Health see Raphael, Ariel
Hell see Pasiel
Home see Cahatel
Hope see Phanael
Hunters, Hunting see Anixiel, Dirachiel
Hurricane see Zaapiel

Imbecility see Akriel
Impulsiveness see Caliel
Infertility see Akriel
Injury see Alimon
Innocence see Haniel
Intellect see Asaliah
Israel, Jewish people see Gabriel, Michael, Zakzaki'el

Jupiter see Baraqiel, Sachiel
Justice see Soterasiel

Knowledge see Raphael, Uriel

Leo see Ol
Liberty see Terathel
Libra see Haniel, Jael
Libraries and archives see Harael
Light see Gabriel, Terathel

Lightning see Baraqiel
Longevity see Eiael
Lost objects see Rochel
Love see Adriel, Theliel, Rahmiel, Raphael
Lucidity see Hakamiah

Magistrates see Ielahiah
Mankind see Metatron
Marriage see Amnixiel
Medicine see Raphael, Asaph
Meditation see Iahhel
Memory see Zadkiel
Merchants see Amnixiel
Mercury see Madan, Michael, Raphael
Mercy see Angels of Mercy, Munka, Zehanpuryu
Minerals see Och
Moon see Gabriel, Haniel, Opanniel
Morality see Pahaliah
Music see Israfil and under Song

Nature see under Angels of the Presence
Night see Lailah
North see Zabdiel
Nurses see Raphael

Obedience see Mitzrael
October see Barakiel
Orators see Meheil
Order see Sadriel

Patience see Achaiah
Peace see Cassiel
Persia see Dubbiel
Perspicacity see Achaiah
Philosophers see Iahhel, Poiel
Pisces see Baraqiel, Pasiel
Poetry see Radweriel, Uriel
Prayer see Gabriel, Guardian Angels, Michael, Raphael, Sandalphon
Prayers of the sorrowful see Pesagniyah
Problem solving see Achaiah

Prostitution see Agrat bat Mahlat
Protection from weapons see Alimon
Punishment see Hutriel

Rain see Matriel
Renewal see Aladiah
Repentance see Michael, Penuel,
Raphael, Salathiel, Suriel
Reptiles see Iaoel
Revelation see Ariel
Rome see Samael

Sagittarius see Michael
Saturn see Cassiel, Sabathiel
Science see Raphael, Hariel
Scholars see Lauviah, Meheil
Scholarship see Harael
Scorpio see Baraqiel, Josel
Sea see Cahatel, Rahab
Seamen see Anixiel
Secrets of Nature see Achaiah
Sensitivity see Umabel
Serenity see Cassiel
Ship building see Damabiah
Showers see Zafiel
Silence see Dumah
Singing see Asaph, Heman, Jeduthun
Snakes see Gabriel
Snow see Shalgiel
Solutions see Jeliel
Song see Sandalphon, Asaph, Heman,
Jeduthun
South see Sariel
Spring see Sealtiel
Stars see Kokabiel
Steadfastness see Thrones
Storm see Zakkiel
Streams see Nahaliel
Stupidity see Ansiel, Arariel,Pathiel,
Peniel, Zuriel
Summer see Tubiel
Sun see Galgliel, Gazriel, Michael, Och,
Raphael, Angels of the Sun

Taurus see Haniel, Tual

Tears see Saldalphon
Terror see Zewaiel
Theology see Pahaliah
Thieves see Mefathiel
Thunder see Ramiel, Remiel, Uriel
Travel see Elemiah
Treasure see Parasiel
Tuesday see Phaleg
Turkey see Jeliel

Universities see Harael

Vegetation see Erelim
Venus see Haniel, Amael
Virgo see Nuriel, Voil
Visions see Ramiel

War see Michael, Gadreel, Phaleg
Water see Arariel, Asaph, Azariel, Mael,
Michael, Taliahad
Wealth see Eliphamasai, Saranana
West see Samael
Whirlwind see Rashiel, Zamiel, Zavael
Wind see Ruhiel, Azael
Wisdom see Damabiah
World see Michael
Wrath see Hemah
Writers see Meheil